READINGS ON EQUAL EDUCATION
(Formerly *Educating the Disadvantaged*)

READINGS ON EQUAL EDUCATION

Volume 16

EDUCATION OF HISPANICS IN THE UNITED STATES:
POLITICS, POLICIES, AND OUTCOMES

Volume Editors
Abbas Tashakkori
Salvador Hector Ochoa

Managing Editor
Elizabeth A. Kemper

AMS PRESS, INC.
NEW YORK

READINGS ON EQUAL EDUCATION
VOLUME 16
Education of Hispanics in the United States:
Politics, Policies, and Outcomes

Copyright © 1999 by AMS Press, Inc.
All rights reserved

ISSN 0270-1448
Set ISBN 0-404-10100-3
Volume 16 ISBN 0-404-10116-X
Library of Congress Catalog Card Number 77-83137

All AMS Books are printed on acid-free paper that meets the guidelines for performance and durability of the Committee on Production Guidelines for Book Longevity of the Council on Library Resources.

AMS PRESS, INC.
56 EAST 13TH STREET
NEW YORK, NY 10003-4686 USA

Manufactured in the United States of America

This volume is dedicated to our families
who have enriched our lives and work:

Marylyn Sines, Cyrus & Mitra Tashakkori

and

Maricela, Victoria Vianey, Aaron Rafael,
Jose Maria & Gloria Ochoa

Con todo nuestro amor
Abbas & Hector

CONTENTS

VOLUME 16

ALFREDO ARTILES is an Assistant Professor at the UCLA Graduate School of Education and Information Studies. Dr. Artiles' scholarly interest is on how constructions of "difference" (on the basis of ethnicity) influence how educational systems address the needs of culturally diverse students. He has focused on how the construction of "difference" is ubiquitous, specifically, the over representation of ethnic minority students in special education. His scholarly work has concentrated on the nature, evolution, and prevention of over representation, as well as teacher learning for student diversity in general education. Dr. Artiles work has been published in prestigious journals such as *Exceptional Children, Review of Research in Education, Elementary School Journal*, and *Journal of Special Education*. He serves on the editorial boards of several journals including, *Exceptional Children, Learning Disabilities Research & Practice, Remedial and Special Education*, and *Comparative Education Review*. Dr. Artiles has worked as a consultant and made presentations at professional conferences in the U.S.A., Latin America, Europe, and Africa.

ANGELA L. CARRASQUILLO is the Chair of the Curriculum and Teaching Division at Fordham University's Graduate School of education. She is also coordinator of the TESOL program and the doctoral program in Language, Literacy, and Learning. She is nationally known in the area of second language and bilingual education and has published extensively in these area. Dr. Carrasquillo's latest books include: *Teaching Reading in Spanish to the Bilingual Student* (1998);, *Language Minority Students in the Mainstream Classroom* (1996); *Puerto Rican Students in the United States* (1995); *Teaching English to Speakers of Other Languages* (1994); *Hispanic Children and Youth in the Unites States* (1994); *Parents and Schools* (with L. London, 1993); and *Whole Language and the Bilingual Learner* (with C. Hedley, 1993).

RAYMOND E. CASTRO is currently the chair of Chicano and Latino studies and director of the Center for the Study of Latino Families and Children at Sonoma State University. He is the former principle investigator of the Latino Development Projects at the Tomás Rivera Center. As an undergraduate, Dr. Castro attended UCLA. He received his doctorate with an emphasis in education social policy from Harvard University in 1976. Dr. Castro is author of numerous articles on language and language policy in the United States.

GLORIA CUADRAZ is Assistant Professor of American Studies Program and Arizona State University, West in Phoenix. Her areas of interest include sociological and interdisciplinary study of education (with emphasis on graduate education); Chicana/o studies using autobiography and biography; race, class, and gender studies; and qualitative methodologies. She is currently completing a book tentatively titled, *A Fluke of History: The Making of a Chicana/o Generation in Higher Education* (Temple University Press). She has published "The Chicana/o Generations and the Horatio Alger Myth" in *Thought and Action: NEA Higher Education Journal* (1997); Experiences of Multiple Marginality: A Case Study of Chicana Scholarship Women" in *Race/Ethnicity Diversity in Higher Education* (1996); and co-authored an article about her own scholarship trajectory in"From Scholarship Girls to Scholarship Women: Surviving the Contradictions of Race and Class in Academe" in *Explorations in Ethnic Studies* (1994). In 1997, Dr. Cuadraz was one of seven featured faculty members in the nationally acclaimed PBS video, *Shattering the Silences: Minorities Break Into the Ivory Tower*.

RICHARD A. FIGUEROA is Professor of Education at the University of California at Davis, and has been a member of the faculty since 1974. His research has concentrated on two areas: psychological testing of minority children and the education of students labeled "learning handicapped." In his most recent book, *Bilingualism and Testing: A Special Case of Bias*, Dr. Figueroa and Dr. Guadalupe Valdes (Stanford University) demonstrate how tests and testing are biased against bilingual individuals. In his current research program, he and his colleagues are investigating why the reductionist pedagogical paradigm for learning disabled, bilingual pupils does not work and how a holistic-constructivist paradigm might "cure" learning disabilities with bilingual children and help to reconstruct the current system of special education.

EUGENE GARCÍA is Dean of the Graduate School of Education and Professor of Education at the University of California, Berkeley. He served as a faculty member at the University of Utah, the University of California, Santa Barbara, Arizona State University, and the University of California, Santa Cruz, before joining the faculty at the University of California Berkeley. Dr. García is involved in various community activities and has served as an elected member of an urban school board. He has published extensively in the area of language teaching and bilingual development, authoring and/or co-authoring over 140 articles and book chapters, along with eight book-length volumes. He holds leadership positions in professional organizations and continues to serve in an editorial capacity for psychological, linguistic, and educational journals, He also serves regularly as a proposal panel reviewer for federal, state, and foundation agencies. He served as a Senior Officer and Director of the Office of Bilingual Education and Minority Languages Affairs in the US department of Education from 1993 to 1995. He is current conduction research in the area of effective schooling for linguistically and culturally diverse student populations.

MILDRED GARCÍA is Associate Vice Provost and Associate Professor in the Social and Behavioral Science Department at Arizona State University West. In addition, she serves as Associate Director of the Hispanic Research Center at Arizona State University. She received her doctorate in Higher Education from Teachers College, Columbia University. She is the chairperson of the Board of the *Journal of Higher Education* and is a board member of the American Association of Higher Education. Her research has concentrated on at-risk students and under represented faculty, staff, and administrators. As well and the implications for policy and practice. Her most recent publication is editor and author of *Affirmative Action's Testament of Hope*.

WILDA LAIJA is a doctoral candidate in school psychology at Texas A&M University. She worked as a district level bilingual school psychologist for five years in California and was chairperson of a district level committee on issues pertaining to bilingual students and special education. She has supported the improvement of programs for minority students and has shown this by organizing services and speaking at conferences pertaining to these issues. Her research interests include improving services for minority children and youth, and bilingualism and its role in primary and secondary language development, cognitive development, and achievement.

ELIZABETH A. KEMPER is a doctoral candidate and research assistant at Louisiana State University, in the department of Educational Leadership and Research. A former high school teacher, her research interests include educational policy implementation, school restructuring, and equal education. She also served as managing editor for this volume.

RAYNOLDO F. MACIAS is a faculty member and Chair of the UCLA César E. Chávez Center for Interdisciplinary Instruction in Chicana and Chicano studies. He is the author, co-author, and editor of six books and over three dozen research articles and chapters on topics including bilingual education, teacher supply and demand, Chicanos and schooling, adult literacy, language choice, and analyses of national language survey data. His work has appeared in journals such as the *NABE Journal*, the *International Journal of the Sociology of Language*, and the *Annual Review of Applied Linguistics*. His current research activities are in language policy/politics/demography, adult literacy, and teacher studies. He is a regular consultant to state policy making bodies, and served on the California Commission for Teacher Credentialing advisory committee on specifying professional development opportunities for Cross-Cultural, Language, and Academic Development (SB 1969), and Teacher Credentialing for the 21st Century (SB 1422).

AMAURY NORA is Professor of Higher Education in the College of Education at the University of Houston. His research focuses on college persistence, the role of college participation on diverse student populations across different types of institutions, the development of financial aid models that integrate economic theories and college persistence theories, graduate education, and theory building and testing. His inquires have not only contributed to traditional lines of research on college persistence bu have opened research on women and minorities in community colleges. Nora has been a Visiting Professor at the University of

Michigan at Ann Arbor and Pen State University. Currently he is serving as program chair for the 1999 annual meeting of ASHE. Nora has published numerous book chapters and article in journals including *Research in Higher Education, The Review of Higher Education, The Journal Of Higher Education, Educational and Urban Society, Handbook of Theory and Research,* and *Educational Record,* He had served on the editorial boards of *Research in Higher Education, The Review of Higher Education, The Journal of Higher Education,* and *The Journal of College student Retention: Research, Theory, and Practice.*

SALVADOR HECTOR OCHOA is an associate professor of educational psychology at Texas A&M University, where he holds a joint appointment in school psychology and special education. Dr. Ochoa is the Director of Training of the Doctoral School Psychology Program at Texas A7M University. He is also program coordinator of the graduate program in Bilingual Special Education and co-program coordinator of the Educational Diagnostician program. Dr. Ochoa's research pertaining to bilingual assessment, social status, and educational programming issues of Hispanic students has been published in the following journals: *Journal of School Psychology, The Journal of Special Education, Learning Disabilities Research & Practice, The Journal of Psychoeducational Assessment, Learning Disability Quarterly, Bilingual Research Journal, The Journal of Educational Issues of Language Minority Students,* and *Diagnostique.*

YOLANDA N. PADRÓN is a Professor in the Curriculum and Instruction Department at the University of Houston where she teaches courses in the areas of bilingual and second language education. She currently serves as Co-Program Director and Principal Researcher, Integrated Reforms, National Center for Research on Education, Diversity, and Excellence (CREDE). Dr. Padrón's research has focused primarily on students' bilingual cognitive strategies in the areas of reading, mathematics, and parent education, teacher training programs and bilingual/bicultural education, capitalizing on her years as a classroom teacher when she taught limited English proficient students and English-monolingual students. She has published in journals such as *TESOL Quarterly, Educational Horizons, Journal of Education for Students Placed at Risk, Hispanic Journal of Behavioral Sciences, Journal of Educational Research, Journal of Social Psychology, Journal of Educational Equity and Leadership,* and *The Reading Teacher.* In 1997, she was Co-Recipient of the Career Contribution to Quantitative Research in Technology and Teacher Education from the Society for Technology and Teacher Education. In addition, she has been editor for the "Research and Field Practices" section of the *Journal of Educational Equity and Leadership* and has been on the Editorial Advisory Board for *National Reading Conference Yearbook, The Reading Teacher,* and *The Bilingual Research Journal.*

MARCO PORTALES is Professor of English at Texas A&M University, College Station. He has held positions as English undergraduate Director, Executive Assistant the Presidents at Texas A & M, and had ben elected to two year appointments as program chair, secretary and president of the Society for the Study of Multi-Ethnic Literature of the United States (MELUS). His next book, tentatively titled *Crowding Out Latinos: Mexican Americans and Public Consciousness,* is expected to be out at the end of 1999.

LAURA I. RENDON is Professor of Educational Leadership and Policy at Arizona State University. She has authored or c–authored more then 60 book chapters, journal articles, and research publications on topics of diversity, assessment of educational partnerships, community college students, transfer and retention of minority students. Rendon has co-edited two books, *Education a New Majority: Transforming America's Educational System for Diversity* (1996) and the *ASHE Ethnic Racial Diversity Reader* (1996). Rendon is associate editor of *The Journal of Minorities in Science and Engineering* and *VOCES: Journal of Chicana/Latina Studies.* She is also on the editorial boards of *About Campus* and *The National Teaching and Learning Forum.* Rendon received the Outstanding Latino Faculty In Higher Education Award (1997) from the Hispanic Caucus of the American Association for higher education and the Outstanding Research Award (1996) from the College of Education, Arizona State University. She is currently the president of ASHE.

YOLANDA RODRIGUEZ-INGLE is the assistant director of Corporation and Foundation Relations at the University of Texas at El Paso, and is presently completing her Ph.D. in education at the Claremont Graduate school. Her main research activities have centered on teacher supply and demand, the impact of teacher assessment and certification practices, the preparation of teachers, and the effect of population demographic changes in the quality of education. Co-authored publications include: Glimpses of innovation: Efforts to increase Chicano/Latino teachers in the southwest; Reshaping teacher education in the southwest: A response to the needs of Latino students and teachers; Learning communities in teacher education programs; *Resolving a Crisis in Education: Latino Teachers for Tomorrow's Classrooms* (with Raymond E. Castro); and, *The Education of Teacher: a Bibliography* (with Magaña and Macias).

NADEEN T. RUIZ is Professor of Education in the Bilingual Multicultural Education Department at California State University, Sacramento. Dr. Ruiz also co-directs the Optimal Learning Environment (OLE) Migrant Education Project, a staff development program that focuses on effective literacy instruction for bilingual migrant children throughout California. The OLE project is also involved in a collaboration with Mexico, helping Migrant special and general education teachers enhance the literacy development of Mexican children. Her research interests include language and literacy development of bilingual students, deaf students, and students with learning disabilities.

ABBAS TASHAKKORI is a Professor of Educational Research Methodology in the Department of Educational Leadership, Research and Counseling at Louisiana State University. He has a Ph. D. in social psychology from the University of North Carolina-Chapel Hill. He has taught psychology at the University of North Carolina-Chapel Hill, Shiraz University, and Stetson University, and has taught research methodology, measurement, and statistics at the Louisiana State University. He has been a post-doctoral fellow of the Carolina Population Center and the University of North Carolina-Chapel Hill, and a visiting scholar at the Texas A&M University. He has published extensively on minority youth, adolescent self-perceptions and attitudes, and gender issues in cross-cultural and multi-cultural contexts. He is also interested in program evaluation and alternative research methodologies in social and behavioral sciences. His most recent work is entitled *Mixed Methodology: Combining the Qualitative and Quantitative Approaches* (Sage Publications, 1998). He is currently co-editing the *Handbook of Mixed Method Research in the Social, Behavioral, and Health Sciences.*

CAROLYN J. THOMPSON is a visiting Assistant Professor of Higher Education in the School of Education at the University of Missouri-Kansas City. Her research interest focus on issue related to under represented faculty, the socialization of under represented students into and through college and university settings and policy issues related to both. Complementing her role as university faculty are her prior professional experiences which include working on state-level education policy reform, as a policy analyst with the Education Commission of the States, and teaching and counseling in secondary schools. She has served as a member of the SUNY Press editorial Board, and the Advisory Board of ASHE-ERIC Higher Education Reports.

LAURIE R. WEAVER is an Assistant Professor of bilingual and multicultural education at the University of Houston-Clear Lake. Formerly she taught bilingual and ESL classes in Texas and Mexico. Her areas of research include teacher preparation for working with culturally and linguistically diverse students and literacy development of language minority students. She received her B.A. cum laude in Spanish from Kalamazoo College in 1982, her M.S. in elementary education from the University of Houston-Clear Lake in 1988, and her Ed.D. in Curriculum and Instruction specializing in bilingual education from the University of Houston in 1995.

Introduction

Policies, Politics, and
Hispanics' Educational Attainment

Salvador Hector Ochoa and Abbas Tashakkori

> ... despite thirty years of educational reforms, Latino students continue to
> lag behind students from the dominant culture... On measures of reading
> and writing proficiency, Latino students are twice as likely as Anglo
> students to score at below basic levels. The drop-out rate remains very
> high, with over 40 percent of Latinos over the age of nineteen years having
> no high school diploma. The proportion of Latino students attending
> segregated schools remains high, particularly in large urban school
> districts where Latino student enrollments are concentrated. Finally, the
> proportion of Latino students enrolled in colleges and universities and
> those who graduate from high school prepared for admission to higher
> education remains low. As a body of scholarly research begins to evolve,
> it appears that these have been chronic over at least the past thirty years.
> (Darder, Torres, and Gutierrez, 1997, p. xiii)

The idea for this book emerged from our early discussions
regarding the plight of Hispanic children and youth in the United
States, as well as from the life experiences and professional
exposure of the two editors. We have both experienced life as
minority group members, and have both learned to think and speak
in a second language. The same is also true for most of the
contributors to this book. Professionally, both of us have had
experience with Hispanics and other minorities in educational
settings. One is a social psychologist with experience in multicultural research and educational program evaluation, the other has
a doctorate in school psychology with extensive research and

professional practice dealing with Hispanic children. Both of us have observed how Hispanic and other bilingual children struggle with the challenge of learning and thinking in a second language; moreover, both of us are concerned about public stereotypes that Hispanic children are not smart enough to learn.

In 1994, the median age of the United States Hispanic population was 10 years younger than the non-Hispanics, while the percentage of Hispanics over the age of 25 with high school diplomas was 30% less than the rest of the population. As reported by Perez and De La Rosa Salazar (1997), while the percentage of African Americans who completed high school increased by 12% between 1970 and 1990, there was a 3% decrease for Hispanics (the non-Hispanic white percentage increased by 2%). This disparity in educational attainment, combined with the fastest rate of population growth point to serious negative consequences for the United Stated as a whole. In spite of these clearly alarming trends, relatively little attention has been paid to its prevention.

The problem is highly complex and multifaceted. Education is one of the fastest and most efficient means of social mobility; and yet Hispanics lag far behind other sectors of the population in educational outcomes. We shared and discussed these concerns in the context of constant media attention regarding the abolishment of some educational programs for Hispanic students in K-12 and higher education.

In trying to predict how the education of Hispanics was going to change as well as the impact of these changes, we have asked the assistance of a group of highly competent scholars. In each chapter of the volume, these scholars try to answer some variation of four general questions:

1) What has been the historical nature of educational access and outcomes for Hispanics in the United States, and how has it evolved?

2) What is the status of educating Hispanics in the midst of recent controversies regarding minority issues in the United States?

3) Given current demographic trends, what educational outcomes can be predicted for Hispanics in the next decade?

4) What policy and curriculum changes are needed to improve future outcomes for Hispanic students?

Although the chapters in this book are separated into K-12 and higher education, there are certain themes common across the divisions. These major themes include the examination of the past and present status of Hispanics' education, changes in laws and national policies affecting Hispanics, issues pertaining to language of instruction, and Hispanics in the teaching profession. A brief discussion of how each chapter fits into these themes follows.

Historical Trends & Current Status
of Hispanic Education

In our opinion, an examination of history is the first step in understanding why any current situation exists. Chapter One of this book examines the historical roots of the inequalities in the access of Hispanics to public education. Although the major focus of the chapter is on Mexican-Americans (by far, the largest segment of the Hispanic population in the United States), many of the issues that are raised in that chapter are also applicable to other Hispanic-American populations. Laija and Ochoa demonstrate the historically deep-rooted inequity in the access of Hispanics to quality education. Moreover, they also point to the slow progress made towards achieving total access.

The search for understanding the state of education among Hispanics continues with Carrasquillo in the second chapter. She skillfully examines the K-12 education of Hispanics, and presents ample insights into the crisis in their public education. Her constructed profile of Hispanics demonstrates that despite the changes in the last three decades, the educational attainment of Hispanics is still far from the optimal level for social mobility and self-sufficiency. Chapter Eight provides insights regarding the status of Hispanics in higher education. An examination of these chapters will demonstrate that although the current status of education among Hispanics is better than in the past, there still is much inequity regarding access to quality public and higher education.

Changes in Laws & Policies Impacting Hispanics Education

During the last three decades, a strong move has materialized to use litigation and legislation as a vehicle to change policy and public opinion towards Hispanics and other minority groups.

Chapters Seven and Nine review these legal changes and their effect on K-12 and higher education for Hispanics. At the time these chapters were being prepared, strong challenges existed to the affirmative action programs, especially with regard to college admission and financial aid.

Eugene Garcia provides an in-depth analysis of the legal and policy issues regarding language minority children in Chapter Seven. He presents a detailed overview of the federal policies regarding the access of Hispanics (and other minorities) to quality public education, including numerous legal challenges to historic inequities. He also examines state-level initiatives regarding the education of language minority children. Following these, Garcia presents a number of questions regarding the access of language minority children to quality education.

Marco Portales, in Chapter Nine, examines the impact of recent legal changes on the access of Hispanics to institutions of higher education. He argues that although legal change has improved the access of Hispanics to junior colleges and to less prestigious institutions of higher education in Texas, the access of Hispanics and African Americans to top-ranked schools is still very limited. He concludes that recent legal changes as a result of the *Hopwood* case have diminished some of the progress that was achieved in gaining access over the last decade. He also provides a variety of recommendations for improving the access of Hispanics to top ranked institutions of higher education.

Language of Instruction & Program Placement

The major thread linking all Hispanic subgroups is their language. Similar to other first and second generation immigrants, many Hispanics use their native Spanish language as their primary source of communication at home, while they use English in school and in the workplace, at least most of the time. The process of acquiring a second language is not an easy one for many first generation immigrants. In Chapter Four, Weaver and Padron skillfully address many of the controversies regarding bilingual education programs and their impact on educational outcomes. They review three types of bilingual programs (transitional, maintenance, and two-way) and discuss the effect of these programs on student achievement. They provide evidence to suggest that maintenance and two-way bilingual programs are effective with respect to academic outcomes. These two programs, however, are not frequently used in school settings. Weaver and Padron also explain the impact of providing instruction in the child's first language on educational outcomes.

The educational outcome of many language minority students is their failure to attain high levels of academic success. Figueroa and Artiles, in Chapter Five, examine different variables that lead to the disproportionate placement of Hispanics in special education classes. Legal, psychological, and educational consequences of these placements are then discussed, and the effects on the students who are placed in these programs are demonstrated. They conclude that both educational access and outcomes are affected by such placement. By incorrectly placing bilingual children in special education programs, they are deprived of more challenging educational opportunities. This results in language minority children falling behind in their educational attainment, as well as the potential of forming negative self-perceptions regarding their competencies.

Placement on the positive side of the exceptionality continuum into gifted and talented programs has a pattern opposite to special education. In Chapter Six, Figueroa and Ruiz provide a glimpse of the under-representation of Hispanics in these programs, and the reasons behind this trend. They view the source of the issue as the placement criteria for entrance into gifted and talented programs, especially the over-reliance on intelligence tests and the failure to take a variety of criteria into consideration for placement. They advocate the necessity of enriching the quality of classroom instruction for all children, instead of a small proportion who meet the criteria for placement in gifted programs. Providing a challenging learning environment which provides the opportunity for individualized learning makes gifted programs unnecessary.

Hispanics in the Teaching Profession

A study of education among Hispanics could not be limited only to the recipients of schooling. Hispanic K-12 teachers and university faculty are important parts of this picture for at least three reasons: a) they can function as an effective means of providing quality education to Hispanic students, b) they provide role models for these students, and c) they demonstrate potential future life experiences for Hispanic children. With regard to this last point, Hispanic educators' status, job satisfaction, and problems would be representative of the future outcomes of their Hispanic students. Chapters Three and Nine examine the status of Hispanic teachers and higher education faculty.

In Chapter Three, Macias, Castro, and Rodriguez-Ingle demonstrate the disparity among the proportion of Hispanics in the United States population, percentage of Hispanic students in public (K-12) schools, and the proportion of Hispanic teachers in such schools. They also provide an in-depth analysis of the number of Hispanic teachers who graduated in 1998 from different teacher-education institutions in the southwest. Based on these, and a variety of other analyses, they conclude that the small proportion of Hispanic teachers in K-12 schools poses a problem both to the Hispanic population and the education community as a whole. Consequently, they provide suggestions regarding how to lessen this problem in the future.

In Chapter Ten, Garcia and Thompson point to the disparity among the proportion of Hispanics in the population, Hispanic students in institutions of higher education, and the Hispanic faculty in these institutions. Based on their own observations and experiences, as well as reports of other scholars, they discuss critical factors that affect Hispanic faculty members' success of obtaining employment, promotions, and tenure. Moreover, they discuss the status of Hispanic (and other minority) faculty in these institutions. They provide recommendations for changing the hiring process, mentoring, communicating the reward structure, and providing professional development opportunities for Hispanic faculty.

Examining Micro-Level Factors Impacting Educational Outcomes for Hispanics

The strands connecting all of the chapters in this book are threefold: 1) legal statutes and changes towards improving the educational opportunities for minorities, 2) federal, state, and local policies for providing access to quality education for minorities, especially for bilingual children, 3) political forces/movements that have affected and/or are currently affecting these opportunities. In the last chapter of the book, Chapter Eleven, Tashakkori, Ochoa, and Kemper discuss additional components of the problem including Hispanic students' educational aspirations, beliefs, self-perceptions, and behavioral intentions. Much of the student information is based on our analysis of the survey data collected nationally by the United States Department of Education (NELS-88 project). We discuss the issues of access, the mediating/mitigating variables, and educational outcomes. In the last section of Chapter 11, we summarize the issues pertaining to the education of Hispanics in terms of pull and push factors. Pull factors are the ones that make education attractive and accessible to Hispanics and other minority children. Push factors are individual and family attributes, attitudes and aspirations that motivate Hispanic children to continue their schooling and achieve at school.

Historically, many of the attempts to improve the education of Hispanics and other minorities in the United States have focused on the legal and policy changes comprising the pull factors. Obviously, there have been improvements due to the impact of such policies and laws. On the other hand, there has also been political resistance to these changes, and to attempts at empowering minorities. A part of the failure to enhance the educational attainment of Hispanic children and youth might be attributable to this resistance and to the ineffective implementation of new policies and laws. On the other hand, a larger part of the failure might be attributable to lack of attention by some school personnel to the above-mentioned push factors. In the last pages of this volume, we argue that for these attempts to be successful, policies should incorporate the individual and family-level push variables.

Hispanics are a very heterogenous group, consisting of different races, ethnicities, and national backgrounds. The only common thread between all of them is their language. Although historical origin (Spain) and religion (Catholicism) is common to some Hispanics, it does not universally apply to all. Reference to different groups of Hispanics is not uniform either. Hispanics of Mexican origin are referred to as Chicanas (females) or Chicanos (male or plural). Some authors refer to Hispanics as Latinos. Our contributors each had their own preferences, and we had lively discussions with them regarding these preferences. However, for the sake of uniformity and consistency in this book we decided to use the United States census label of Hispanic, instead of other nomenclature. We had to convince our contributors to allow us to use a uniform terminology (except when a specific subgroup was being discussed, or another source was being quoted). We appreciate their willingness to allow us to do this.

References

Darder, A., Torres, R. D., and Gutierrez, H. (1997). *Latinos and education: A critical reader.* New York: Routledge.

Perez, S. M., and De La Rosa Salazar, D. (1997). Economic, labor force, and social implications of Latino educational and population trends. In Darder, Torres, and Gutierrez (Eds.), *Latinos and education: A critical reader.* New York: Routledge.

SECTION I.

The Political And Legal Status of Hispanic Education in the United States: Past History and Current Trends

CHAPTER 1

Historical Roots of Politics and Policies Regarding the Education of Hispanics: The Mexican American Experience

Wilda Laija & Salvador Hector Ochoa

Introduction

American culture has promoted education as a means of getting ahead and becoming successful in life. The probability of attaining this success has typically required one to have access to quality education. However, a number of current controversies regarding the education of Hispanics in the United States, such as propositions 187 and 227 in California, cast doubt on the wide-spread availability of such opportunities.

Educational literature and research during the late nineteenth and first half of the twentieth century focused primarily on European immigrant children. The educational needs of Mexican and Mexican American children, however, were only marginally addressed. There are few articles pertaining to Mexicans or Mexican Americans in the National Education Association's journal in the first half of the twentieth century. Most articles in journals and magazines in the early part of the century document perceptions or historical facts in regards to the Mexican American population. Educational studies and historical documentation did not begin in earnest with this population until the 1930s.

The primary focus of this chapter is to review the historical literature pertaining to factors which have significantly influenced the educational attainment of the Mexican American population in the Southwest beginning in the latter part of the 1800s. The

1

historical factors from the nineteenth and early twentieth century will be compared to the current state of affairs in an attempt to illustrate major changes, or lack of changes, in opportunities for Mexican Americans in the Southwestern states during the last century. In particular, this review will examine psychosocial variables and schooling factors which continue to have an impact upon Mexican American opportunities for advancement.

Historical Factors Impacting
The Social Mobility of Mexican Americans

In our opinion, several critical psychosocial variables have impacted Mexican American's opportunities for advancement with respect to their abilities to obtain educational access. These factors include: a) legacy of Mestizaje (me-stee-zo), b) denial of rights, c) lack of English skills, and d) immigration. The focus of this section is to illustrate how significantly these historical factors have affected the educational achievement and attainment of the Mexican American population.

Legacy of Mestizaje
The legacy of Mestizaje is often not recognized, although its repercussions continue to be felt. A consequence of the Spanish colonization of Mexico was the transformation of many native Mexicans into Mestizos. The term Mestizos describes people who are of both Native American (Indian) and Spanish descent. At the time of the colonization, Mestizos had a higher status than the native dark skinned Mexicans of Indian descent, but lower status than the lighter skinned Spaniards. The differentiation in skin tone resulted in discrimination toward this group by both Spaniards and early European settlers. Neo-nativism, along with social Darwinist thought, contributed to the belief that Mexicans were culturally and racially unacceptable as equals to the early European settlers in the Americas (Miranda, 1990). Mestizos, due to their indigenous background, became part of a stratified society in which they were often subservient. Race conscious Americans in the early nineteenth century made reference to the fact that Mexicans were Indians in spite of their Spanish surnames (Miranda, 1990). Attitudes towards Indians affected Mexican American's acceptance among non-Hispanic whites.

Miranda (1990) explains that the discrimination and racism against Mexicans at this point in history were due to an assumption made by non-Hispanic whites that Mexicans and Indians were enemies of "American" civilization. It is important to note that the term Mexican American is a relatively new term. Some Mexican Americans at the time were addressed as "Mexicans" and this term was often associated with negative connotations, which continues to this day (the terms Mexican and Mexican American will be used in this chapter to reflect the terms used by original sources). At the turn of the century, Miranda (1990) indicates that the majority of Americans perceived the Mexican American way of life to be not only inferior, but un-American, foreign, and alien to the more secular and individualized Eurocentric heritage.

Denial of Rights
Despite the fact that their ancestors inhabited the Southwestern states, the Hispano-Mexican heritage of the Southwest continues to be undervalued. When the United States acquired the Southwest as part of the Treaty of Guadalupe Hidalgo (also known as the Gadsden Purchase) in 1848, it guaranteed a) property rights to all Mexican residents, b) retention of their Catholic faith, Spanish language, cultural traditions (Dinnerstein, Nichols, & Reimers, 1979), c) right to vote, and d) a promise of fair treatment in all endeavors (Miranda, 1990). These promises, however, were not kept. Mexican Americans were displaced from their properties, as their ancestors had been, their political power was eliminated due to increased non-Hispanic white majority, and they were targets for discrimination (Meier & Stewarat, 1991).

Cultural and racial antagonism continued over the next century. The popular nativist practices of the nineteenth century American way of life ignored the guarantees made to the Mexican population of the Southwest in 1848 (Miranda, 1990). Mexican Americans were demoted and accorded the status of foreigners or immigrants in their native land. Mexican Americans in the Southwest found themselves with few rights. For example, in Texas, Mexican Americans were segregated in theaters, not given service in some restaurants, and were barred from many public and educational facilities (Dinnerstein, Nichols, & Reimers, 1979).

One of the main criticisms Americans had of the Treaty of Hidalgo was that Mexicans were not interested in education, since Mexico had not established a public education system. It is important to note, however, that the first schools in America were in Mexico and South America, prior to the arrival of Europeans to the continent (Weinberg, 1977).

Lack of English Skills

Mexican Americans were also targeted due to their inability to speak English. Since Americans viewed the ability to speak English as fundamental to their participation in American society, they often viewed the monolingual Mexican American as culturally and linguistically impoverished (Jenks, Lauck, & Smith, 1922; Woofter, 1933). In a 1921 study of 1,081 Mexican families in Los Angeles, Bogardus reported that 55% of the men and 74% of the women could not speak English (Sedillo, 1995). Education was believed to be the most potent force toward Americanizing and inculcating American ideals in immigrants (Miranda, 1990). Few opportunities to address their lack of English proficiency resulted in many Mexican Americans being marginalized by mainstream society.

Immigration

In the United States, Mexican immigration has historically been due to increased labor needs in agriculture, mines, and railroads, and lack of economic opportunities in Mexico. The Mexican American population doubled every ten years from the early twentieth century to 1940 (see Jenks, Lauck, & Smith, 1922). The Mexican population increased proportionately faster in each of the five Southwestern states (Arizona, California, Colorado, New Mexico, and Texas) than did the total U. S. population during the period of 1910 to 1930 (Reynolds, 1933).

Mexican and Mexican American families, who were for the most part laborers, migrated to where they could find employment. Mexicans were often employed because they could be hired for lower wages than other immigrants or American born workers would accept. As a result, the Mexican immigrants were generally at the bottom of the economic ladder. For example, the immigration commission found the wages paid to "Mexicans" to be the lowest of any laborer who worked on the railroads in the early part of the twentieth century. This was often twenty-five percent less than that paid to the Japanese (Jenks, Lauck, & Smith, 1922). Moreover, Schermerhorn (1949) indicated that "the job ceiling for most Mexicans [was] low and rigid" (p. 453).

Realization and recognition of inequality and discrimination became more prevalent in the 1960s. Before the 1960s, the "deplorable situation of the Mexican American was little known outside the Southwest; within the area it was accepted as the natural order and had been ignored for decades" (Carter & Segura, 1979, p. 14). After the civil rights movement of the 1960s, changes concerning inequality resulted primarily from litigation. This is especially true with regard to issues pertaining to education.

Historical Educational Factors Impacting Educational Equity

To some extent, public schools can be perceived as political institutions in which the degree of schooling received by a group is dependent upon their political power and social status (Weinberg, 1983). Mexican Americans' political and social status during the latter part of the nineteenth century and the beginning of the twentieth century was clearly reflected by their lack of educational equity. According to Weinberg (1977), the first study of the education of Mexican American children in Texas was conducted by Manuel in 1928. This study revealed that:

- Mexican Americans represented 13% of the school population.
- 40% percent of Mexican Americans were not attending any school.
- Nearly half of the Mexican American students were in the first grade and only one in twenty-five were in high school.
- Classrooms in Mexican American Schools were far more crowded than classrooms attended by non-Hispanic white children.
- The school year was often shorter for Mexican-American students, sometimes only half as long as that for other children.
- Schools were often segregated, with Mexican-American students receiving inferior physical facilities.
- Teachers in Mexican American schools frequently received the same salary as those in Non-Hispanic white schools, but taught many more children.

- Per-pupil teaching costs were lower in Mexican American schools.

The following sections examine in greater detail many of the factors revealed in Manuel's 1928 study with regard to the educational equity of Mexican American children (Manual, 1934). These include: a) school segregation and unequal access, b) factors associated with school attendance, initial placement, retention, and dropout, c) lack of financial resources, d) quality of teachers, e) perceptions regarding Mexican Americans' academic achievement and intellectual functioning, and f) instruction in a non-comprehensible language.

School Segregation and Unequal Access

Historians have documented that Mexican children were required by law to attend school, but their opportunities for educational equity were not the same as they were for the non-Hispanic white children (Miranda, 1990; Schermerhorn, 1949; Cooke, 1948). Mexican American children in Texas were not consistently permitted to be enrolled in some school districts. In the Sonora and Bastrop districts, Mexican American students were not permitted to register in high school (Weinberg, 1977). Weinberg's historical analysis noted that non-Hispanic white farmers in Nueces County outside of Corpus Christi did not want Mexican Americans to receive a great deal of education. To further this agenda, many of the opposers sat on the school boards to prevent Mexican Americans from attending school.

When Mexican American students did attend school, they were required to attend "Mexican schools," which were often segregated classrooms or schools that focused on instilling American values. While segregation of African-American students was stated in the law, no such legislation existed for Mexican American children. School officials did have the power, however, to classify schools and many states used this power to segregate Mexican American children from other children (Weinberg, 1983).

Not only did government offices promote segregation, but professional organizations of teachers, administrators, and non-Hispanic white parents actively collaborated to maintain the "racial order" (Reynolds, 1933; Weinberg, 1977). Planned deprivation became a norm of educational practice, and racial and ethnic barriers were accepted by school faculty and administrations as inevitable limitations on educational opportunity (Weinberg, 1977).

Reynolds (1933) conducted a study on the "education of Spanish-speaking children in five Southwestern states" in order to prepare a report for the United States Office of Education. She reported that segregation was often observed in the various Southwestern states. In addition,

> the problem of location and adequacy in type and number of school buildings and rooms for Mexican pupils is affected by the prejudice by the staff and parents, who do not want their children to go to school where Mexican children attended. (1933, p. 5)

It should be noted that Mexican American students were bused to segregated school even though there were other "Anglo schools" closer to their homes. When non-Hispanic white children found themselves living closer to a Mexican American school, they would readily transfer to an non-Hispanic white school and were provided with transportation (Weinberg, 1977).

During the 1920s, segregated schools became the norm in the southwestern states. Schools in Mexican American sections of the Texas cities became "Mexican schools." Between 1922-1923 and 1931-1932, the numbers of such schools doubled from twenty to forty in the state of Texas (Weinberg, 1977). According to Weinberg (1977), by 1920 a pattern had emerged in Texas to promote separate schooling in greatly inferior facilities for Mexican American students. These separate schools did not incorporate the children's cultural heritage or Spanish, and had a shorter school year.

In 1948, Mexican American parents in the Texas counties of Bastrop, Caldwell, and Travis, brought a class action suit to Federal district court to abolish separate schools for their children. This case, *Delgado v. Bastrop Independent School District* case, resulted in the declaration that segregation was in violation of state law and of the Fourteenth Amendment (Garcia, 1989). Separation was specifically approved for only first grade. Thereafter, separate placement could only take place following the administration of "scientific and standardized tests, equally given and applied to all pupils" (Weinberg, 1977, p. 168). School districts throughout Texas continued to violate the rulings delineated in *Delgado*.

California also segregated its Mexican American students. California, like Texas, had no law requiring segregation of

Mexican American children (Cooke, 1948). As of 1930, California school law stated that trustees had the power to establish separate schools for Indian children and for children of Mongolian descent (Weinberg, 1977). Many school officials interpreted this to include Mexicans of Indian descent and subjected Mexican Americans to segregation.

In 1928, California's Mexican American population was 65,572, and just under one-tenth of all students attended public and private schools in the state. During this period, the enrollment of sixty-four schools in eight counties was 90-100% Mexican American (Weinberg, 1977). Many school districts in San Bernardino County, Orange, Los Angeles, Imperial, Kern, Ventura, Riverside and Santa Barbara had segregated schools or segregated classes, even though they did not report them as such (Weinberg, 1977; Cooke, 1948).

Segregation was challenged in 1928 in the Charlotte schools in Atascosa County, California (Weinberg, 1977). A Mexican American girl was denied enrollment in a non-Hispanic school based on "ethnic grounds" which were attributed to irregular attendance and language difficulties. An appeal to the state superintendent of public instruction resulted in the local board being directed to admit the student.

Mexican Americans in California were not legally seen as being of the "white" race until the *Mendez v. Westminster School District* case in 1943. This decision gave a sense of empowerment to Mexican American parents. A group of parents sued school districts in Orange County, California, and demanded that their children be admitted into non-Hispanic white schools, and that the segregation of Mexican American children be declared illegal (Weinberg, 1977). Judge McCormick ruled that "segregation of pupils of Mexican ancestry was not permitted either under the Constitution or under the Statues of California; that it was not possible to single out a class for segregation" (Cooke, 1948, p. 420). In addition, the judge indicated that the only possible grounds upon which segregation could be justified is language difficulty determined by testing individual children. Educational separation could only be made for lower grades (Cooke, 1948). An important determinant in this case was that noted anthropologists testified and demonstrated that in any meaning of the term "race," the Mexican American belonged to the same group as the non-Hispanic white.

It should be noted, however, that some middle class and lighter skinned Mexican American children were permitted to enroll in non-Hispanic white schools in the various Southwestern states. Wealthier Mexican Americans could afford to send their children to private Spanish language schools, usually taught by Mexican teachers from Mexico (Weinberg, 1977). Some Mexican American children also attended private Catholic and Protestant schools (Weinberg, 1977).

Another factor which contributed to the continued segregation of Mexican Americans was the fact that they often lived in colonies. This was primarily due to the low income level of many Mexican American families and the resulting inability to afford better housing. The colony lifestyle was often criticized and perceived as voluntary segregation, even though colony living was due to social and economic factors, not necessarily to choice.

The unequal treatment of Mexican American students was exhibited in various ways. In addition to segregation, Mexican American children were denied equal instructional time. In California, Mexican American children received instruction for only five hours, while the usual school day was six hours. "The five hour school day was clearly a violation of the state school law" (Phillips, 1931, p. 495). Another issue was the unequal quality of facilities and materials. School facilities were almost uniformly inferior for Mexican American students. Students enrolled in rural schools often encountered more inequalities than students enrolled in city schools. Furthermore, school facilities for Mexican Americans were often either not present or inadequate. In California, *Newsweek* reported the following about Mexican American children in their April 14, 1947 issue:

> In the elementary schools of Fresno, for example, 2,560 children were jammed into double classes, sitting in aisles and corridors, huddled in reconverted rest rooms and, in one case, an old school kitchen. In Los Angeles, 20,000 boys and girls were limited to half sessions. Another 50,000 throughout the state faced the same handicap to learning. (California's Children, 1947, p. 93)

As reported by teachers and outside observers, teaching materials for Mexican American children were often conspicuously deficient in both amount and appropriateness (Reynolds, 1933).

Barriers to Full Utilization of Educational Experiences
Several other factors affected the degree to which Mexican American children could benefit from their educational experience. Reynolds (1933) obtained information from the United States Bureau of the Census and compared Mexican American and non-Hispanic white school attendance for ages 6-15 for two cities in states of Arizona, California, Colorado, New Mexico, and Texas. Information revealed that 38-39% of the Mexican American students were attending school. In contrast, the percentage of non-Hispanic white students attending school ranged from 71-96%. Many Mexican American children had to work in the fields and do other types of labor in order to help their families. Reynolds (1933) indicated that 84.3% of the Mexican American children stayed out of school to work. Mexican American children lost 64.8% of school time due to work as compared to a 14.1% time loss for other children (Reynolds, 1933).

Hispanic student's lack of attendance was often blamed on parents and attributed to their low value of education and their migratory habits. The reality for many Mexican Americans was that they had to migrate where they could find employment. In addition, many families needed the extra income their children could earn and were encouraged to work instead of attend school. This resulted in residential and educational instability for Mexican American children.

Another factor which limited the maximization of educational benefits to Mexican American students was how they were initially placed in the educational setting. A regular practice in the Texas public school system was to automatically place Mexican American children, regardless of age and ability, in first or second grade for two or more years (Weinberg, 1977). Manuel's (1934) study revealed that in Texas

> Nearly half of the Spanish speaking children who were enrolled at all were in the first grade, nearly three fourths in the first three grades, and only three or four percent in high school. In the third grade, the Spanish speaking child was about three years older than the English speaking child. (p. 695)

Another issue affecting the education of Mexican American students was the frequency of being retained. Weinberg's (1977) review of historical educational records found that in Texas, 22% of Mexican American children, as compared to only 7% of non-

Hispanic white children, repeated the first grade and in California, the corresponding percentages were 10% and 6% respectively.

Given the combination of the aforementioned obstacles, it is not surprising that the dropout rate for Mexican Americans was very high. Reynolds reported in 1933 that a survey distributed in 1930 reflected that "Mexicans" in Arizona, California, Colorado, New Mexico and Texas comprised only 17% of the student enrollment in grades 5 to 8. In addition, the majority of the Mexican American students reached the compulsory age limit of 16 before they reached the fifth grade. During the 1930s, Mexican children had the highest dropout rate among all groups in South-western schools (Miranda, 1990). The dropout rate among Mexican American students approached 100% until about 1950 (Weinberg, 1977).

Lack of Financial Resources

Funding was an additional obstacle for Mexican Americans in obtaining an education. In New Mexico and Texas, taxes were not charged for the appropriation of schools for minority children. Given that most Mexican Americans were of low economic resources, the schools, where available, were not in very good condition. A year after the civil war, Texas, created an educational fund for "white schools" only. Due to pressure from African American leaders during reconstruction, Texas was finally compelled to create a statewide system of schools. Public schools were funded through property taxes, which reflected the surrounding communities' socioeconomic status.

Even after Texas was forced to create a statewide educational system, the denial of equal allocation and distribution of financial resources to schools was prevalent. Texas school districts often collected monies for Mexican American students and would transfer these monies to benefit non-Hispanic white schools. This, according to Weinberg (1977), was admitted by some school administrators and appeared to be an open practice. "A special irony lay in the fact that the state school funds used to discriminate against Mexican American children in Texas was based largely on land taken from Mexico in 1836" (Weinberg, 1977, p. 163).

Quality of Teachers

While there were many willing and capable teachers working with Mexican American children, quite a few were untrained and, given the degree of discrimination, ashamed to be working with this group. Bogardus (1930), a well known sociologist, described teachers in the "Mexican schools" as

> sympathetic, patient, and encouraging. Often they are highly sacrificial and work overtime without extra pay in behalf of their friends, the Mexican.... But, even so, they will report that the Mexican children are greatly handicapped in comparison with the average American child. (p. 79)

Many teachers working with Mexican American students were unqualified and many received their first years of training with this group. Once they had experience, many would transfer to "white schools." Training and teaching performance was not an issue with teachers who taught Mexican American children, since it was believed that Mexican American children were less capable of learning and less interested in school than their non-Hispanic white counterparts (Schermerhorn, 1949).

Teachers were usually unacquainted with the traditions of Mexican American children and often had little sympathy for their customs. Contacts with the public school system often led Mexican American children to question the traditional ideals which their parents were striving to instill in them (Woods, 1956). This type of experience often caused cultural conflicts for second and third generation Mexican American children (Carrasquillo, 1991).

> The contrast between the symbols acquired at home and those acquired in school may create sharp behavioral conflicts that require selective change and adjustment. In the classroom, the structure of academic tasks, the use of power by authority figures, the role of teachers and principals, and the behavior of mainstream peers all send minority students indirect messages about their own incompetence and the lack of value of their home culture and language. (Trueba, 1989, p. 36)

Misconceptions of Mexican Americans' Intellectual Ability

While the educatability of European immigrants was never an issue, Woofter (1933) indicates that "grave doubts were expressed as to the educatability of the Negro, the Indian, and the Mexican" (p.164). These ideas were supported by those who believed that color groups had inferior mental capacities and by those who opposed the education of minority children. At the turn of the century, educational opportunity mirrored social perceptions.

It is interesting to note that historical literature on minority education often documents perceptions that Mexican American students were "retarded academically" due to poor abilities (Baruch, 1946; Higham, 1981; Mitchell, 1937; Wilson, 1952; Woods, 1956). Reynolds' (1933) report to the United States Department of Education indicated that "over a period of several years few Mexican pupils promoted from primary grades were able to do work assigned to them in the upper grades" (p. 36). Various studies (Manuel, 1934; Reynolds, 1933) that examined the academic achievement of Mexican American children found that they performed comparable to their non-Hispanic white peers in math, but did poorly in reading.

Mexican American students' low academic achievement was largely attributed to "low intelligence" and low potential. Various studies were done on the intellectual abilities of Mexican American students. In a study conducted by Garth (1928) and presented to the American Association for Advancement of Science in 1927, 1,004 Mexican children from Texas, New Mexico, and Colorado were administered tests. Garth's results indicated that Mexican children were on average 1.1 years younger mentally than white children and had a median IQ of 78.1. Caution, however, should be given to these results since the IQ test (i.e., National Intelligence Test – a verbal test for grades 3-5) in this study was later described by Mitchell (1937) as not being desirable for "measuring the relative intelligence of races." Similarly, Reynolds (1933) reported that among Mexican American students tested in Los Angeles on the Binet Intelligence Scales, the mean intelligence quotient was 91.2 while the mean for non-Hispanic white children was 105. These results should be viewed with caution due to methodological flaws.

Weinberg's (1977) review of the literature found that in fourteen San Antonio schools studied during 1925, intelligence quotient scores were found to be strongly related to language. In a study done by Mitchell (1937), Mexican American children's IQ scores were higher when intelligence tests were administered in Spanish rather than English. This trend of higher IQ scores on Spanish tests versus English tests was evident at all grade levels examined, with a 13.22 mean IQ point difference between Spanish and English test administration. As research in this area increased, it was recognized that language, economic, and cultural factors were the larger contributors of Mexican American students lack of success, rather then inborn mental deficiencies (Trueba, 1989; Shah & Bhayana; 1978; Ryan & French, 1976).

Instruction in a Non-Comprehensible Language
    The lack of English language skills was seen as a significant handicap in schools. This not only affected children's ability to learn, but also their ability to socialize with others. While educators were aware that Mexican American children were being taught in a language they did not understand, they continued to emphasize English only instruction (Weinberg, 1977). Moreover, "students were punished, even humiliated publicly, for using it [the Spanish language] on school grounds" (Weinberg, 1977, p. 153). Mexican American children were regarded as handicapped because they were perceived as not being able to learn either English or Spanish proficiently. In addition to learning the English language, school programs for Mexican American children during the 1930's emphasized vocational, manual arts, health, hygiene, and the adoption of American core values, such as cleanliness, thrift, and punctuality (Carter & Segura, 1979).

Current Trends in Psychosocial
Variables and Schooling Factors

    The civil rights movement, judicial cases, and legislation during the last half of the twentieth century have raised awareness that Mexican Americans were not historically afforded the same educational opportunities as non-Hispanic whites. In spite of these positive events, there must still be improvement for Mexican Americans to achieve educational equity. The four historical psychosocial variables identified earlier in the chapter remain relatively unchanged and continue to significantly affect Mexican Americans' opportunities for advancement.

Current Status of Psychosocial Variables
    Few individuals would argue that, collectively, the psychosocial variables of Mestizaje (i.e., both skin color and indigenous descent), denial of rights, English language ability, and immigration status affect one's ability for advancement in the United

States. In varying degrees, some Mexican Americans continue to be affected by all or some of these psychosocial factors.

Mexican Americans continue to reside primarily in Arizona, California, New Mexico, and Texas, with the majority (73%) living in California and Texas (Valdiviesco, 1990). Mexican Americans are still among the poorest minorities. According to the U.S. Bureau of the Census (1990), 31.4% are poor. The number of Mexican Americans living below the poverty line increased from 1988 when it was estimated that about 25% of these families lived below the official poverty line (Valdiviesco, 1990). This poverty rate is more than two and a half times as high as the rate for non-Hispanics.

Mexican Americans continue to hold lower-status occupations when compared to the United States population as a whole and are employed most heavily in blue-collar jobs (41% as compared to 27% of the total population), farm work, and service occupations (Valdiviesco, 1990). Moreover, comparatively fewer Mexican Americans hold white-collar jobs (35% as compared to 57% of the total population) (Valdiviesco, 1990). In addition, Mexican Americans are the least well educated group. Meier and Stewart (1991) indicate that while education by itself explains 45% of the variation in Hispanic incomes, it plays a more important role for Mexican Americans in finding employment than for non-Hispanic whites.

Discrimination continues to affect Mexican Americans, as perceptions about Mexican Americans influence social and/or political agendas (Meier & Steward, 1991). In addition, the issue of skin color has not disappeared. The legacy of Mestizaje continues to exist and affect Mexican Americans in terms of social perceptions and equal opportunities. Lighter skinned people, including lighter skinned Mexican Americans, continue to have more opportunities with respect to education, employment, and upward mobility (Penaloza, 1995; Miranda, 1990). Bartolome (1994) indicates that studies of structural factors show that there are "discriminatory practices aimed at students from groups perceived as low status" (p. 203). Moreover, there is evidence that some teachers indicate a preference for lighter-skinned Latino students (Bartolome, 1994).

Civil rights for Mexican Americans continues to be a struggle. Proposition 227 in California, which mandates abolishment of the bilingual education program, appears to be in direct conflict with the *Lau v. Nichols* 1974 Supreme court case. The Supreme Court in *Lau v. Nichols* indicated that providing language minority students the same facilities, textbooks, teachers, and curriculum as other students was not enough towards providing equal education. The court specifically stated that school districts must provide special assistance to students in a language they can understand, as well as teaching English, to ensure that language minority youth are provided meaningful opportunity to participate in educational programs. Failure to provide these services to students is a violation of the Civil Rights Act of 1964 (Cortes, 1986).

Language issues continue to challenge the Mexican American population. The 1987 passage of Proposition 63 in California declared English to be the official language of the state, thus denying many citizens freedom of language. The 1990 census indicates that out of the 31 million non-English speakers in the United States, the majority, 17 million, are Spanish speakers (U.S. Bureau of the Census, 1990). Out of the 17 million Spanish speakers, four and one-half million do not speak English well or at all (U.S. Bureau of the Census, 1990). Yet, they are expected to learn and speak English exclusively.

In 1994, Proposition 187 raised the question of equal rights for education, health, and other social services in California. While initially the focus of this proposition was on illegal immigrants, the anti-immigrant sentiment eventually led to include legal resident immigrants. The difference between this event and previous animosity against immigrants was that politicians were not the only ones wanting to limit immigration. Organized labor and many traditional defenders of minority civil rights helped create the momentum for Proposition 187 (Goldenberg, 1996). In addition, almost one-third of California's Hispanics supported Proposition 187 (Goldenberg, 1996). Negative sentiments towards immigrants continue to exist among the majority population and among second, third, and fourth generation Hispanics who fear loss of jobs and opportunities.

Immigration continues to be a significant factor for some Mexican Americans. While a large proportion of the Mexican American population has been in the United States for centuries, others are first or second generation residents who continue to have ties with Mexico. In 1994, of the Hispanic population with origins in Mexico, 62.3% were born in the United States and 36.2% were born in Mexico (Goldenberg, 1996).

Current Status of Schooling Factors
"In a nation that prides itself on the ideal of upward social mobility, the ability to rise above one's social origins is heavily dependent on attaining a quality education" (Meier & Stewart, 1991, p.2). Public schools continue to be political institutions which are affected by public opinion and socio-economic factors. Current information reflects that this has not changed drastically within the last century, as Carrasquillo will illustrate in the following chapter. Many Mexican American children continue to experience unequal educational and achievement opportunities and continue to lag significantly behind non-Hispanic white and other Hispanic groups as well (Meier & Stewart, 1991; Carrasquillo, 1991; Valdiviesco, 1990; Trueba, 1989).

Factors which have historically affected Mexican Americans' equal educational opportunity continue to exist in the 1990s and are likely to continue to negatively affect opportunities. School segregation continues to be present in the experience of many Mexican American children. For example, Espinoza and Ochoa (1986) found that,

> California Hispanic students, even in the earliest grades, are highly concentrated in segregated schools where the average achievement level is seriously lower than in schools attended by Anglo students. This same pattern holds through all the grade levels....[A] student of above average potential in a Hispanic neighborhood would be very likely to attend a school with less challenging classmates and lower than average expectations than a similar Anglo student. If the well-established trends toward increased isolation of Hispanic students have continued to operate since the late 1970's, the pattern may well be more extreme today. This may well point to one of the key mechanisms by which educational inequality is perpetuated and by which talented students are denied the opportunity for equal preparation for college. (p. 95)

Other factors, such as teacher preparation, access to core curriculum, and funding continue to be relevant in the quality of education Mexican American students receive. The curriculum provided and teacher expectations of Mexican American children are often considerably lower than for the general student population (Orfield, 1988 as stated in Wells, 1989). In addition, less qualified and experienced teachers work in low-income neighborhoods (Orfield, 1988 as stated in Wells, 1989). Meier & Stewart (1991) indicate that when bilingual programs were first implemented, not enough bilingual teachers were trained. Thus, bilingual programs in practice became remedial programs which stigmatized children, not the enrichment programs which they were intended to be.

With respect to funding, Hispanic students are prone to attend schools with traditionally lower funding bases. McLeod (1994) indicates that "studies in California and Texas found that as the proportion of Hispanic students increased, per-pupil expenditures....decreased" (p. 28). Additionally, the distribution of funds from programs designed to assist minority students has been questioned. Trueba (1989) states that "all the money spent by the government from 1968 to date has reached only a fraction of the eligible student population"(p. 35).

Academic achievement for Hispanic students continues to be a major problem which is reflected in lower levels of educational and occupational attainment. "Many students read two or more grade levels below grade placement and comparatively few score at advanced levels on standardized tests" (Sosa, 1990, p.2). Academic grouping into lower-ability group classes is a phenomenon that affects Mexican American students more than African-American and non-Hispanic white students (Meier & Stewart, 1991). This has primarily been an artifact of bias standardized testing, especially when considering students for compensatory or special programs. Historically, a disproportionate number of Hispanic students have been placed in special education classes.

In 1986, Hispanic students were 13% more likely to be in classes for the educable mentally retarded than non-Hispanic whites, 52% less likely to be in classes for the gifted, three and one-half times more likely than the average student to be placed in bilingual classes, 10% more likely to be suspended, 43% more likely to be expelled (Meier & Stewart, 1991). Mexican Americans, as well as other Hispanics, are disproportionately assigned to lower academic groups, kept out of higher academic settings, and punished more frequently (Meier & Stewart, 1991).

Hispanics continue to have the highest high school dropout rate among the three groups. The estimated dropout rate in 1995 for Hispanics was 11.6%, while the dropout rate was estimated to be 5.1% for non-Hispanic whites and 6.1% for African-Americans (U.S. Census, 1990). This indicates that Hispanic students are twice as likely to dropout of high school than non-Hispanic whites or African Americans.

While certain bilingual education programs have been found to be effective when compared to English immersion instructional programs (Ramirez, 1991; Thomas & Collier, 1995; and Willig, 1985) , only a few students have access to instruction in their native language. Meier and Stewart's study found that in 1986, only 18.2% of Hispanics in the districts surveyed were enrolled in bilingual classes (1991). Moreover, Wells (1989) stated that even in schools with predominantly Hispanic student enrollment, approximately 84% of Hispanic students were not receiving the bilingual education they were legally eligible for under the Civil Rights Act of 1964.

While many Mexican American students have had success in various programs at micro levels (i.e., in maintenance or dual language programs based at individual sites, Thomas & Collier, 1995), Mexican Americans as a group have not had much success at macro levels, which involve equal and consistent opportunities in various settings for all students. Discrimination, lack of social acceptance, segregation, inadequate appropriation of school facilities. and deficient curriculum, materials, teachers, and funds continue to affect opportunities for equal educational attainment among many Mexican Americans (Carrasquillo, 1991; Meier & Stewart, 1991; Trueba, 1989).

Conclusion

A country's educational system reflects its society, its views, and its perspectives. It was not until the second half of this century that the general society became more cognizant regarding concerns associated with the education of Mexican American and other minority children. Psychosocial variables and schooling factors affecting the Mexican American population have not changed significantly in the last century and continue to play a significant role in educational access. Mexican American children continue to experience and suffer the same hardships as their parents and grandparents. The historical review presented in this chapter illustrates that there continues to be a gap between Mexican American students and students from the majority culture with regard to educational attainment and advantages.

Educational inequality is alive and well in America, albeit more subtle than in the first half of this century. Segregated schools, ineffective programs and teachers, inappropriate materials and curriculum, funding factors, and discriminatory discipline practices continue to be prevalent in public education for Hispanic children. It is imperative that educators, legislators, parents, and the general public understand that the historical psychosocial variables and school factors which impact upon the education of Mexican American and other minority school age children have not yet dissipated. The disparities in opportunities and performance experienced by Mexican American and other minority children make it imperative for educators and the general public to learn from the past in order to provide equal access for all students in the future.

References

Bartolome, L. I. (1994). Teaching strategies: Their possibilities and limitations. In McLeod, B. (Ed.), *Language and learning* (pp. 199-224). Albany, NY: State University of New York Press.

Baruch, D. W. (1946). *Glass house of prejudice.* New York: William Morrow and Company.

Bogardus, E. S. (1930). The Mexican immigrant and segregation. *The American Journal of Sociology, 36,* 74-80.

California's children. (1947, April 14). *Newsweek, 31(15),* 93.

Carrasquillo, A. L. (1991). *Hispanic children and youth in the United States: A resource guide.* New York: Garland Publishing, Inc.

Carter, T. P. & Segura, R. D. (1979). *Mexican Americans in school: A decade of change.* New York: College Entrance Examination Board.

Cooke, W. H. (1949). The segregation of Mexican-American school children in southern California. *School and Society, 67(1745),* 417-422.

Cortes, C.E. (1986). Schooling language minority students. In, Beyond language: Social and cultural factors in school language minority students (p3-34). Sacramento CA: California State Department of Education.

Dinnerstein, L., Nichols, R. I., & Reimers, D. M. (1979). *Natives and strangers.* New York: Oxford University Press.

Espinosa, R., & Ochoa, A. (1986). Concentration of California Hispanic students in schools with low achievement: A research note. *American Journal of Education, 95(1),* 77-95.

Garcia, A. M. (1989). A Mexican-American community's struggle for educational equality. *The Journal of Ethnic Studies, 17(3),* 133-139.

Garth, T. R. Intelligence of Mexican school children. *School and Society, 27,* 791-794.

Goldenberg, C. (1996). Latin American immigration and U.S. schools. *Social Policy Report: Society for Research in Child Development, Vol. 1 (1).* 1-29.

Higham, J. (1981). Integrating America: The problem of assimilation in the nineteenth century. *Journal of American Ethnic History, 1(1),* 6-25.

Jenks, J. W., Lauck, W. J. & Smith, R. D. (1922). *The immigration Problem: A study of American immigration conditions and needs.* New York: Funk & Wagnalls Company.

Lau v. Nichols, 414 U.S. 563 (1974).

Manuel, H. T. (1934). The educational problem presented by the Spanish-speaking child of the southwest. *School and Society, 40,* 692-695.

McLeod, B. (1994). Linguistic diversity and academic achievement. In McLeod, B. (Ed.), *Language and learning* (pp. 9-44). Albany, NY: State University of New York Press.

Meier, K. J. & Stewart, J. (1991). *The politics of Hispanic education: Un paso pa'lante y dos pa'tras.* New York: State University of New York Press.

Mendez et al. Vs. Westminister school District et al, 161 Federal Reporter (1943).

Mexican exodus. (1939, July 31). *Newsweek, 14 (5),*11.

Miranda, G. E. (1990). Mexican-Americans in the history of the United States. In A.J. Wrobel & M. J. Eula (Eds.), *American ethnics and minorities: Readings in ethnic history* (pp.71-89). Dubuque, IA: Kendall/Hunt Publishing Company.

Mitchell, A. J. (1937). The effect of bilingualism in the measurement of intelligence. *The Elementary School Journal, 38,* 29-37.

Penalosa, F. (1995). Toward an operational definition of the Mexican-American. In A. S. Lopez (Ed.), *Historical themes and identity: Mestizaje and labels* (pp.411-422). New York: Garland Publishing, Inc.

Phillips, H. (1931, September 1). The school follows the child. *The Survey, 96,* 493-495.

Ramirez, J. D. (1992). Executive summary. *Bilingual Research Journal, Vol. 16: (1&2).* 1-62.

Reynolds, A. (1933). The Education of Spanish-Speaking Children: In five Southwestern States. In U. S. Office of Education, Bulletin No. 11-15. Washington, D. C.: United States Government Printing Office, Publication # I16.3.

Ryan, J. J. & French, J. R. (1976). Long-term grade predictions for intelligence and achievement tests in schools of differing socio-economic levels. *Educational and Psychological Measurment, 36.* 553-559.

Schermerhorn, R. A. (1949). *These our people: Minorities in American culture.* Boston: D. C. Heath and Company.

Sedillo, A. (1995). *Historical themes and identity: Mestizaje and labels.* N. Y.: Garland Publishing Inc.

Shah, M. A. & Bhayana, K. M. (1978). Effect of socio-economic status and intelligence on acquisition of English language. *Psycho-lingua, Vol. VIII, I.* 43-48.

Sosa, A. (1990). Making education work for Mexican-Americans: Promising community practices. (Digest EDO-RC-90-2). Kentucky: ERIC Clearinghouse on Rural Education and Small Schools Institute for Urban and Minority Education.

Thomas, W. P. & Collier, V. P. (1995, September). *Language Minority Student achievement and Program Effectiveness.* Unpublished summary of ongoing study.

Trueba, H. T. (1989). *Raising silent voices: Educating the linguistic minorities for the 21st century.* Boston: Heinle and Heinle Publishers.

U.S. Bureau of the Census (1990). Current Population Survey (Annual high school dropout rates by sex, race, grade, and Hispanic origin: 1990,301). Washington, DC: U. S. Government Printing Office.

U.S. Bureau of the Census (1990). 1990 Census of Population (Detailed language spoken at home and ability to speak English: 1990, CPHL-133). Washington, DC: U. S. Government Printing Office.

U.S. Bureau of the Census (1990). 1990 Census of Population (Language use and English ability, persons 5 to 17 years, by state: 1990, CPHL-96). Washington, DC: U. S. Government Printing Office.

U.S. Bureau of the Census (1998). 1990 Census of Population (Poverty by race-ethnicity including unrelated persons: March 1996,Ethnic & Hispanic Statistics Branch, PPL-72). Washington, DC: U. S. Government Printing Office.

Valdiviesco, R. (1990). Demographic Trends of the Mexican-American Population: Implications for Schools (Digest EDO-RC-90-10). Charleston, WV: ERIC Clearinghouse on Rural Education and Small Schools.

Wang, P. H. (1974). The immigration act of 1924 and the problem of assimilation. *The Journal of Ethnic Studies, 2(3),* 72-76.

Weinberg, M. (1977). *A chance to learn: The history of race and education in the United States.* Cambridge, MA: Cambridge University Press.

Weinberg, M. (1983). *The search for quality integrated education: Policy and research on minority students in school and college.* Westport, CT: Greenwood Press.

Wells, A. S. (1989). Hispanic education in American: separate and unequal. (Digest EDO-UD-89-9). New York, NY: ERIC Clearinghouse on Urban Education, Institute for Urban and Minority Education.

Willig, A. C. (1985). A meta-analysis of selected studies on the effectiveness of bilingual education. *Review of Educational Research, 55(3),* pp. 269-317.

Wilson, H. E. (1952). Intercultural education and international relations. In, *One America: The history, contributions, and present problems of our racial and national minorities* (pp.578-582). New York: Prentice-Hall, Inc.

Woods, F. J. (1956). *Cultural values of American ethnic groups.* New York: Harper & Brothers, Publishes.

Woofter, T. J. (1933). *Races and ethnic groups in American life.* New York: McGraw-Hill Book Company, Inc.

CHAPTER 2

Profile of Hispanic Students in
United States Public Schools

Angela L. Carrasquillo

Introduction

The United States is a country of great linguistic and cultural diversity, which is evidenced most clearly among young and school-aged children. The diversity of language, customs, traditions, values, and ways of learning that students bring to a learning situation continues to inspire educators to meet increasing challenges in their role as educators. As we approach the beginning of the twenty-first century, educators are critically analyzing the changes or reforms that need to be undertaken in order to prepare themselves to educate all children, including those of Hispanic ancestry. The challenges Hispanic children and youth present to educators require programmatic and curricular reforms, as well as new leadership roles, all of which focus on providing educational equality and academic excellence.

This chapter provides a demographic profile of kindergarten through twelfth grade Hispanic students in United States public schools, describes their general educational characteristics, and lists general recommendations to assure educational equality and opportunities.

Hispanic Students in the United States:
A Demographic Overview

The Hispanic population within the United States continues to grow faster than the rest of the population as a whole. As the nation strives to motivate and engage students of all ages and grades to achieve their maximum intellectual and academic potential, educators have become concerned about the ability of schools to educate the increasing numbers of Hispanic students. The nation's ability to achieve national education goals is dependent upon its ability to educate students of different ethnic backgrounds, especially the limited English proficient, the African American, and the Hispanic. United States Census Bureau data shows that African American, Asian, and Hispanic populations are growing faster than the non-Hispanic white population (United States Bureau of the Census, 1996). In 1992, the United States Bureau of the Census projected that an increase in births among Hispanic women living in the United States, coupled with massive immigration, would increase the Hispanic population in the United States. Hispanics are projected to number 31 million in the year 2000, 63 million in 2030, and 88 million by 2050. By then, nearly one in four Americans may be Hispanic, and half of the United States population will be made up of African Americans, Hispanics, Asians and Native Americans.

The rapid growth of the Hispanic population in the 1990s is a continuation of trends over the past twenty years. In 1996, there were 28 million Hispanics living in the United States, of which 18 million were Mexican, 3.1 million Puerto Rican, and 4.05 million Cuban, Dominican, or South and Central American. As a result, about one in ten Americans today is Hispanic. However, the total United States population has grown much slower, increasing by only six percent. Two reasons for the rapid increase of the Hispanic population are higher birth rates for Hispanics than for non-Hispanics, and high levels of immigration (about 2 million Hispanic immigrants entered the United States between 1990 and 1994). One of the reasons for the increase in the foreign-born Hispanic population is family-based immigration, which refers to immigrants who become permanent residents and bring their relatives to the United States.

Although the Hispanic population in the United States is concentrated in six states, California, New York, Texas, Florida,

New Jersey and Illinois, almost every state has counties with substantial numbers of Hispanics. In New York State, for example, Westchester County, which traditionally was a non-Hispanic white ethnic county, has experienced a strong Hispanic mobility in cities such as Tarrytown, Yonkers, Yorktown, and Haverstraw. In addition, Miami is not the only Hispanic city in Florida; cities such as Orlando and Jacksonville are experiencing an influx of Hispanics. Orlando has a growing Puerto Rican population, many of whom are professionals who could not find employment in their area of specialization in Puerto Rico and work for entertainment agencies such as Disney World and Universal Studios.

There are demographic, social, and economic factors which have impacted upon the lives and schooling experiences of Hispanic children in the United States. Analysis of Census data published in September 1995 (Statistical Brief) and March 1996 (Current Population Survey) indicate the following:

- Hispanics are a young population. In 1994, their median age was 26 years, 10 years younger than non-Hispanic whites. Among Hispanic groups, the median age ranged from 24 years for persons of Mexican origin to 43 years for those of Cuban descent. In 1996, 36% of the Hispanic population (10.3 million) were under the age of 18.
- In 1994, over one-third (39%) of Hispanics were born outside the United States, compared with 3% of non-Hispanic whites.
- More than half of all Hispanics have a high school diploma, and have made gains over recent decades in high school completion rates. Slightly over five in ten Hispanics, age 25 and over, were high school graduates in 1994, compared to more than four in ten in 1980. About 9% of Hispanics held bachelor's degrees in 1994.
- Most Hispanic families have married heads of household, 68% of Hispanic families were married couples in 1994; another 25% were maintained by a woman with no husband present. For non-Hispanic families, the corresponding figures were 79% and 17%, respectively.

- Hispanics are twice as likely to be poor (31%) as non-Hispanics (13%). Poverty rates for Hispanic families are more than twice as high as for non-Hispanic families. In 1993, about 27% of Hispanic families (compared to about 11% of non-Hispanic families) were poor. Among Hispanic groups, poverty rates ranged from an apparent low of 17% for Cuban families, to 35% for Puerto Rican families.
- In 1996, 47% of Hispanics lived in households with yearly incomes of less than $25,000 compared to 24% of non-Hispanic whites. Puerto Rican families have the lowest income; 48% of Mexicans lived in households with less than $25,000 compared to 55% for Puerto Rican households.
- Unemployment rates vary among Hispanic groups. In 1994, unemployment ranged from 7% for Cubans to as high as 14% for Puerto Ricans. Overall, 11% of Hispanics and 6% of non-Hispanic whites were unemployed.
- The occupational distribution of Hispanics has representation in a range of occupations: managerial (14%), technical/administrative support (27%), service occupations (22%), farming/forestry/fishing (5%) production/ craft/repair (11%) and operators/ laborers/fabricators (22%).
- Poverty among certain groups of Hispanic children is higher than the rates for all Hispanics. For example, 66% of Puerto Rican children live in households with incomes of less than $25,000.

The growth of Hispanic student enrollment has had an enormous impact on educational systems and on the quality of education offered to students. Hispanic children make up a significant percentage of the overall public school population in the United States (Carrasquillo, 1991; Lara, 1994). Thirty-six percent of the Hispanic population is under age 18, and consists of 11.9% of United States public school students. New York City is a living example of the challenges that lie ahead for educators. In 1996, there were 1075,605 students enrolled in public schools in New York City. Of those, 37% were Hispanics, 36% were African Americans, 16% were non-Hispanic whites, and 10% were Asian. This student demographic trend is evident in other large urban areas such as Los Angeles, California; Dade County, Florida; Hartford, Connecticut; and Chicago, Illinois. In addition to New York City, disparities between non-Hispanic white and Hispanic students are especially pronounced in California, the state with the largest Hispanic population.

Hispanic Students' Academic Achievement and Educational Attainment

More rigorous levels of academic achievement will be required for students to meet educational, social, economic, and professional demands of the twenty-first century. Significant progress has been made in the last twenty years with regard to improving the social conditions of schooling, increasing high school graduation rates, and steady but small improvements in achievement within the core academic subject areas. Since the 1989 Education Summit and the adoption of Goals 2000 in 1990, the National Goals Panel have presented reports to measure progress towards the national educational goals through the year 2000. Available data (National Education Goals Panel, 1996) of prenatal care, birth weight, children's health index, children's nutrition, family-child language, and school learning activities tend to indicate limited learning opportunities and limited preschool participation for all United States school children.

National Education Goals Panel data indicated that in 1992 few students in the United States were able to demonstrate competency with content or skills within challenging subject matter (mathematics, reading, science, and foreign languages). In its 1996 report, the National Educational Goals Panel found that national educational performance is still far short of the ambitious goals set for the year 2000 (National Educational Goals Panel, 1996). The reported data revealed that, in general, most American students did not attain the expected high school completion rate of 90%. The Panel also found the following negative trends: a large gap between minority students (especially Hispanics) and non-Hispanic white high school graduates; 18-24 year-old Hispanics and African Americans were as far behind non-Hispanic whites in their age group as the proportion who had completed high school in 1995 and in 1994, and the gap in pre-school attendance between children from high-income and low-income families is still about 28%.

Education Week's report card on the 1994 condition of public education in the United States found that only three in ten of all fourth graders were reading at a proficient or advanced level. Nearly seven in ten eighth graders with the best records in mathematics cannot meet the mathematics proficiency level (Education Week, 1996). However, the public school system as a whole is making some strides towards improving schooling experiences for students. The National Goals Panel (1996) found positive social and educational trends such as: (a) fewer infants being born with one or more health risks, (b) more students receiving degrees in math and science, and (c) fewer incidents of in-school threats and violence.

Although all public school students are not performing at desired performance levels, Hispanics and African Americans are still far behind non-Hispanic white students. No matter what criterion is used (grades, tests scores, dropout rates, college acceptance rates), Hispanic students as a group do not perform as well in school as their majority group counterparts in school. High school completion for Hispanics dropped from 31% to 29%. Unfortunately, school failure still persists among a disproportionate number of Hispanic students. Data summarized by Wagoner (1997) from various national reports on the condition of public schools in the United States present the following facts:

- According to Census Bureau statistics (1993), the high school completion rates in 1993 for non-Hispanic whites twenty five years or older were 81.5% compared to 53.1% for Hispanics.
- Although the levels of educational attainment of Hispanic students as measured by such factors as high school graduation, daily attendance records, persistence rates, and levels of academic proficiency are increasing, dropout rates continue to be a major problem. In 1993, the average national dropout for Hispanics was 30.7%, almost two and a half times that of African Americans and more than four times that of non-Hispanic whites. (U.S. Department of Education, 1994). In 1994, the dropout rate was 11% for all groups in the United States, 8% for non-Hispanic whites, 14% for blacks, and an alarming 28% for Hispanic students (National Goals Panel Report, 1994, p. 42). In 1999, the dropout rate is still high for African Americans as well as for Hispanic students. In some school districts,

the dropout rates exceeds the national average. For example, in California, Hispanics have the highest dropout rates of all ethnic groups. In Chicago, Boston, New York, and Philadelphia school districts, the dropout rate for Puerto Ricans has been as high as 70% (Nieto, 1995). Reasons for dropping out vary, with an alarming number of youths citing pregnancy and conflicts with jobs.

- Hispanics have the lowest levels of educational attainment of any major population group. For example, in 1994, 13% of fourth grade Hispanic students were able to read at the proficient level, showing great disparities between non-Hispanic whites and Hispanics. In California, about a quarter of the non-Hispanic white public school fourth graders read proficiently, and were more than four times as likely to do so as their Hispanic classmates, only 6 % of whom read proficiently. In three other states with large Hispanic population (New York, Texas, and Florida), 31 to 39% of non-Hispanic white public school students read proficiently, two to three times more than Hispanic children.

The overall academic profile of Hispanic students sends mixed messages. It is encouraging to see that the significant declines which all groups experienced in the early 1980s were counteracted by some recovery during 1990, 1992, and 1995. The fact that Hispanic students made small but steady gains in reading, science, and mathematics achievement was also encouraging. But recent national reports (National Educational Goals Panel, 1994, 1996; Children's Defense Fund, 1997; National Center for Educational Statistics, 1995,1996) are not so encouraging for any ethnic group, especially African Americans and Hispanic. There is a large gap between Hispanic student achievement and that of non-Hispanic whites. Another sad fact is that although Hispanic students are making steady and small academic progress, their dropout rate is still high and their high school completion rate has declined in recent academic years.

Barriers to Hispanic Students' School Performance

In educating Hispanic students, educational policy makers, administrators, and teachers face many challenges today. Hispanic infants born in 1995 will enter the first grade in the year 2001. Will the nation be able to say that Hispanic students are as ready to learn when compared to any other group of six year-olds? Failure to recognize that the Hispanic student population is diverse in aspects such as language, culture, English proficiency, educational backgrounds and preparation, and grade and age when first enrolled in school, will seriously hinder the academic achievement of Hispanic students. Case studies by Hodgkinson (1991) and Wong-Filmore (1991) indicated various factors which act as barriers to high academic achievement of a significant number of Hispanic students such as: socioeconomic factors, variety of language backgrounds, English proficiency, and educational inequalities in the provision of school experiences.

Variety of Language Backgrounds and English Proficiency

Hispanic students in the United States reflect a variety of language backgrounds and language proficiencies. There is a misconception that most Hispanic students in United States schools speak Spanish as their primary language. In New York State, for example, of the 480,594 students identified as Hispanic in 1996, only 28% were identified as limited English proficient (New York State Department of Education, 1997). Some Hispanic students speak only English, some are bilingual in English and their native language (Spanish), and still others either do not speak English at all or have limited English-speaking skills. A final group show equal deficiencies in both English and Spanish. It is then fair to say that Hispanic students show various degrees of language proficiency. For simplicity, these students can be grouped into three broad language proficiency areas: the proficient bilingual, the partial bilingual, and the limited bilingual.

Proficient bilingual Hispanic students are those individuals who show well-developed competencies in both their native and English language, and have attained an approximately equal level of proficiency in both languages. It is assumed that these students can communicate and achieve goals in English and their native (Spanish) language. Partially bilingual Hispanic students usually attain native-like proficiency in the full range of understanding, speaking, reading, and writing in one language, usually a language other than English, but achieve less than native-like skills in some or all of the skill areas in English. Limited bilingual Hispanic students either show deficits or are at an early stage of development in both languages, especially in vocabulary, language usage and functions, as well as the processing and usage of both languages creatively.

Some Hispanic students have neither the experience nor the opportunity to function in all-English classrooms. However, because they were born in the United States, or because they show some level of oral English communicative skills, they are placed in classrooms in which they are required to use more abstract academic English then they have yet mastered. Their limited English proficiency (LEP), coupled with a curriculum that is often non-stimulating, results in lack of academic success. The United States is currently experiencing an increasing representation of LEP students in schools, placing unprecedented demands on teachers, administrators, and educational policy makers. Particularly striking has been the growth rate of Hispanic LEP students.

There is a growing influx of immigrant Hispanic students with little or no education in their home countries. Chronologically, they mainly fall into the upper elementary and middle school levels; they are semi-literate and sometimes pre-literate in their own language and do not understand, speak, read, or write English. They may have experienced separation from family, physical deprivation, or other hardships. These Hispanic students are at the greatest risk of not succeeding academically, dropping out, or not graduating from high school. The New York State Department of Education (1997) conducted a survey of LEP students with interrupted formal schooling and found three main characteristics of these students. First, they came from a home where a language other than English is spoken and enter a school in the United States after grade two. Second, upon enrollment, they have had at least two years less schooling than their peers. Third, they function at least two years below expected grade level in reading and mathematics.

On the national level, identified LEP students' enrollment population increased by 56% between 1985 and 1992 (U.S. Department of Education, 1993). There are between 2.3 million and 3.5 million school age children and youth in the United States who are LEP students (Lara, 1994; United States Department of Education, 1993). It has been repeated in the literature that LEP students show language characteristics that are different from English proficient students (Carrasquillo & Rodriguez, 1996). These language characteristics may affect Hispanic students' academic success in all-English classrooms. Success in building capacity for the educational system to address the needs of the LEP student population will require collaboration and concerted efforts at the federal, state, and local levels. While some progress has been achieved, still more initiatives remain to be put in place.

Socioeconomic Factors

In 1971, ten million children in the United States were poor; in 1995, 14 million children, or one in five, were poor. Moreover, the youngest children, those under age six, constitute the largest portion of the growth in poverty, from 3.5-5.7 million children, or one in four (Children's Defense Fund, 1997). Of 14.8 million children in female-headed households in 1992, 54% were poor. The National Center for Children in Poverty (1990) indicated that of the 21.9 million children under six years of age, 5 million (23%) were living in poverty. In 1996, 53% of Hispanic children lived in households with income of $25,000 a year, or less.

Other factors affecting children include the loss of private health coverage for children of working parents, increasing inequalities in family income, and the need for adequate child care. The data provided by the Children's Defend Fund (1997) indicates that many children, especially minorities, will enter school in the twenty-first century unable to meet the National Educational Goal of "readiness to learn." Garcia (1993) indicated that although less than 30% of all children under six years of age were Hispanic, over 50% of the children living in poverty were Hispanic.

Hispanic children in the United states are three times more likely to be poor than children in comparable non-Hispanic families. Poverty translates into poor housing, isolated neighbor-hoods, poor nutrition, and lack of health insurance. In general, the parents of language minority students have a hard time getting access to health care. For example, Hispanics suffer from in-creased incidences of asthma, diabetes, tuberculosis, certain cancers, and AIDS; yet, they are less likely than other Americans to report a regular source of medical care. This is largely because they work in industries and occupations which are less likely to provide health care benefits (Carrasquillo, 1991; Children's Defense Fund, 1997; Garcia, 1993).

Inequality of Educational Experiences

A main reason for Hispanic students' low academic performance is that their education is not specifically included as a facet of the United States educational system. Large numbers of Hispanic students continue to receive instruction that is substandard to what mainstream non-Hispanic white students receive, and are disproportionately enrolled in special education programs, vocational courses, and lower track classes. Hispanic students are also under-represented in high track and college preparatory programs. In many instances, these students are not expected to meet the same high standards as "mainstream" children. A large number of Hispanic students attend schools in urban cities, which traditionally have less money, fewer resources, poorer facilities, more inexperienced teachers, fewer qualified teachers, greater management problems, and high turnover rates among teachers and administrators. Many Hispanic students tend to be enrolled in educational "tracks" which prepare students for neither college nor stable employment. For example, a high percentage of Hispanic youth are in non-academic tracks which do not offer the required courses, especially in mathematics and science, to enter college.

Hispanic students are highly under-represented in college preparatory and gifted and talented programs. Hispanic students are encouraged to take fewer years of course work in mathematics, physical sciences, and social studies than non-Hispanic white students . Even in subjects in which the years of course work are similar, the content of the courses differs substantially. For example, although Hispanic high school students are as likely as non-Hispanic white students to have taken three years or more of mathematics, they are less likely to have taken algebra, geometry, trigonometry, or calculus and more likely to have taken general and business math (National Center for Education Statistics, 1996; United States Department of Education, 1994).

The placement of Hispanic students in vocational courses occurs earlier in their school career, and the programs differ substantially in kind and content for non-Hispanic white students. For example, Hispanic students are often assigned to vocational programs that train specifically for low-status occupations (cosmetology, building maintenance, clerical jobs), while other vocational programs prepare students for managerial training and business finance (Carrasquillo, 1991; Lara, 1994; Nieto, 1995). The enrollment of Hispanic students in academic programs is unequally distributed. In addition, there is no coordination among programs designed for students who need compensatory educational services. Federal programs such as Bilingual Education, Title 1, and Migrant Education offer fragmented services to students, thus only partially meeting their academic needs. The beneficiaries of Title 1 education (supplementary educational services for educationally and economically disadvantaged children in kindergarten through twelfth grades) included about 27% of Hispanics in 1994 (U.S. Department of Education, 1994).

Achieving Educational Equality

What needs to be done? The social, economic, ethnic, and linguistic diversity of the school population necessitate systemic educational reform. School reforms must address Hispanic students' linguistic, cultural, and cognitive characteristics, as well as provide appropriate and effective teaching and learning practices to educate all students according to their needs, characteristics, and strengths. Because students of Hispanic ancestry traditionally experience less success in school, there is a need for educational policy makers, parent advocacy groups, and educators to provide physical access to the same schools and instructional programs as other students. The following solutions respond to specific Hispanic students' educational needs and opportunities.

Establish High Expectations for Student Achievement
Educators need to prove that they have high expectations for Hispanic students. How can the moderate gains in the achievement profiles of Hispanic students be explained? One possible explanation is that teachers and instructional programs are beginning to acknowledge and respond to these students' academic needs and motivation.

However, these small successes are not enough to prepare these students to meet the high academic standards of the twenty-first century. Educators need to challenge these students in the classroom and outside of school, to empower them and their parents to take ownership and responsibility for their own learning. Perhaps writers, such as myself, have contributed to educators' low academic expectations of Hispanic students. On several occasions, I have identified the learning deficits of

Hispanic students with the purpose of informing educators that the ways they are teaching are not producing academic success. Thus, there is a need to advocate for appropriate educational experiences and expectations for these students. High expectations are necessary to provide students with a challenging curriculum, effective instructional strategies, qualified teachers, availability of school resources, and a highly focused self-esteem program, to motivate students to learn and stay in school.

Implement a Focused Academic Curriculum
    The education of Hispanic students requires a highly focused academic curriculum. Hispanic students can greatly benefit from the movement toward higher standards for all students. All students need to be skillful in mathematics, reading, writing, science, language arts, history, music, and art. All classrooms should adopt curriculum frameworks which focus on the development of a community of learners and problem solvers. Academic performance may be the result of curriculum differences that already exist between non-Hispanic white and Hispanic students in elementary and secondary schools. For the most part, these students are not enrolled in similar kinds of courses, nor are they receiving equal status instruction. It is not surprising then, that there is variance in their academic achievement.
    Curriculum is the outcome of deliberate decisions and interrelated plans which students undertake under the guidance of the school, for the purpose of making impacts in their academic and cognitive development (Tyler, 1992; Marsh & Willis, 1995). All educators are involved in making decisions about curriculum content and teaching by constantly monitoring and adjusting ends and means. A challenging school curriculum encourages the active participation of learners in their own learning and provides them with opportunities to internalize the criteria for making decisions and judgments. Ideally, development of the intellect, learning to learn, decision making, creativity and problem solving become the subject matter of instruction. Thus, the content selected becomes a vehicle to practice the thinking processes and skills and the provision of learning experiences are the activities which offer opportunities for students to reach the objectives specified. Tyler (1992) asserted that learning experiences must be selected so that students have sufficient opportunities to experience and complete the tasks required of them successfully.

School academic content must provide a multicultural curriculum that is integrated throughout the curriculum, rather than taught in isolated, fragmented, units on special occasions. The concept of culture can be seen as a continuum, with people demonstrating characteristics ranging from traditional roles to more contemporary ones. The curriculum thus includes content that looks at the customs, folklore, values, and language of diverse people and cultures which make up the United States, and those groups represented in the classroom. The most fundamental aspect in this process is that all members of the school, the school district, and the community understand that although not every student in the educational setting is proficient in English, the educational experiences provided to all students should emphasize a first class curriculum.

Reconceptualize Methods of Teaching Students

It is imperative that in meeting the educational needs of Hispanic students, those responsible for instruction in schools must have the authority and competency to make that vision a reality. Teachers are undoubtedly the major participants in students' learning. Successful teaching requires pedagogical and content area knowledge and a deep understanding of the student population. If we require changes in curriculum standards, teachers will need to improve their knowledge of content and teaching methodology.

Teachers have many factors to consider when planning and delivering instruction to students, especially for those who may not be from their own ethnic or socioeconomic background. Teachers must consider their own philosophy of education (child centered, teacher centered, constructivist), the content to be taught, how this content will be organized and presented, the strategies they will use, and the materials needed to present the content. Teachers must have background knowledge in how Hispanic students learn, how to motivate them, and how to approach Hispanic parents to become more involved in their children's education.

Teachers must be able to reflect upon the learning process occurring in the classroom, and the goals and objectives they have set up for their students. Teachers must be knowledgeable about classroom management and how to integrate everyone into the process of learning. Stanz (1994) defined successful teachers as those with a "deep personal commitment to their subject area, having clear instructional objectives and goals and establishing an environment which encourages interaction and activity" (p. 5). It is expected that by the year 2000 the United States teaching force will have sufficient professional skills to instruct and prepare *all* American students. However, the current situation is that teachers, especially those working in districts with large numbers of language minority students, remain unprepared or uncertified. It is ironic that the best qualified and prepared teachers are not placed in schools with the greatest educational and instructional needs.

To meet the unique needs of all students, instruction may have to be organized differently, perhaps around individual students' work or sub-groups within the class. Organizing the school curriculum by subject areas (i.e., the history class, the science class, the French class) has proven to be unsuccessful in challenging Hispanic students on the basis of effort, ability, and level of development. These students may feel overwhelmed and lost within all of these academic subjects. Perhaps, curricula will have to be rethought around integrated themes of subject areas, as well as around the individual and collaborative experiences of students themselves.

Conclusion

Setting high expectations for all children will increase educational equality, provided that appropriate, high-quality instruction and other essential resources are available. The United States school population is diverse, not only in terms of ethnicity, race, and language, but also in terms of socioeconomic, academic, and educational backgrounds. This diversity challenges educators to look at the forces which inhibit students, especially Hispanic students, from becoming successful learners and professionals. Appropriately addressing the diversity within the Hispanic school population is critical to the implementation of school and instructional strategies to raise academic standards and academic performance. We may not change the immediate academic achievement of Hispanic students. However, as educators, we can improve the expectations we have for these students, offer them a highly focused curriculum, and provide them with excellent learning and teaching opportunities.

For decades, it has been said that Hispanic students are not performing at the same rate as their non-Hispanic white counterparts. But the United States educational system has failed to provide school experiences to change the failure rate of these students. The message for educators and educational policy makers is to look at *all* students opportunities to learn, readiness to start schooling, school facilities, learning environment, quality of school curricula, and preparation and competency of teachers. Required learning opportunities and experiences for these students should be based upon educational reforms provided in Goals 2000 and reinforced by the emphasis on academic standards in all subject areas at the local, state, and national levels.

Every national educational reform has entailed a redefinition of roles and responsibilities at all levels. Individuals involved in the education of public school students must participate in the development of a common vision for the nation's children. The United States national educational objectives for students foresees a structured educational system that will hold all students to high common academic standards. The idea behind these objectives is the implementation of academic standards to improve teaching, provide additional and richer learning experiences, which should result in greater success for all students. This vision will include eliciting public and professional participation, creating state plans, developing content and performance standards, and providing guidance to school districts towards meeting defined goals.

The school curriculum should be tailored to students' needs and strengths to provide rich opportunities for literacy development across the curriculum. The curriculum must include comprehension of content, critical thinking, problem solving, reading, and writing development, with an emphasis on collaborative learning and problem solving activities. It should provide a variety of subject areas with the objective of moving students to the most challenging processes and skills. For example, students at the high school level should have the opportunity to not only take Algebra, and Geometry but also Calculus and Trigonometry. Students should be involved in learning experiences and activities related to their aspirations and interests. This is in direct conflict with the traditional academic emphasis placed upon Hispanic students to acquire merely basic English skills to the exclusion of other subjects.

Educators need to deliver instruction taking into consideration Hispanic students' linguistic levels, cultural diversity, and learning styles, and see these characteristics as strengths rather than deficits. For those Hispanic students who are not proficient in English, the curriculum also needs to provide access to challenging content while the students are acquiring English. This reconceptualization requires that educators carefully find ways to meet the needs of Hispanic students in achieving content standards in subject matter areas such as mathematics, science, social studies, English language, reading, and writing. Programs must be designed and administered to provide opportunities for the implementation of language and culturally enriching curricula, challenging content with high expectations for all students, and extracurricular support systems. School principals, content area supervisors, as well as teachers need to plan and develop approaches to meet the unique needs of Hispanic students.

Hispanic students must be provided with the opportunity to learn the same challenging content and high level skills that school reform movements advocate for all students. High expectations for Hispanic students include the implementation of challenging school experiences emphasizing problem-situated learning, judgment, organization, and collaboration. These school activities/experiences typically involve more than one content area, reflecting the interdisciplinary nature of learning in the real world. At the same time, teaching must be a team effort in which teachers' talents, knowledge, and skills are used to the maximum. In this way, all students have access to at least one teacher who is top notch in each area. Local school districts should specifically address the recruitment, training, and development of teachers and aides to provide effective instruction for all students. Staff training should not only revolve around certification requirements, but focus on content areas, instructional methodology, theories of learning, students' diverse learning characteristics, and motivational strategies.

References

Carrasquillo, A.L. (1991). *Hispanic children and youth in the United States*. New York: Garland.

Carrasquillo, A.L., Rodriguez, V. (1996). *Language minority students in the mainstream classroom*. Clevedon, England: Multilingual Matters

Children's Defense Fund (1997). State of America's children: Yearbook. Washington, DC: Author.

Education Week. (1996). *Quality counts: A report card of the condition of public education in the 50 states.* : DC: Author.

Garcia, E. E. (1993). Language, culture and education. In L Darling-Hammond (Ed.). *Review of research in education* (pp. 51-98). Washington, DC: American Educational Research Association.

Hodgkinson, H. (1991). Reform vs reality. *Phi Delta Kappan, 73,* 8-16.

Lara, J. (1994). Demographic overview: Changes in student enrollment in American schools. In K. Spangenberg-Urbschat & R. Pritchard (Eds.), *Kids come in all languages; Reading instruction for ESL students* (9-21). Newark, DE: International Reading Association.

Marsh, C. & Willis, G. (1995). *Curriculum: Alternative approaches, ongoing issues.* Englewood Cliffs, NJ: Simon & Schuster.

National Center for Children in Poverty (1990). Five million children: A statistical profile of our poorest young citizens. New York: Columbia University.

National Center for Education Statistics (1996). Vocational education in the United States: The early 1990s. Washington, DC: Government Printing Office.

National Center for Education Statistics (1995). Language characteristics and academic achievement : A look at Asian and Hispanic eight graders. Washington, DC: Government Printing Office.

National Educational Goals Panel (1996). The national education goals report. Washington, DC: Author.

National Educational Goals Panel (1994). The national education goals report. Washington, DC: Author.

New York State Department of Education (April 14, 1997). Building capacity: Addressing the needs of limited English proficient students, Albany, NY. Mimeographed.

Nieto, S. (1995). A history of the education of Puerto Rican students in U.S mainland schools: "Losers", "outsiders' or "leaders". In J. A. Banks & C. A. M. Banks (Eds.), *Handbook of Research on multicultural education* (pp. 388- 411). New York: Macmillan.

Stanz, C. (1994). *Classrooms that work: Teaching and learning generic skills.* Center focus, 1-5.

Tyler, R. (1992). The long-term impact of the Dewey school. *The Curriculum Journal, 3*(2),125-129.

United States Bureau of the Census (1996). Current population reports. Washington, DC: Government Printing Office.

United States Bureau of the Census (September, 1995). Statistical brief Current Population Reports. Washington, DC: Government Printing Office.

United States Bureau of the Census (1992). Population projections of the United States, by age, sex, race, and Hispanic origin: 1992-2050. Current Population Reports, P25-1092. Washington, DC: Government Printing Office.

United States Bureau of the Census (1993). Press release. CB9318. Washington, DC: Government Printing Office.

United States Department of Education (1994). Digest of education statistics. Washington, D. C.: U.S Government Printing Office

United States Department of Education (1993). Descriptive study of services to limited English proficient students. Washington, D. C.: Planning and evaluation Service.

Waggoner, D. (March, 1997). From the editor. *Number and Needs. 6*(2), 1-6.

Wong-Fillmore, L. (1991). Language and cultural issues in the early education of language minority children. In S. Kagan (Ed.). *The care and education of America's young children: Obstacles and opportunities. Ninetieth Yearbook of the National Society for the Study of Education, Part II* (pp. 30-49). Chicago, IL: University of Chicago Press.

SECTION II.

Issues of Access and Outcomes in the Elementary and Secondary Education of Hispanic Children

CHAPTER 3

Looking for Needles in a Haystack:
Hispanics in the Teaching Profession

Reynaldo F. Macías, Raymond E. Castro, &
Yolanda Rodríguez-Ingle

Introduction

Over the last two decades, colleges and universities around the United States have begun to recognize that there is a proportionately low representation of Hispanic[1] teachers in the teacher workforce. In addition, there is a need to instill in all educators a professional competency to teach *all* students. Some colleges and universities have adopted or developed programs to affirmatively address these issues by attempting to reduce barriers to access (including discriminatory practices), or by enhancing retention and completion rates of minorities throughout the educational pipeline (K-12, undergraduate, and professional education). In addition, there has been a growing movement to retain Hispanic teachers in the classroom and in the profession, and to develop alternative routes to teacher certification.

This chapter was designed to answer the questions:
(1) What is the distribution of Hispanic teachers in the profession today?
(2) What problems are there regarding access, preparation, and credentialing of Hispanic teachers? What strategies are there to address these problems?
(3) What are the working conditions and environments of Hispanic instructional personnel?

47

One should keep in mind the limited data sources in this area of research; there are national sources of data on the race and ethnicity of teachers, but little with much historical depth. There are few studies on the racial and ethnic composition of those who would become teachers, and even fewer work condition studies that have included and identified Hispanic teachers specifically.

Hispanic Teacher Representation in the United States

The composition of the United States population has been changing rapidly, particularly during the 1980s and 1990s. As seen in Table 1, the population has become more racially diverse with an increasingly larger and more varied immigrant segment. This is the result of differential rates of natural increase across the races as well as a more equitable system of immigration from nations from around the world since 1965. The previous national quota system favored applicants from western and northern Europe. This growth and diversification of the general population has been reflected in the school age population, as seen in Table 2. However, while the public school student enrollment has reflected this diversity, the national teaching force has become predominately more non-Hispanic white and female (Tables 3 & 4).

U.S. Census Bureau (1996) projections reflect a continued diversification of the national population, particularly the school-age cohorts. In their periodic population projections, the Census Bureau develop low, middle, and high series of population projections, typically over a 50 year span. These conservative Census Bureau projections tell us several things regarding the probable composition of our nation's population. The Bureau projects that the numerical dominance of the non-Hispanic white population will decrease to possibly less than half of the school age population in a little more than one generation. Net immigration may continue with an 80% minority contribution to the population growth. After 2020, Hispanics may contribute more net growth to the U.S. population than all other groups combined. The U.S. Census Bureau projects a continued disproportionate concentration of the foreign born in California over the next two generations, a state in which 40% of the Hispanic population resides. The implications for ethnic and language diversity for the country are staggering.

Table 1. Growth of the U.S. Population, by Race & Latino Origin, 1970-1996[2]

	1970*	1980		1990		1996	
	N	N	1970-80	N	1980-90	N	1990-96
Total U.S.	203,212,000	226,546,000	11.5%	248,718,000	9.8%	265,284,000	6.7%
White	178,098,000	180,906,000	1.6%	188,306,000	4.1%	193,978,000	3.0%
Black	22,581,000	26,142,000	15.8%	29,275,000	12.0%	31,912,000	9.0%
Am.Ind, Eskimo, Aleut	n/a	1,326,000	–	1,796,000	35.4%	1,954,000	8.8%
Asian/Pacific Islander	n/a	3,563,000	–	6,988,000	96.1%	9,171,000	31.2%
Total Non-Latino	194,139,000	211,937,000	9.2%	226,365,000	6.8%	237,015,000	4.7%
Hispanic	9,073,000	14,609,000	61.0%	22,354,000	53.0%	28,438,000	27.2%
Mexican	4,532,000	8,740,000	92.9%	13,496,000	54.4%	18,039,000	33.7%
Puerto Rican	1,429,000	2,014,000	40.9%	2,728,000	35.5%	3,123,000	14.5%
Cuban	545,000	803,000	47.3%	1,044,000	30.0%	1,127,000	8.0%
Other Hispanic	2,566,000	3,051,000	18.9%	5,086,000	66.7%	6,149,000	20.9%

Data Source: General Race, U.S. Census Bureau, 1998. pp. 14-19, Tables 12, 19; Latino, Del Pinal & Singer, 1997, p. 13, Table 3.

Table 2. Ethnic Diversity of Population by Selected Age & Race, 1980-90[1]

	1980			1990		
	5-17	18-24	25-64	5-17	18-24	25-64
White	35,653,000	22,752,000	87,564,000	31,236,400	18,437,150	98,322,650
Black	7,112,000	3,791,000	11,001,000	7,098,250	3,632,450	14,334,050
Asian/Pacific Islander	821,000	460,000	1,898,000	1,400,500	879,200	3,857,600
American Indian	378,000	215,000	590,000	428,850	252,300	796,300
Hispanic: Mexican	2,568,000	1,346,000	3,304,000	3,697,400	1,985,850	5,969,450
Puerto Rican	577,000	297,000	806,000	604,300	392,150	1,173,500
Cuban	143,000	100,000	461,000	145,750	90,200	542,450
Other Hisp.	720,000	440,000	1,382,000	937,050	601,850	2,427,000
Total population	48,046,000	29,438,000	107,105,000	45,627,000	26,288,200	127,495,950

Data Source: 1980 and 1990 Census. Public Use Micro-Data Samples (PUMS).

These changes have begun to show themselves in our public schools, and will continue into the future. The National Center for Education Statistics (NCES) also does projections of the age cohorts underlying the school enrollments of the nation. The Center projections for 5 to 17 year olds between 1993 and 2020, indicate a decline in the non-Hispanic white population and a growth for the African American, Hispanic and other groups (Table 3).

Table 3. Percentage change in the population of children, aged 5-17 years, by race, 1993-2020

	1993-2000		2000-2020	
	5-13 years	14-17 years	5-13 years	14-17 years
Non-Hispanic white	2.8%	10.1%	-11.2%	-10.3%
African American	12.9%	11.5%	15.4%	20.0%
Hispanic	29.8%	23.8%	47.0%	60.6%
Other	32.5%	45.1%	67.2%	73.3%

Data Source: NCES, 1997. *Condition of Education.* Washington, DC: USGPO, p. 3, Table 1.

Table 4. Ethnic diversity of public school enrollments and teacher labor force, 1990-91

	Enrollments		Teachers		Ratio
	N	%	N	%	%
American Indian	409,342	1.0%	17,301	0.7%	67.8%
Asian/Pacific Islander	1,379,231	3.4%	25,952	1.0%	30.2%
Hispanic	4,714,221	11.5%	80,046	3.1%	27.2%
African American	6,614,471	16.2%	233,893	9.2%	56.7%
Non-Hispanic white	27,719,311	67.9%	2,188,975	86.0%	126.7%
Totals	40,836,576	100.0%	2,546,167	100.0%	100.0%

Data Source: American Association of Colleges for Teacher Education, 1994, p. 7.

In fall 1996, California Hispanic students became the plurality within public school enrollment, at 44%. In addition, the 1.38 million limited English proficient student enrollment was 24% of the state's total school enrollment. Over the last several years, about half of the Hispanic and almost half of the Asian and Pacific Islander enrollment was limited English proficient (LEP). If this LEP proportion of the growing Hispanic, Asian, and Pacific Islander enrollment continues during the next 30 to 50 years, the need to address their English language proficiency will become a concern for all public school systems.

These projected demographics, particularly in the southwestern states, have created a struggle in producing more Hispanic and minority teachers, as well as preparing all teachers to teach effectively in classrooms with diverse ethnic enrollments. This phenomenon could easily be ignored, except Hispanics and other minorities often bring qualitative, "value-added" competencies and sensitivities to the teaching profession, due to their familiarity with the cultural and class backgrounds of minority students. In addition, many minority teachers bring bilingual competencies which greatly facilitate teaching, learning, communication, and interaction. These competencies and skills have been visibly absent from the liberal arts and professional education of the teaching profession, making personal, qualitative competencies all the more important.

There is a growing body of literature that points to the value, and need for a cultural fit, or synchronization, between students and teachers (see Losey, 1995, for a partial review). That is, the need to match the social and economic status, as well as the ethnicity, culture, and language of students and teachers for at least part of the twelve to sixteen years of schooling has a positive effect on the schooling of all students, but particularly those of under-represented minority groups. This is especially critical for students identified as being "at-risk" in school settings where the presence of minority role models in the teaching profession is noticeably absent (Castro, 1989; Galguera, 1998). While this need not take place in every classroom, there should be enough exposure to overcome the negative effects of a segregated teacher workforce.

Synchronization provides a number of benefits to minority and at-risk students. Meier (1993, as cited in The Tomás Rivera Center, 1993) identified seven positive effects that Hispanic teachers have on Hispanic elementary and secondary students: (1) fewer Hispanic students placed in educable, mentally retarded classes; (2) more Hispanic students identified as gifted; (3) lower rates of corporal punishment, out-of-school suspensions, alternative education assignments, and expulsions of Hispanic students; (4) lower Hispanic drop-out rates; (5) lower grade-retention rates of Hispanics; (6) higher Hispanic student scores on standardized math tests; and (7) higher Hispanic student scores on standardized communication tests. These effects were significantly correlated with the percent of the Hispanic teachers in a school, and provide support to the general value of diversifying the teacher work force.

Distribution of Hispanics in the Teaching Profession

The number of Hispanic teachers in the national teacher workforce is relatively small, amounting to about 4% in 1993-94, which was little changed from the previous decade as shown in Table 5. Non-Hispanic whites amounted to 87% of the teacher workforce, while African Americans accounted for 6.8%, and the other racial groups combined amounted to less than 2%. From one perspective, that of population parity, the teacher labor force in the country is very segregated and dominated by non-Hispanic whites. From another perspective, that of a comparison with the racial breakdown of the student enrollment, non-Hispanic whites were over-represented as teachers by 27%, while African American teachers were under-represented by 43%, and Hispanic teachers by 72%.

Table 5. Ethnic diversity of the teacher work force, the U.S., 1993-94

Race	N	%
Non-Hispanic white	2,228,641	87.2%
African American	173,793	6.8%
Asian/Pacific Islander	30,669	1.2%
American Indian	17,890	0.7%
Hispanic	104,787	4.1%
Totals	2,555,781	100.0%

Data Source: National Center for Education Statistics. 1996.

This suggests that in the future, minority and non-Hispanic white students alike will see fewer minority teachers over the course of their schooling. The effects of having fewer minority teachers in the classrooms are most visibly manifested in the lack of role models for minority students and limited experience for non-minority students to come in direct contact with minority teachers as professionals and as authority figures (The Commission on Minority Participation in Education and American Life 1988). The Task Force on Teaching as Profession sponsored by the Carnegie Corporation (Carnegie Forum on Education and the Economy, 1986) emphatically proposed that schools be staffed by a diverse teacher work force, "we cannot tolerate a future in which both [non-Hispanic] white and minority children are confronted with almost exclusively [non-Hispanic] white authority figures in the school."

Lack of exposure to minority teachers is further exacerbated because these teachers are concentrated in schools with predominately urban and minority student populations (NCES, 1993). In 1988, 64% of non-Hispanic white teachers in the nation were working in schools with less than 20% minority enrollments, whereas about 64% of African American and Hispanic teachers were working in schools with greater than 50% minority enrollments (Ibid.). This means that non-Hispanic white students in predominantly non-Hispanic white schools have a very low probability of coming in contact with minority teachers, much less Hispanic teachers, in their 13 years of K-12 schooling.

Table 6. Diversity of the teacher work force, by credential, California, 1994-95

	Total Persons		Credentials		Authorizations	
			Elem.	H.S.	Bilin-gual	ESL
	N	%	%	%	%	%
Non-Hispanic white	182,247	79.8%	79.4%	80.3%	48.3%	63.3%
African American	11,937	5.2%	5.3%	5.7%	2.9%	2.3%
Asian/Pacific Islander	10,381	4.5%	4.8%	4.4%	8.0%	3.9%
Amer. Indian	1,783	0.8%	0.7%	0.9%	0.5%	0.7%
Hispanic	20,980	9.2%	9.7%	8.5%	40.1%	29.6%
Totals	228,299	100.0%	100.0%	100.0%	100.0%	100.0%

Data Source: Special Tables from the California Dept. of Education, CA
                        Basic Educational Data, 1996.

In addition to the concentration of minority teachers in high minority schools, there has long been a need for teachers trained and credentialed (or licensed) to teach in bilingual and English as a second language classrooms. In 1988, over half (52%) of those authorized to teach in such situations were non-Hispanic white; 36% were Hispanic (NCES 1993). In California in 1995, the distribution was not much different. About half (48%) of the credentialed bilingual teachers were non-Hispanic white and almost a third (29.6%) were Hispanic (see Table 6). This pattern varies by state, however, and we should be reminded that these data reflect credentials and authorizations obtained by teachers, not actual teaching assignments. In Texas there is a much higher proportion of credentialed bilingual teachers who are Hispanic than in California.

Problems & Strategies Regarding Access & Preparation of Hispanic Teachers

The shortage of minority teachers has been documented extensively in several key national policy reports and articles. Organizations such as the American Council on Education (1988), the National Governors' Association (1991), the American Association of Colleges for Teacher Education (1988), and the Education Commission of the States (1990), to name a few, have documented the necessity for a comprehensive analysis of the recruitment, retention, and certification of minority students for the teaching profession. There is a consistent reference to a need for commitment on the part of educational institutions to target a cadre of minority applicants for the teacher pool to better reflect diversity and equity in the teaching profession. The significant decrease of minority teacher candidates entering the teaching profession, and the simultaneous dramatic increase of minority student enrollment at the K-12 level, has compounded the problem and stimulated efforts to focus on the recruitment of minorities into the teaching profession. The policy and political pressures created with the demise of Affirmative Action programs, and policies designed to increase the numbers of racial minorities in colleges and universities, have added to the challenges in diversifying the teaching profession.

Unlike the southern states which have "Historically Black Colleges and Universities" (HBCUs) to aid in the production of African American professionals, including teachers, there are no regions of the country with colleges and universities dedicated to the higher education of Hispanics. Southwestern four-year colleges and universities have been primarily dominated by individuals of non-Hispanic origin, and do not have a similar history or legacy of traditionally Mexican or Hispanic colleges.[3] Only in the Commonwealth of Puerto Rico are there colleges and universities run by and for Hispanic students, with either English or Spanish as the language of instruction, or in some cases both. These institutions, however, tend to prepare teachers for Puerto Rican public schools where the principal language of instruction is Spanish.

Teaching has historically been one of the few professions somewhat open to those few Hispanics who were able to secure access to post-secondary institutions. However, in recent years fewer minorities, including Hispanics, have chosen to enter into the education profession. Some of the reasons for this decline include: (1) the relatively small percentages of minority students in the teacher preparation pipeline (Macías, 1989); (2) obstacles linked to competency testing (Pritchy, 1987); (3) lack of recognition and rewards for teachers (Boyer, 1983); (4) negative public image about teaching (Alston, 1988); (5) minority student preference for other professions because of higher salaries and greater prestige (Garibaldi, 1987; Alston, 1988); (6) existence of few minority teacher role models; (7) limited number of comprehensive recruitment plans; and (8) lack of financial support for Hispanic students to attend college.

Heading this list is the limited educational pipeline. Participation in higher education has been a key to giving individuals opportunity and access to higher income levels and a better standard of living. Hispanics have higher drop-out rates in K-12 schooling and lower retention and completion rates in higher education than other groups. Non-Hispanic whites reached an average of twelve years of schooling in the early 1950s, while the nation as a whole achieved this average number of school years in the early 1970s. African Americans reached an average of twelve years of schooling in the early 1980s, while Hispanics have yet to achieve this threshold. Furthermore, junior and community colleges attract the largest share of Hispanic students who participate in higher education. A high percentage of the students enrolled in community colleges do not continue their education by transferring to a four year institution. Minority students continue to complete their undergraduate degrees at rates far lower than their non-Hispanic white counterparts.

Recruiting, Assessing, and Preparing
Pre-Service Hispanic Teachers

The Tomás Rivera Center (TRC) carried out a series of studies between 1987 and 1993, that described the state of Hispanic teachers and teaching, primarily in the southwestern United States, and identified innovative programs and practices in the teacher preparation process at selected colleges and universities in the United States with a particular focus on improving the access of Hispanics to the teaching profession (Tomás Rivera Center, 1993). One study surveyed 46 colleges in the five southwestern states (Arizona, California, Colorado, New Mexico and Texas), specifically to collect and analyze data on intervention programs aimed at (1) recruiting, (2) preparing, and (3) certifying Hispanic teachers (see Rodríguez-Ingle & Macías, 1990).

The analysis of data and information gathered from the survey of the 46 major producers of Hispanic teachers in the five southwestern states[4] revealed eight general findings (see Rodríguez-Ingle & Macías, 1990):

- There were no programs in the Southwest that included a complete range of integrated effective practices (recruitment, assessment and placement) of Hispanic teachers.
- The five southwestern states in general did not track the number, areas of expertise, or employment activity of graduates from institutions that prepare teachers.
- There existed a wide range of special intervention activities among the five states in terms of the preparation of Hispanic teachers, with a concentration of activity in California and Texas;
- While examples of innovative practices were identified, institutional representatives had a better understanding of the problems or barriers than of the actual strategies required to improve the access of Hispanics to the teaching profession.
- Where innovations did exist in the various teacher preparation programs, little or no evaluation data existed on the effectiveness of these programs, and/or the programs had been too recently adopted to produce such information.

- The most significant numbers of Hispanic teachers were produced by public, state, non-research institutions (i.e., California State University, Los Angeles), but the best completion rates for Hispanic student teacher candidates were most evident at small private colleges.
- The production of significant numbers of Hispanic teacher graduates did not necessarily reflect the adoption of innovative polices and practices, but rather, the process often reflected the demographics of an institution's service area and/or the practices of feeder schools.
- Institutions of higher education increasingly recognized the value of building partnership efforts involving community colleges and school districts in the recruitment, preparation, assessment, and certification of Hispanic and other minority teachers.

These eight general findings also showed that there was a soft data base to work with in this area, and that information development may be a prerequisite in promoting institutional change to improve the number of Hispanic teachers in the southwest. In addition to the general findings among the 46 colleges and universities, several problems and strategies were identified in the recruitment, assessment and preparation of Hispanic teachers.

All of the institutional respondents agreed that they had a teacher supply problem in their state both for Hispanics and non-Hispanics alike, as well as in some specialized areas, such as math, science, or bilingual education. The most frequently mentioned problem areas related to teacher supply were: (1) assessment issues; (2) low salaries; (3) lack of interest in teaching as a career choice; (4) competition with career options in other lucrative fields; (5) very few minority teacher role models; (7) limited number of comprehensive recruitment plans; and (8) lack of financial support to initiate and implement recruitment activities targeted to specific population groups. These responses can be organized and summarized into three steps or phases reflecting the teacher pipeline: recruitment, assessment, and preparation (Rodríguez-Ingle & Macías, 1990).

Recruitment

Recruitment, or the outreach and targeting of potential teacher candidates, varied according to the institution and credentialing program. There were five critical stages in a student's schooling pointedly related to career decisions: (1) high school, (2) freshmen/sophomore undergraduate level, (3) junior/senior undergraduate level, (4) community/junior college level and, (5) the graduate student level. The institutions concentrated their outreach efforts at each of these points involving university students, counselors, alumni and teacher role models who visited the junior and senior high schools in their immediate geographic service areas.

First and foremost, the lack of financial aid for college was cited as an important barrier in the recruitment of potential Hispanic teachers into the pipeline. More than any other single factor, limited financial aid for Hispanic and other minority undergraduate students, accounted for their relatively high drop-out rate or their decisions not to pursue college. Financial support was imperative for candidates in undergraduate programs, coordinated fifth year programs with undergraduate education, and alternate certification routes. Over sixty percent of the institutions (n=28) cited Title VII bilingual programs as one of the few programs that supported Hispanic teachers. One-third of the respondents (n=15) went so far as to say that bilingual programs were the only recruitment effort on their campuses that attracted and supported Hispanic teacher candidates.

   Strategies and Programs for Recruitment. Effective recruitment efforts in California and Texas centered around the adoption of cross-institutional collaborative approaches. This involved policies, procedures and practices for connecting institutions of higher education with community colleges, school districts, and other educational agencies, in order to achieve better institutional articulation (development of programs and activities that facilitated the transfer of students from one institutional setting to the next level of the teacher preparation continuum).

Partnerships between institutions of higher education and school districts gave potential teacher candidates individual and specialized attention through special summer programs and/or future teacher clubs. These collaborative efforts and the experience they provided for individuals with an interest in teaching, paved the way for teacher candidates to enter the educational pipeline. In addition, there was also mention of practices which match potential students with members of college faculty and/or mentor teachers in school districts as a way of solidifying mentoring relations.

Effective approaches aimed at the recruitment of prospective Hispanic teacher candidates took a variety of forms. For example, partnership arrangements between institutions of higher education were essential in order to ensure the transfer of students from one institution to another and augment the number of Hispanics in the educational pipeline. Other partnerships between institutions of higher education and school districts were vital in the early identification (i.e., junior high or high school levels) of potential teacher candidates. Comprehensive advising and monitoring of student performance throughout the college entrance phase ensured the retention of potential teacher candidates. In addition, these efforts required incorporating a comprehensive assessment component to diagnose the strengths and weaknesses of potential teacher candidates and to provide intervention assistance in defining and providing solutions to perceived problem areas. Most recruitment efforts have recognized that recruiting Hispanic and other minority students to teaching requires intensive individualized attention and active efforts within the early identification phase. Recruitment efforts, for example, were likely to be effective in increasing the number of students at the pre-collegiate level, if they adopted a future teacher club approach in order to give students a positive image of the teaching profession and an opportunity to become engaged in the process of teaching.

Assessment

The five southwestern states each had a required entry-level test to enter a teacher preparation program. In addition to an entry test, any student applying for certification was required to perform satisfactorily on a basic skills examination. The screening function of standardized tests limited the supply of Hispanic teacher candidates since there were lower pass rates for minority teacher candidates than for non-Hispanic white teacher candidates.

Most institutions, particularly public sector colleges, identified teacher testing requirements as a major barrier for Hispanic students interested in teaching. More than half of the institutional representatives that were interviewed (n=25) stated that Hispanics have difficulties fulfilling the assessment requirements. Although respondents cited some possible reasons why Hispanics have difficulties on the tests (e.g., poor preparation in high school), there were no commonalities as to student performance in the three basic skill areas: math, reading, and writing/composition. Some students had difficulty with reading and composition, while others did poorly on the math portions of these tests. Only a few institutions had integrated tutorial or remediation activities within the schools of education.

       Strategies and Programs for Assessment. A number of programs have instituted a variety of test preparation activities (e.g., tutorials and workshops) to help Hispanic students become more comfortable with testing environments and to better meet testing requirements. Early diagnosis and identification of likely problem areas represent positive approaches for assisting students to pass the required tests. Once problem areas were identified, remediation or further skill building activities helped students prepare for the next testing date. Also useful was distinguishing between test-taking skills as a general issue and the development of English language and math knowledge (or "basic skills"). Often the development of test taking skills had an immediate and positive impact on subsequent test results.

       In addition, many respondents recommended that the purpose of assessment practices pertaining to teacher candidates be reexamined, and redirected by the teacher credentialing agencies. It was underscored by the survey respondents that the purpose of assessment needed to emphasize identification and diagnostic functions, not screening or gate keeping functions. The negative consequence of the screening process needs to be significantly reduced or eliminated. Because the currently adopted tests are suggestive of the kind of preparation (i.e., counseling and instruction) students receive prior to testing, and because that preparation differs according to socioeconomic status, it is important that the pre-service teacher assessment process reflect this fundamental difference. A realignment of the important linkages between teacher preparation and assessment, therefore, must take place.

Teacher Preparation
      Better preparation of prospective teachers to relate more effectively to a diverse student population was an area identified

by respondents as critical. Most college faculty, and as a result most teacher candidates, need to be exposed to materials and methods that work with a culturally diverse student population. Most institutional efforts to sensitize or orient students in this direction (e.g., a multicultural education course) were sorely inadequate. A mandated or required multi-cultural course for all teacher candidates was not sufficient to make teacher candidates fully aware of the realities of classroom life with children from diverse backgrounds. As a result of this limited experience, most teacher candidates were neither well prepared nor sensitive to the needs of the culturally diverse student populations found in their classrooms.

Strategies and Programs for Teacher Preparation. Effective approaches for helping Hispanic students meet credentialing requirements took a variety of forms, but for the most part they shared the following characteristics:
(1) early student identification and assessment;
(2) systematically consistent counseling for personal support and academic advising;
(3) variety of tutorial and remediation activities so that different learning styles could be recognized and accommodated within the teacher preparation curricula;
(4) one-to-one relationships with college faculty and practicing teacher mentors;
(5) careful and consistent monitoring of student academic progress;
(6) creation of a team or "family group" working environment for student teachers (e.g., student teacher clubs);
(7) personal monitoring, support help, sensitivity and caring attention;
(8) involvement of all student teachers in the kind of curriculum offered in bilingual programs;
(9) clinical and field experience in classrooms with high concentrations of Hispanic students;
(10) exposure to a critical mass of Hispanic faculty and other appropriately trained or expert staff who can infuse the preparation process with appropriate cultural information and also serve as successful role models; and

(11) appreciation of the role of culture in the entire preparation
process, including the curriculum, teaching practicum,
counseling, tutorials, and other support services.

School districts, together with community colleges and four-
year institutions, also need to develop processes for assessing and
building the basic skills of Hispanic and other minority students
who have not reached their academic potential. The underlying
premise to this approach is that a much larger pool (including
many of those labeled "at risk") of potential teacher candidates
exists that is not being tapped. The students in this pool require
early identification and consistent attention throughout their
educational experience via contact with faculty and staff that can
effectively reflect the cultural background and social experience
of these students.

Promising Practices

While the information gathered suggests that there were promising practices, there was no evidence to document the effectiveness of such practices. Many of the promising practices, as
described in the report, were not new. In fact, the California
Postsecondary Education Commission (1986), the Minority
Engineering Program (MEP) (Landis, 1988), and the Holmes
Group (1989), have documented similar practices as being
essential components for improving the recruitment, retention, and
academic preparation of minorities in postsecondary institutions
in general.

It is important to keep in mind that the most significant part
of a promising practice or problem solving strategy is its faithful
execution. The 46 colleges and universities involved in this
survey showed an inverse relationship between the number and
percentage of Hispanic graduates. As shown in Table 7, if the
university had a high number of Hispanic graduates, then these
graduates represented a small proportion of their total teacher
graduates (e.g., California State University, Los Angeles). If the
university had a high percentage of Hispanic teacher graduates,
then the institution graduated a small number of teachers (e.g.,
New Mexico Highlands).

Other solutions rest with the availability of alternative options
for teacher certification. All of the states in the Southwest have an
alternate teacher certification program. Each state varied in how
and who was eligible to participate in these programs. Alternative

certification approaches have a significant role to play, especially when they are used to tap alternate pools of potential teachers (e.g., career changers who have math or science skills). These approaches, however, also need to begin addressing the training of teacher candidates to work effectively with a culturally diverse population. One such alternate pool for the increase of Hispanic teachers are teaching assistants or paraprofessionals.

Table 7. Southwest Colleges and Universities with Significant Production of Hispanic Teachers, 1988.

State	Institution	Total Teacher Grads	Hispanic Teacher Grads	
			N	%
Arizona	Arizona State University	470	46	9.8%
Arizona	Northern Arizona University	200	8	4.0%
Arizona	University of Arizona	326	39	12.0%
California	Biola University	470	20	4.3%
California	Cal Poly Pomona	423	29	6.9%
California	Chapman College	674	65	9.6%
California	Claremont Graduate School	86	17	19.8%
California	CSU, Bakersfield	212	13	6.1%
California	CSU, Chico	528	18	3.4%
California	CSU, Dominguez Hills	246	21	8.5%
California	CSU, Fresno	582	43	7.4%
California	CSU, Fullerton	489	35	7.2%
California	CSU, Hayward	372	12	3.2%
California	CSU, Long Beach	593	33	5.6%
California	CSU, Los Angeles	1,268	204	16.1%
California	CSU, Northridge	541	39	7.2%
California	CSU, Sacramento	604	25	4.1%
California	CSU, San Diego	560	45	8.0%
California	CSU, San Bernardino	707	37	5.2%
California	CSU, San Jose	645	41	6.4%
California	CSU, Stanislaus	488	30	6.1%
California	Loyola Marymount Univsity	154	22	14.3%
California	Mount Saint Mary's .	69	23	33.3%
California	National University	2,129	82	3.9%
California	UC Berkeley	80	2	2.5%
California	UC Irvine	245	18	7.3%

State	Institution	Total Teacher Grads	Hispanic Teacher Grads	
			N	%
California	UC San Diego	107	18	16.8%
California	UC Santa Cruz	130	11	8.5%
California	Univ. of the Pacific, Stockton	182	25	13.7%
California	Univ. of Southern California	238	35	14.7%
Colorado	Adams State College	165	25	15.2%
Colorado	Metropolitan State College	321	22	6.9%
Colorado	Univ. of Northern Colorado	1,243	68	5.5%
New Mexico	Eastern New Mexico Univ.	72	10	13.9%
New Mexico	NM Highlands University	17	16	94.1%
New Mexico	NM State University	88	24	27.3%
New Mexico	University of New Mexico	86	16	18.6%
New Mexico	Western New Mexico Univ.	20	8	40.0%
Texas	Corpus Christi State Univ.	196	51	26.0%
Texas	Laredo State University	78	67	85.9%
Texas	Pan American University [a]	450	378	84.0%
Texas	Southwest Texas State Univ.	552	55	10.0%
Texas	Sul Ross State University	151	63	41.7%
Texas	Texas A & I [b]	231	131	56.7%
Texas	University of Houston	723	43	5.9%
Texas	UT Austin (&Tributaries)	611	67	11.0%
Texas	UT El Paso	307	168	54.7%
Texas	UT San Antonio	205	45	22.0%
Totals		19,334	2,313	12.0%

a - This university has merged with the University of Texas system, and is now known as University of Texas, Pan American.

b - This university has merged with the Texas A&M system and is now known as Texas A&M University, Kingsville.

Several states, including California and Texas have incentives or support career ladder programs for paraprofessionals to gain their teaching credentials. A much greater proportion of school para-educators are minorities, have generally made some commitment to working in schools, and work in their minority communities in what are often "hard-to-staff" schools. In a survey of all paraprofessionals in the Los Angeles Unified School District in 1992, 44% of the respondents were of Mexican origin, while another 12.5% were of other Hispanic national origins. Nearly two-thirds indicated they aspired to become teachers (see Table 8). Many of these paraprofessionals were also bilingual, and many were already taking steps to complete their teacher certification requirements (see Haselkorn & Fideler, 1996, for a more detailed discussion of this option to increase and diversify the teacher workforce).

Table 8. Paraprofessional Aspirations to Become a Teacher, by Race, LAUSD, 1992

Race/ethnicity	Aspire to be a Teacher					
	Yes		No		No Answer	
White, Anglo, Euro-American	462	49.4%	420	44.9%	54	5.8%
African American	488	55.5%	302	34.4%	89	10.1%
Asian, Asian American, Pacific Islander.	166	58.7%	99	35.0%	18	6.4%
Mexican, Mexicano, Chicano	1,632	68.8%	598	25.2%	143	6.0%
Cuban	29	67.4%	11	25.6%	3	7.0%
Puerto Rican	20	55.6%	15	41.7%	1	2.8%
Central/ South American	479	82.0%	80	13.7%	25	4.3%
Other	49	71.0%	18	26.1%	2	2.9%
No Answer	46	51.1%	28	31.1%	16	17.8%
Totals	3,371	63.7%	1,571	29.7%	351	6.6%

Data source: Macías, R. & M. Lavadenz. In press. Paraprofessional Survey, 1992.

Work Conditions, Aspirations and Attitudes

The difference in representation between Hispanic students and Hispanic teachers in the nation as a whole brings dramatic attention to some fundamental problems. This gap between student and teacher representation reflects underlying problems concerning the recruitment and preparation of Hispanic teachers. Despite the complexity of issues related to Hispanic teacher preparation, practices already exist to address the problem of under-production of Hispanic teachers. We cannot conclude this discussion, however, without examining the issue of Hispanic teacher retention.

While preparation issues surface as significant contributors to the pattern of under-representation, teacher attrition figures highlight another important aspect of the problem. A recent survey of teachers, conducted by the NCES (1996) documented the attrition rate for public school teachers at 6.6% during the comparison period of 1993-95 (see Table 9). This attrition rate is approximately the same for both non-Hispanic white (6.5%) and African American (6.6.%) teachers. Yet, while the rate of attrition for Hispanic teachers had been lower during two prior survey periods, it was 9.1%, or almost 50% higher than that of other groups, for the most recent comparison period. What accounts for this significant group difference in teacher retention? A glimpse at the attitudes of practicing teachers helps to reveal some answers to this question.

Table 9. Attrition Rates in U.S Public School Teachers., by Race, 1987-95

Race of teachers	1987-88 to 1988-89	1990-91 to 1991-92	1993-94 to 1994-95
Total public school teachers	2,387,174	2,553,474	2,555,781
National attrition rate	5.6%	5.1%	6.6%
Non-Hispanic white	5.7%	5.1%	6.5%
African American	5.1%	6.1%	6.6%
Asian/Pacific Islander	4.2%	7.0%	2.4%
American Indian	3.1%	1.7%	3.5%
Hispanic	2.9%	4.4%	9.1%

Data Source: National Center for Education Statistics. 1996.

In 1988-89, researchers from the National Center for Education Statistics (NCES,1991) surveyed teachers who cited dissatisfaction with teaching as a reason for leaving the profession. When asked to identify specific areas of dissatisfaction, teachers pointed to inadequate support from administration as the undisputed primary reason for feeling dissatisfied. This study of teacher attitudes was replicated in 1991-92 and 1994-95 (see Table 10). In all three years the teachers identified other key issues as reasons to feel dissatisfied with teaching. Student discipline problems, poor student motivation and low salaries surfaced as among the most important reasons. Despite these common complaints, the issue of inadequate administrative support was identified as most critical. Only in 1994-95 was the administrative support issue not identified as the number one reason for teacher dissatisfaction. Yet, in this same year, the teachers created a new reason to feel dissatisfied: lack of recognition from the administration. This issue seems an extension, or at least a complement, to the concern for lack of support. All of which suggests that working conditions matter a great deal in the issue of teacher retention and administrative support and recognition matter most.

The NCES survey of teacher attitudes paints a helpful but incomplete picture of the issues behind the teacher retention dilemma. More helpful still would have been information about the nature and type of administrative support required and teacher data disaggregated by race and ethnicity. We should note that attitudinal data on Hispanic teachers are virtually nonexistent. To find hints of material that respond to these information needs, we turned to the only survey that focused on Hispanic teacher attitudes concerning working conditions (Monsivais,1990).

Table 10. Reasons for Leaving the Teaching Profession in U.S. Public Schools, 1987-95.[a]

Reasons for leaving the teaching profession	1987-88 to 1988-89	1990-91 to 1991-92	1993-94 to 1994-95
Inadequate support from administration	30.2%	24.9%	15.3%
Poor student motivation to learn	20.3%	18.8%	17.6%
Intrusions on teaching time	--	10.8%	4.5%
Lack of control over own classrooms	2.5%	9.5%	4.9%
Student discipline problems	9.0%	9.4%	17.9%
Inadequate time to prepare lesson plans	--	5.5%	2.1%
Poor opportunity for professional advancement	9.4%	5.3%	3.5%
Lack of influence over school policies & practices	7.9%	4.3%	6.6%
Lack of community support for schools	--	3.0%	--
Unsafe working environment	1.1%	2.8%	
Interference from others regarding what I taught	--	2.0%	--
Class size too large	3.5%	1.4%	1.2%

Reasons for leaving the teaching profession	1987-88 to 1988-89	1990-91 to 1991-92	1993-94 to 1994-95
Generally poor working conditions	4.4%	1.2%	
Poor salary	8.2%	0.7%	10.7%
Lack of professional competence of colleagues	1.6%	0.4%	--
Lack of recognition and support from administration	--	--	13.8%
Lack of resources & materials/equipment for classroom	--	--	1.7%

a - Rates of base year teachers who reported "dissatisfaction with teaching as a career," as one of three main reasons for leaving the profession, Public Schools in the U.S., 1987 thru 1995.
Data Source: National Center for Education Statistics, 1996.

In 1989-90 the authors participated in a survey of teacher attitudes among the members of the Association of Mexican American Educators (AMAE). Actual codeable returns from Hispanic teachers numbered 156 or about 12% of the total group membership. Respondents were mostly women (77%) and bilingual (73%); their teaching experience averaged 11 years, most of which occurred at the K-6 level (70%). In response to questions related to work environment, 76% of the teachers indicated that they worked in a "low-wealth" school, providing indirect evidence that limited resources make such things as poorly maintained facilities a working conditions issue. Beyond the low-wealth status of their schools, 79% of participants considered over-crowded classrooms to be a moderate or serious problem.

The most telling responses in the survey grapple with the issues of peer expectations of students and job assignments for Hispanic teachers. When asked about the attitudes of non-Hispanic teachers, a disturbing 65% of respondents believe that fellow teachers have lower expectations for Hispanic students for non-Hispanic white students. Due in part to this belief, 53% of Hispanic teachers felt that they were typecast into activities related to Hispanic students and that these assignments increased their workload beyond that of other teachers.

Our interpretation of this last observation was not that Hispanic teachers are unwilling to provide special assistance to Hispanic students, but that the inclination of peer teachers to underestimate the potential of Hispanic students created undue burdens for Hispanic teachers. This last observation from Hispanic teachers concerning peer expectations and job assign-ments allows us to return to the perceived need for increased administrative support. Increased administrative support, when provided strategically, should address the professional develop-ment of non-Hispanic teachers concerning the needs of Hispanic students. This support also can provide Hispanic teachers with a sense of balance in terms of assigned tasks as well as a feeling of recognition and appreciation for their work. But this work must begin soon. The AMAE respondents indicated that over half (51%) would be leaving the teaching profession within the next five years. Of these, 24% concluded that they likely would seek an occupation outside of education.

The National Commission on Teaching and America's Future (1996) has emphasized that:

> High-poverty urban and rural schools face persis-tent hurdles in hiring the teachers they need, and across the nation there is a critical need for many more teachers who reflect the racial and cultural mix of students in schools. Yet many school districts do little to recruit teachers or to keep good ones in the profession. They treat teachers like easily replaceable, interchangeable cogs in a wheel, meeting most of their personnel needs with last-minute scrambles to put warm bodies in class-rooms. (p. 8)

Preparing and retaining good teachers, the Commission main-tained, was the central strategy for improving our schools. Insufficient representation of Hispanics and other minorities in the classroom, serves as a glaring reminder of our society's struggle with social and economic inequities. A commitment to increasing the number of minority teachers will do much to address these inequities by providing students with teachers who can increase their chances for academic success.

Conclusions & Recommendations

Teacher supply and demand issues, coupled with educational reform and school improvement concerns, are critical issues in public schooling. This shortage of teachers in particular areas (i.e., math, science, bilingual education, foreign language) is exacerbated as states, and possibly the Federal government, attempt to reduce the student to teacher ratios through classroom size reduction strategies. While the number of teachers will grow, there is no indication it will diversify.

Yet, a serious public recognition of the segregated nature of the national teaching force, in favor of non-Hispanic whites, is obviously lacking. Aggressive recruitment of minorities into teaching, and greater cooperation among all institutions, can be a positive force in identifying, recruiting, retaining and certifying a greater number of minority and Hispanic teachers. However, this goal needs to be embraced by the public, and by educational policy makers alike. Restricting access to the teacher profession under the guise of raising quality and standards while not addressing the fundamental problems of workforce segregation, allows our public school systems to be collaborators in the dis-education of all our youth. Racial and ethnic diversity and the need for cross-cultural mutual understanding is a pre-requisite for twenty-first century global citizenship. The lack of Hispanic teachers is not only the problem of the Hispanic community, it is the nation's problem as well.

Efforts to restructure the educational system can have an impact on the nature of the teaching profession. If these reforms lead to improved achievement for all students, they help improve minority student access into the educational pipeline. There are specific actions that local school districts, colleges of teacher education, teacher certification boards, and teacher recruitment and selection offices can take to ensure a highly talented cadre of minorities who will choose teaching over other professions. Early preparation of minority students to be college-ready, and, thus, potential teacher candidates, is intimately tied to broader efforts to restructure the educational system. Energy and resources might best be expended on the early recruitment and intensive training of minorities who wish to teach and better prepare them for meeting state certification requirements. We should also focus on retaining teachers in the profession and specifically in the classroom.

Why Hispanic teachers? The reality of the demographic changes in our society and public school enrollments dramatically argue for a concerted effort to prepare teachers to deal more effectively with all of the youth of this society, and to prepare them for the realities of the changes in the world. The need for Hispanic teachers and other minority teachers should not be evaluated as a self-serving posture that teaching is the only way for minorities, and in particular for Hispanics, to gain employment. This is not the issue. Students should not have to come in contact with Hispanic teachers as if they found needles in a haystack. The U.S. teaching workforce should not be the province of one racial group (or of women alone). The diversification of the teaching workforce not only benefits all students but it strengthens the nation's public school system as well.

Notes

1. The editors greatly appreciate the willingness of the authors to allow us to use the term Hispanic when not specifically referring to subgroups, for the sake of uniformity and consistency throughout the book.

2. Data for 1970, for non-Hispanic whites and African Americans, include Hispanics of those races. This decennial census also did not provide for self-report of Hispanics, which were counted only in certain states by surname matches, or other means.

3. During the early 1970s there was an alternative school movement among Chicano communities that included the establishment of several Chicano colleges, Colegio Jacinto Treviño (TX), Juárez-Lincoln Center (affiliated with Antioch College) (TX), and Deganawidah-Quetzalcoatl (DQ) University (CA). The first two institutions did not last the decade, while the latter has struggled as an Indian-Chicano college in northern California with a small enrollment. In the mid 1980s, the Hispanic University (CA) was established, and is now located in San José, CA, with a focus on undergraduate and teacher education.

4. The states' teacher credentialing body was contacted for a list of the teacher preparation institutions and any demographic information that was available on their graduates. This list was used to select as many or all of them for a semi-structured telephone interview with the head of the teacher preparation program for that institution, or their recommendations of who might be able to provide us with the needed information. The interview protocol consisted of over 32 stimulus items, allowing for free follow-up questions and elaborations. In some instances

as many as three or four individuals from an institution were interviewed to compile the screening information; data on recruitment and admissions; their teacher preparation practices; and post-partum/exit relations with their graduates.

References

Alston, D. (1988, March 15). Recruiting minority teachers: state policies and practices. *Capital Ideas.*

American Association of Colleges for Teacher Education (1988). *Teacher education pipeline: Schools, colleges, and departments of education enrollments by race and ethnicity.* (Pre-Publication). Washington, DC: AACTE.

American Association of Colleges for Teacher Education (1994). *Teacher education pipeline III: Schools, colleges, and departments of education enrollments by race, ethnicity, and gender.* Washington, DC: AACTE.

American Council on Education (1988). *One third of a nation. A report of the commission on minority participation in education and American life.* Washington, DC: ACE.

Boyer, E. L. (1983). High school: A report on secondary education in America. New York: Harper & Row.

California Postsecondary Education Commission (1986). *A background for expanding educational equity* (March). A Technical Supplement to the Report of the Intersegmental Policy Task Force on Assembly Concurrent Resolution 83, Expanding Educational Equity in California's Schools and Colleges.

Carnegie Forum on Education and the Economy (1986). *A nation prepared: Teachers for the 21st century.* The Report of the Task Force on Teaching as a Profession. New York, NY: Carnegie Corporation.

Castro, R. (1989). *Improving the access of Latinos to the teaching profession. Executive summary.* Claremont, CA: The Tomás Rivera Center.

Castro, R. (1997). *Mandate for excellence.* Sacramento, CA: California Dept. of Education.

Castro, R. &. Rodríguez-Ingle Y. (1993). *Learning communities in teacher education programs: Four success stories.* Claremont, CA: The Tomás Rivera Center.

Castro, R. & Rodríguez-Ingle Y. (1992). *Missing teachers.* Claremont, CA: The Tomás Rivera Center.

Education Commission of the States (l990). *New strategies for producing minority teachers.* Denver, CO: ECS.

Galguera, T. (1998). Student attitudes toward teachers' ethnicity, bilinguality, and gender. *Hispanic Journal of Behavioral Sciences , 20* (4), 411-428.

Haselkorn, D. & Calkins, A. (1993). *Careers in teaching handbook.* Belmont, MA: Recruiting New Teachers, Inc.

Haselkorn, D. & Fideler E. (1996). *Breaking the glass ceiling: Para-educator pathways to teaching.* Belmont, MA: Recruiting New Teachers, Inc.

Holmes, B. & Rosaur, R. (l987). General information relative to the recruitment and retention of minority teachers. *ECS Working Papers.* Working Paper TE-87-6. Denver, CO: Education Commission of the States.

The Holmes Group (1989,January). *Work in progress: The Holmes Group one year on.* East Lansing, MI: The Holmes Group.

Landis, R.B. (1988,May). The case for minority engineering programs. *Engineering Education.*

Losey, K. (1999). Mexican-American students and classroom interaction: An overview and critique. *Review of Educational Research, 65* (3), 283-318.

Macías, R. (l989). *Bilingual teacher supply and demand in the United States.* Claremont, CA: The Tomás Rivera Center and USC Center for Multilingual, Multicultural Research.

Macías, R. & Lavadenz, M. (in press). *Para-Educators: Who they are, what they do.* Los Angeles, CA: USC Center for Multilingual, Multicultural Research.

Meier, K. J. (1993). *Latinos and representative bureaucracy: Testing the Henderson Hypothesis.* University of Wisconson-Milwaukee. (Unpublished manuscript.)

Monsivais, G. (1990). *Executive summary: Latino teachers: Well educated, but not prepared.* Claremont, CA: Tomás Rivera Center.

National Center for Education Statistics (1993). *America's teachers: Profile of a profession.* (NCES 93-025). Washington, DC: US GPO.

National Center for Education Statistics (1996). *Schools and staffing in the U.S.: A statistical profile, 1993-94.* (NCES 96-124). Washington, DC: US GPO.

National Center for Education Statistics (1997). *Condition of education, 1997.* (NCES 97-388). Washington, DC: US GPO.

National Commission on Excellence in Education (1983). *A nation at risk: The imperative for education reform.* Washington, DC: U.S. Government Printing Office.

National Commission for Excellence in Teacher Education (1985). *A call for change in teacher education.* Washington, DC: American Association of Colleges for Teacher Education.

National Commission on Teaching and America's Future (1996). *What matters most: Teaching for America's future.* NY: Author.

National Foundation for the Improvement of Education (1986). *A blueprint for success.* Washington, DC: NFIE.

National Governors' Association (1991). *Results in education: 1987, 1988, 1989, 1990, 1991.* Washington, DC: NGA.

Rodríguez-Ingle, Y. & Castro, R. (1993). *Resolving a crisis in education: Latino teachers for tomorrow's classrooms.* Claremont, CA: The Tomás Rivera Center.

Rodríguez-Ingle, Y. & Macías, R. (1990). *Promising practices and new directions for Attracting Latinos to the Teaching Profession.* Claremont, CA: The Tomás Rivera Center.

Texas Education Agency (1987). *Alternative teacher certification in Texas.* Austin, TX: Division of Teacher Education.

The Tomás Rivera Center (1993). *Resolving a crisis in education: Latino teachers for tomorrow's classrooms.* Claremont, CA: Author.

U.S. Census Bureau (1996). *Population projections of the U.S. by age, sex, race and Hispanic origin: 1995-2050.* (Series P25-1130). Washington, DC: USGPO.

U.S. Bureau of the Census (1998). *Statistical abstract of the United States: 1997. The national data book.* Washington, DC: Author–CD version.

CHAPTER 4

Language of Instruction and its Impact
On Educational Access and Outcomes

Laurie R. Weaver and Yolanda N. Padrón

Introduction

The number of minority students has continued to increase in United States public schools, including an increase in the number of students who speak and understand a language other than English upon entering school. As a result, a variety of instructional programs, including bilingual education, have been promoted as a means by which the needs of non-English speaking students can be met. Research that examines bilingual education, however, has produced mixed results. The purpose of this chapter is to present a discussion on how native language instruction can provide language minority students with better access to educational opportunities. First, we examine the increase in the non-English speaking student population, then we present an overview of various educational programs and policies that address the linguistic needs of language minority students. Next, we discuss native language instruction and its impact on students' academic achievement, beginning with the theoretical foundation for native language instruction and then reviewing research studies that have investigated bilingual education. Finally, implications for the education of language minority students into the next century are discussed.

The Context

The number of minority students, including students for whom English is not their native language, has continued to increase in United States public schools. From 1984 to 1991 the total elementary school enrollment rose 11%; the non-Hispanic white student population increased 5%, the African-American student population increased 17%, and the Hispanic student population increased 45% (Snyder, 1993). There have been numerous projections made for the year 2000, and beyond, indicating that this trend will continue. For example, some of these projections predict that by the year 2000, one third or more of all students enrolled in public schools will be people of color (Cushner, McClelland, & Safford, 1992). Hispanic students, in particular, are becoming an increasing presence in American schools. In 1982 about 73% of the school age population was non-Hispanic white; by the year 2020 it is projected that this percentage will decline to 54.5% (Pallas, Natriello, & McDill, 1989). Conversely, in 1982 Hispanic students constituted 9.3% of the student population less than 17 years of age, but by the year 2020 it is projected that this percentage will increase to 25.3% (Pallas, Natriello, & McDill, 1989). For the year 2026, projections indicate that the student enrollment in grades K-12 will be 70% minority students (García, 1994). According to García (1994), this is the exact reverse of the same student population in 1990.

Linguistic Diversity
Linguistic diversity often accompanies racial and ethnic diversity. Census data for 1990 indicated that there were 9.9 million students from language minority background enrolled in schools throughout the United States (Waggoner, 1994). Projected estimates indicate that the number of school-age children from diverse language backgrounds will reach 3.5 million by the year 2000 (Trueba, 1989; Waggoner, 1994), to 15 million (25%) by the year 2026. These second language learners share one common aspect, the need to become proficient in English (La Celle-Patterson & Rivera, 1994). In order for English language learners to have access to educational opportunities, educational programs will need to consider the unique academic language needs of these students. Otherwise, these students will have a greater likelihood for failure (García, 1994).

Restructuring Education

In the past fifteen years, a number of studies and reports which have sought to identify deficiencies within the U.S. educational system. The initial reports that addressed the need for improving the education included: *A Nation at Risk: An Imperative for Education Reform* (National Commission on Excellence in Education, 1983), *The Paideia Proposal* (Mortimer & Paideia Group, 1982), and *A Place Called School* (Goodlad, 1983). In addition, other efforts such as the National Education Goals, and the development of standards by professional organizations have been a part of the current efforts to restructure education.

This movement to restructure education in the United States indicates that the present systems are not effective and that changes are needed. One of the problems with the restructuring approach is that it seldom addresses language minority students and how to best achieve equity in their education. Development of native language skills in an important factor with regard to the educational excellence of language minority students (Hakuta, 1986). Nonetheless, many second language students do not participate in programs where their native language is used and are enrolled in English-monolingual programs (LaCelle-Patterson & Rivera, 1994).

It is important that second language students receive instruction that meets both their linguistic and academic needs. Discourse strategies, for example, that emphasize student-student interaction are important in enhancing linguistic development (García, 1983). This type of instruction acknowledges the critical role that students play when they are active participants in the learning process (García, 1994). In addition, rather than casting teachers as the experts who bestow knowledge upon their students (Freire, 1970), teachers become the facilitator of learning experiences by providing opportunities for their students to actively participate in speaking, listening, reading, and writing (García, 1992). Such findings suggest that schools must be restructured to meet the needs of the disadvantaged students (Allington, 1994).

Overview of Bilingual Education Programs and Policies

In an effort to meet the educational needs of language minority students, bilingual programs have been implemented throughout the United States. Typically, bilingual education in the United States is designed for elementary-aged students although it is sometimes implemented in middle and high school grades (Richard-Amato, 1997). Bilingual education combines instruction in the students' native and second languages in order to facilitate the students' acquisition of academic concepts and skills while simultaneously acquiring a second language (Ovando & Collier, 1998). These programs vary in their design and implementation. A key aspect of the way in which these programs are differentiated is the way they combine the student's native language and English during instruction (Peregoy & Boyle, 1997).

The three major models of bilingual education typically implemented in the United States are transitional, maintenance, and two-way bilingual education (Ovando & Collier, 1998). Transitional bilingual education emphasizes acquisition of English in order to quickly transition the students to a general education classroom. The native language is used for subject area instruction; however, this is typically for a short time period, that is, two to three years. Transitional programs are the most commonly implemented in the United States (Ovando & Collier, 1998).

In contrast, maintenance bilingual education has as a major goal the continued development of the students' native language through native language instruction for as many years as possible. In addition, students in maintenance bilingual education programs are provided with instruction to facilitate the development of English skills. Thus, there is less emphasis on transferring the students to an all English environment.

Finally, a less frequently implemented program is the two-way program which is also known as dual-language education or bilingual immersion (Ovando & Collier, 1998). In this program, students from two different language groups are instructed throughout the day in two languages with the goal being the development of literacy in both languages as well as the cognitive and academic growth expected of students enrolled in monolingual programs.

Native Language Instruction in the United States

The use of a student's native language for instructional purposes is not a recent educational innovation; in fact, instruction provided in the students' native language have a history dating back to the first establishment of schools in the United States (Crawford, 1995; Ovando & Collier, 1998). Many of the early immigrants settled in ethnic communities and established their own schools. As a result, the students' native language was used as a medium for instruction in schools throughout the 1700s. In addition, missionaries in the southwest employed a bilingual delivery system with the Native Americans with whom they worked.

A rise in the number of immigrants to the United States in the late 1800s, however, led to a rise in xenophobia. Native born Americans were afraid of the supposed disloyalty of the new immigrants and speaking English was linked with being a loyal American. Economic and political tensions in the early 1900s led to a virtual eradication of the use of native language for instruction in United States schools. Throughout much of the early twentieth century, use of a language other than English for instructional purposes was not allowed in schools. In fact, children were punished for speaking their native language even when spoken during non-instructional times (Crawford, 1995).

Changes in immigration, however, have influenced the rise of bilingual education programs. The recent bilingual education movement can be traced to the establishment of the Dade County, Florida, Coral Way Elementary School bilingual program in 1963 (Crawford, 1995; Ovando & Collier, 1998). Designed to meet the needs of Cuban immigrant children, but also allowing for the participation of English-speaking students, this program met with much success. Students in both language groups mastered English reading while the Spanish-speaking students also mastered reading in Spanish. There were many factors that contributed to the success of the Coral Way program, one being that the program was developed as an enrichment program rather than a remedial program. That is, emphasis was placed on mastering a second language while continuing to develop the native language, rather than on replacing the native language with a second language. This is in contrast to the subtractive philosophy, which has been the focus of most bilingual education programs in the past thirty years.

Policies Which Impact Native Language Instruction
Educational policy regarding language minority students has a long history in the United States (see García, Chapter 5, this

volume). The most modern efforts of educating language minority students have emerged as a result of the success of the Coral Way Elementary School program and the rising numbers of non-English speaking students. This has resulted in a number of important pieces of legislation and policies related to instruction in students' native languages. In 1968, the Bilingual Education Act, Title VII of the Elementary and Secondary Education Act, was signed into law (Díaz-Rico & Weed, 1995). The original authorization of this act provided funding for educational resources, teacher training, materials development, and parent involvement. Re-authorizations of this act required schools that received Title VII grants to provide students with native language and native culture instruction (1974), to emphasize a transitional approach to bilingual education (1978), and to emphasize family literacy and include special populations (1984). In general this legislation has focused on providing language minority students with equal access to education.

Both state and federal court decisions have had an impact upon bilingual education. The landmark Supreme Court decision which addressed the issue of access was *Lau v. Nichols* in 1974. The class action suit was filed on behalf of Chinese students enrolled in San Francisco schools, and stated that the children were not receiving an equal educational opportunity because they did not understand the language of instruction. The school system countered that equal educational opportunity was provided because the Chinese-speaking students had the same access to education as was provided to all other students. The Supreme Court, however, stated that equal educational opportunity was not provided by equal access. Rather, the students needed to be provided with the same opportunity to gain from instruction as other students. While the Supreme Court judgment did not specifically mandate the implementation of bilingual programs, it did offer bilingual education as one means by which a school could provide an equal educational opportunity for its non-English speaking students.

The *Lau* decision was followed by the Equal Educational Opportunities Act, passed by Congress in August of 1974. This act provided legislative backing for the *Lau* decision. In 1975 the Office for Civil Rights and the Office of Education issued the *Lau* Remedies. Like the *Lau* decision, the *Lau* Remedies did not mandate the implementation of bilingual education; however, the use of bilingual education was strongly encouraged. School districts which could not show that an appropriate educational program was being offered to their non-English speaking students were faced with the possible loss of federal funds (Ovando & Collier, 1998). All of these legal decisions were aimed at increasing educational access for minorities in the public school system. Legislation, while subject to the political climate of the times, has paved the way for equal educational opportunity to be provided for language minority students through the implementation of bilingual education.

Language of Instruction and Its Impact On Students' Academic Achievement

Recent research indicates that native language instruction accompanied by English language instruction facilitates students' acquisition of concepts and skills as well as their development of English (Collier, 1992; Ramirez, Yuen, Ramey, & Pasta, 1990; Thomas & Collier, 1996). Traditionally, it was believed that native language instruction developed a proficiency which existed separately from English proficiency. The implication was that if native language and English proficiency were separate, what was learned in one language would not transfer to another. Thus, increasing proficiency in the native language was an activity that took time away from developing English proficiency.

Cummins (1988, 1991), however, posited that a "common underlying proficiency" exists in which exposure in either language promotes development of the proficiency that is common to both. In other words, what is taught in the students' native language can be understood and expressed in the second language once the requisite vocabulary has been acquired. Native language instruction, therefore, is not seen as an activity which takes away from the development of English. Rather, development of the native language facilitates the acquisition of English because concepts and skills common to both languages will transfer from one language to the other.

Dual Language Exposure Promotes Proficiency
Royer and Carlo (1991) addressed this in a study designed to examine whether reading skills taught in Spanish transferred to English. By using the sentence verification technique, which is a

measure of listening and reading comprehension, Royer and Carlo measured the Spanish and English reading skills of 49 students when they were in bilingual classes in fifth grade and again in sixth grade. Royer and Carlo found that the students' English reading performance at the end of the sixth grade was highly correlated with reading in Spanish a year earlier. That is, good fifth grade readers in Spanish become good sixth grade readers in English. The researchers posited that this occurred because the students transferred the skills they had learned in Spanish to their English reading.

Troike (1983) also examined the issue of transfer of skills in a study undertaken with thirty sixth grade Mexican immigrant children in Illinois. Half of the students had begun their schooling in the United States; the others had two or more years of schooling in Mexico prior to coming to the United States. Of this second group, all but one scored higher in reading comprehension in English than any of the students who had begun school in the United States. Troike explained this by stating that the skills the students had learned in their native language transferred to English enabling them to become better readers in English.

Cummins (1979) also posited that there is a threshold level of competence that must be acquired in the native language in order for competence to be developed in the second language. Students taught in an additive bilingual environment, where second language acquisition is added to an already well developed native language proficiency, will more easily reach the level necessary for positive cognitive effects to be seen. If, however, students are instructed in a subtractive environment in which the goal is to replace native language competency with second language competency, Cummins posited that negative cognitive effects would be seen. Thus, the lack of native language development would cause language minority students to have difficulty in adequately acquiring both the second language and in acquiring academic concepts and skills. This instructional approach would, therefore, hinder students' access to educational opportunities.

The Language Acquisition Process

Language acquisition is not a quick process. Traditionally, students were exited from bilingual programs after two years during which they had typically mastered oral language skills (Ovando & Collier, 1998). These students often struggled academically despite their oral English skills. Cummins (1988, 1991) stated that it takes on average from five to seven years for a student to gain the English proficiency needed to be able to understand concepts taught in English.

Collier (1989) has indicated that for some students, the level of process of acquiring the level of English needed to benefit from all-English instruction may take up to ten years. Thus, students were being exited from bilingual classrooms when oral skills had been developed but before the necessary reading and writing skills had been acquired. An important distinction can be made between oral language skills, what Cummins refers to as Basic Interpersonal Communication Skills (BICS), and language skills needed to understand and perform academic tasks, or Cognitive Academic Language Proficiency (CALP). According to Cummins, students can master BICS in approximately two years but need more time to develop the language needed for academic success in an all-English environment. This has been supported by research which indicates that growth in English increased over time spent in the bilingual program (Burnham-Massey, 1990; Leyba, 1978; Troike, 1983) and that time spent in a bilingual program was a factor in LEP students reaching grade equivalent performance in English (Leyba,1978).

Research on the Effect of Bilingual Education

During the past 25 years, the impact of bilingual education on academic achievement has been investigated. Results from this research have been mixed; some studies find that bilingual education impedes academic progress while others find that bilingual education facilitates academic progress. The differences in these studies have been attributed to several factors including: different values being given to bilingualism which lead to different interpretation of results, methodological weaknesses, and varying definitions of what constitutes a bilingual program (Cziko, 1992). In addition, Hakuta & Garcia (1989) explain that evaluations of bilingual programs have generally concentrated on examining English language skills and not students' overall academic development.

Research with Conflicting Outcomes

Results from research conducted during the late 1970's and the 1980's indicated that bilingual education was not effective and did not "work" (Crawford, 1997). It is important to note that there was no overall definition of what was meant by effectiveness. Studies often examined the impact of English language development in programs with widely varying amounts of native and second language instruction. Many of these studies did not examine the impact of bilingual education on cognitive and academic growth. In addition, there was no systematic effort to examine programs with similar characteristics (Crawford, 1997).

For example, Danoff (1978) reported the findings of a study conducted by the American Institutes of Research (AIR) which examined United States bilingual education programs. This study compared the achievement of students enrolled in bilingual programs receiving federal funds through Title VII with the achievement of comparable students not in bilingual programs. The students' English oral comprehension and reading abilities were assessed along with Spanish oral comprehension, reading, and math achievement. Results of this study indicated that the Title VII programs did not appear to have a significant impact on the students' achievement. The students in the Title VII programs tended to perform at lower levels than those students in the all-English programs except in the area of Spanish reading. These results are not surprising since, as it was stated earlier, it would take approximately five to seven years before students could gain the proficiency in English needed to understand concepts taught in English (Cummins, 1988).

The AIR study has been criticized because a variety of programs were included, but not differentiated, in the analysis. In addition there was no effort to determine if the programs actually exemplified the characteristics of the program model they purported to typify (Thomas, 1992). The AIR study has also been criticized because it did not take into consideration the initial differences between the groups being compared and only a short time period (five months) passed between pre-test and post-test administration (Gray, 1977; O'Malley, 1978).

In a synthesis of research on the effectiveness of bilingual education, which has since been criticized because of methodological weaknesses, Baker and de Kanter (1981, 1983) found that results were mixed. In their synthesis, Baker and de Kanter (1981) initially found 28 studies that met the criteria they had set for acceptable studies. In their 1983 revision, they included 39 studies. Of these studies, 11 reported that bilingual education had positive effects on English language performance whereas 26 studies indicated that there was no positive effect.

Willig (1985) undertook a meta-analysis of the same studies used in Baker and de Kanter's review and came to a different conclusion. Willig found that the Baker and de Kanter review was affected by methodological weaknesses such as oversimplification in the method of tallying the results of studies and the failure to use rigorous research standards in interpreting the results of all the studies. When statistical measures were used to control for the methodological inadequacies of many of the studies, it was found that there were small to moderate differences favoring bilingual education. These differences were found in tests of reading, language skills, math, and total achievement in English.

In 1987, the United States General Accounting Office conducted a survey of ten experts (U.S. General Accounting Office). The experts were asked to examine research related to the effectiveness of bilingual education. The experts examined the research with regard to the impact of bilingual education on the acquisition of English, achievement in other areas, whether alternative approaches to education for language minority students were viable, and the relationship between bilingual education and high school completion and postsecondary education. The opinions of the experts were not consistent. There were 19 responses that indicated that bilingual education had a positive impact on the education of language minority students while 13 responses were critical. These mixed results may be the result of the experts' using different criteria for determining positive impact.

Research with More Positive Outcomes

Zappert and Cruz (1977) conducted a review of studies related to bilingual education which found that bilingual education was superior. The purpose of the review was to examine studies which compared bilingual and monolingual educational programs. Six criteria which addressed methodological issues were used to select the studies; only 12 studies met the criteria. These studies examined the impact of bilingual and monolingual education on native language development, English language development, native reading and writing, English reading and writing, social studies, and math achievement. Results of the studies indicated that the bilingual programs were either superior to monolingual programs (58%), or that there was no difference between the two programs (41%). Interestingly, the finding that there was no difference between achievement of students enrolled in the two programs was seen as a positive finding. The researchers felt that learning two languages in the bilingual program was a benefit even if the children were not achieving at a higher level in the program (Cziko, 1992).

The results of a study examining the impact of bilingual education conducted in the 1970s were reported by Troike (1978). Troike analyzed the results of studies which examined 12 bilingual education programs throughout the United States. Troike (1978) purposely examined programs determined to be effective programs, that is the programs were predetermined to facilitate academic achievement of the language minority students enrolled. English language development and achievement test data was examined. Troike (1978) found that quality bilingual programs do make a difference. In other words, students enrolled in quality bilingual programs demonstrated both academic growth and acquisition of English.

Two recent studies also found that bilingual education programs do have a positive impact on language minority students' achievement. The Ramírez study (Ramírez, Yuen, Ramey, & Pasta, 1990) was a longitudinal study of 2,300 Spanish-speaking children that provided support for late-exit bilingual education. That is, the study found that students in late-exit programs who received substantial amounts of native language instruction along with gradual implementation of English language instruction showed the greatest growth in math, English language skills, and English reading (Ramírez, et. al., 1990). This was in comparison to students' performances in immersion (all English) and early exit bilingual programs.

The results of a study conducted by Thomas and Collier (1996) indicated that long term exposure to both native and second language instruction is likely to result in academic gains. In this ongoing study, the academic progress of 42,000 students over an eight to twelve year period has been examined. This study compares the impact of five different programs for non-English speaking students: two-way bilingual education, maintenance bilingual education with content-based ESL, transitional bilingual education with content-based ESL, transitional bilingual education with traditional ESL, and ESL pullout. Results have indicated that growth is correlated to amount of native language used for instruction. That is, the longer students receive native language instruction, the better their academic achievement. The most beneficial bilingual education model as indicated by this research is two-way bilingual education. The least beneficial program is pullout ESL, in which students leave the general education classroom for a portion of the school day to receive instruction in English from an ESL teacher.

Implications For The Education of Language Minority Students Into The Next Century

The level of educational attainment of language minority students continues to fall behind that of the total school population (Arias, 1986; Padilla, 1990), and these students have a higher than average rate of school non-completion (Robledo, Cardenas, García, Montemayor, Ramos, Supik & Villareal, 1990). Students with limited English proficiency were not provided with services that met their academic needs during the past sixty years. Rather, students with limited English proficiency were expected to attend classes taught completely in English and were punished for speaking their native language. Their native language was seen as an impediment to English language acquisition and their culture was blamed for their lack of academic success.

The move to restructure education suggests that current school systems are not working and that changes are needed. The current approaches to restructuring, however, do not address equity for all students. The lack of academic success of minority students from any language background has been explained as the result of either the students' faulty genes or their deficient home environment (Darder, 1991). Recently, rather than placing the blame for underachievement on the students, underachievement is seen as the lack of effective educational practices (Reyes & Scribner, 1995; Waxman, 1995). Some of these educational practices have included being denied the opportunity to learn higher-level thinking skills (Foster, 1989) or being tracked into low-level classes based on their perceived lower abilities (Darder, 1991).

Generally, the emphasis for low-achieving students in low track classes has been on remediation and an overemphasis on repetition of content through drill-and-practice (Darder, 1991). In addition, in high track classes, which are more likely to consist of middle and upper class Anglo students, instructional activities tend to develop leadership and decision-making skills (Cushner, McClelland, & Safford, 1992), while low track classes emphasize rule following and memorization of rote facts. In a study by Padrón (1994), it was reported that the type of instruction in schools where there is a large number of language minority students is very passive. Students, for example, are not given much opportunity to interact with one another or with the teacher. It has been suggested that this type of instruction has contributed to the lack of success of diverse students (García, 1994).

It is imperative that language minority students develop proficiency in English if they are to succeed in the United States public school system. In addition, language minority students must also gain the abilities and content area knowledge comparable to their English-speaking counterparts. Clearly, learning a language takes a long time (Cummins, 1988, 1991). As shown by the research, to facilitate the academic success of language minority students, it is important that students continue to develop their native language abilities while increasing their abilities in their second language.

References

Allington, R. L. (1994). The schools we have. The schools we need. *The Reading Teacher, 48*(1), 14-29.

Arias, M. (1986). The context of education for Hispanic students: An overview. *American Journal of Education, 95*(1).

Baker, K., & de Kanter, A. (1981). Effectiveness of bilingual education: A review of the literature. Washington DC: U.S. Department of Education, Office of Planning, Budget, & Evaluation.

Baker, K., & de Kanter, A. (1983). Federal policy and the effectiveness of bilingual education. In K. Baker and A. de Kanter (Eds.), *Bilingual education: A reappraisal of federal policy* (pp. 33-86). Lexington, Massachusetts: Heath.

Burnham-Massey, L. (1990). Effects of bilingual instruction on English academic achievement of LEP students. *Reading Improvement, 27*(2), 129-132.

Collier, V. (1989). How long? A synthesis of research on academic achievement in second language. *TESOL Quarterly, 23*(3), 509-531.

Collier, V. (1992). A synthesis of studies examining long-term language minority student data on academic achievement. *Bilingual Research Journal, 16* (1&2), 187-212.

Crawford, J. (1995). *Bilingual education: History, politics, theory and practice*, 3rd edition. Los Angeles, California: Bilingual Educational Services, Inc.

Crawford, J. (1997). Best evidence: Research foundations of the bilingual education act. Washington DC: National Clearinghouse for Bilingual Education.

Cummins, J. (1979). Linguistic interdependence and the educational development of bilingual children. *Review of Educational Research, 49*(2), 222-251.

Cummins, J. (1988). Language proficiency, bilingualism and academic achievement. In P. Richard-Amato (Ed.), *Making it happen: Interaction in the second language classroom-From theory to practice* (pp. 382-395). New York: Longman.

Cummins, J. (1991). The role of primary language development in promoting educational success for language minority students. *In Schooling and language minority students: A theoretical framework* (3-49). Los Angeles: California: Evaluation, Dissemination and Assessment Center, California State University.

Cushner, K., McClelland, A. & Safford, P. (1992). *Human diversity in education: An integrative approach.* New York: McGraw-Hill.

Cziko, G. (1992). The evaluation of bilingual education: From necessity and probability to possibility. *Educational Researcher, 21*(2), 10-15.

Danoff, M. (1978). *Evaluation of the impact of ESEA Title VII Spanish/English bilingual education program: Overview of study and findings.* Palo Alto, California: American Institutes for Research. (ERIC Document Reproduction Service No. ED 154 634)

Darder, A. (1991). *Culture and power in the classroom: A critical foundation for bicultural education.* New York: Bergin and Garvey.

Freire, P. (1970). *Pedagogy of the oppressed.* New York: Continuum.

Díaz-Rico, L., & Weed, K. (1995). *The cross-cultural, language, and academic development handbook: A complete K-12 reference guide.* Boston: Allyn and Bacon.

Foster, G.E. 1989). Cultivating the thinking skills of low achievers: A matter of equity. *Journal of Negro Education, 58,* 461-467.

García, E. (1983). *Bilingualism in early childhood.* Albuquerque: University of New Mexico Press.

García, E. (1992). Effective instruction for language minority students: The teacher. *Journal of Education,* 173, 130-141.

García, E. (1994). *Understanding and meeting the challenge of students' cultural diversity.* Boston: Houghton Mifflin.

Gray, T. (1977). Challenge to USOE final evaluation of the impact of ESEA Title VII Spanish/English bilingual education programs. Washington DC: Center for Applied Linguistics.

Goodlad, J. (1983). *A place called school: Prospects of the future.* New York: Harper & Row.

Hakuta, K. (1986). *Mirror of language: The debate on bilingualism.* New York: Basic Books.

Hakuta, K.; & García, E. (1989). Bilingualism and education. *American Psychologist, 44*(2), 374-379.

LaCelle-Peterson, A., & Rivera, C. (1994). Is it real for all kids? A framework for equitable assessment policies for English language learners. *Harvard Educational Review,* 64, 55-75.

Lau v. Nichols, 414 U.S. 563 (1974).

Leyba, C. (1978). Longitudinal study: Title VII bilingual programs, Santa Fe public schools, Santa Fe, New Mexico. Los Angeles, California: National Dissemination and Assessment Center, California State University.

Mortimer, J. A., The Paideia Group (1982). *The Paideia Proposal: An educational manifesto.* New York: MacMillian.

The National Commission of Excellence in Education (1983). *A Nation at risk: The imperative for educational reform.* Washington, D.C.: U.S. Department of Education.

The National Council of Teachers of Mathematics (1981). *Curriculum and evaluation standards for school mathematics.* Reston, VA: The National Council of Teachers of Mathematics.

O'Malley, J. (1978). Review of the evaluation of the impact of ESEA Title VII Spanish/English bilingual education programs. *Bilingual Resources,* 1, 6-10.

Ovando, C., & Collier, V. (1985). *Bilingual and ESL classrooms: Teaching in multi-cultural contexts.* New York: McGraw-Hill.

Padilla, A. (1990). Bilingual education: Issues and perspectives. In A. Padilla, H. Fairchild, & C. Valadez (Eds), *Bilingual education: Issues and strategies.* Newbury Park, CA: Sage.

Padrón, Y. N. (1994, April). *Observations of reading instruction for limited English proficient students.* Paper presented at the annual meeting of the American Educational Research Association, New Orleans, Louisiana.

Pallas, A. M., Natriello, G.; & McDill, E. L. (1989). The changing nature of the disadvantaged: Current dimensions and future trends. *Educational Researcher, 18*(5), 16-22.

Peregoy, S., & Boyle, O. (1997). *Reading, writing and learning in ESL: A resource book for K-8 teachers*, 2nd edition. New York: Longman.

Ramírez, J.D.; Yuen, S.; Ramey, D.; & Pasta, D. (1990). *Final report: Longitudinal study of immersion strategy, early-exit and late-exit transitional bilingual education programs for language-minority children.* San Mateo, CA: Aguirre International.

Richard-Amato, P. (1997). *Making it happen: Interactions in the second language classroom-From theory to practice*, 2nd edition. New York: Longman.

Robledo, M. R., Cardenas, J. A., García, Y., Montemayor, A. M. Ramos, M. G., Supik, J. D., & Villareal, A. (1990). *Partners for valued youth: Dropout prevention strategies for at-risk language minority students. Handbook for teacher and planners from the Innovative Approaches Research Project.* Arlington, VA: Development Associates.

Royer, J., & Carlo, M. (1991). Transfer of comprehension skills from native to second language. *Journal of Reading, 34*(6), 450-455.

Snyder, T.D. (1993). Trends in education. *Principal, 73*(1), 9-14.

Thomas, W. (1992). Analysis of the research methodology of the Ramírez study. *Bilingual Research Journal, 16,* (1&2), 213-245.

Thomas, W., & Collier, V. (1996). *Language Minority Student Achievement and Program Effectiveness.* Fairfax, Va.:

92

Center for Bilingual/Multi-cultural/ESL Education, George Mason University.

Troike, R. (1978). Research evidence for the effectiveness of bilingual education. *NABE Journal*, 3, 13-24.

Troike, R. (1983). Bilingual ¡Sí! *Principal, 62*(3), 46-50.

Trueba, H. T. (1989). Sociocultural integration of minorities and minority school achievement. In H. T. Trueba (Ed.), *Raising silent voices: Educating the linguistic minorities for the 21st century* (pp. 1-28). New York: Newbury House.

U.S. General Accounting Office. (1987, March). *Bilingual education: A new look at the research evidence*. Washington DC: Author.

Valadez, C. M. (1992). Education of Hispanic Americans. *Encyclopedia of Educational Research.* (Vol. 6, pp. 592-597). New York: Mac Millan.

Waggoner, D. (1994). Language-minority school-age population now totals 9.9 million. *NABE News, 18*(1), 1, 24.

Walker, C. (1987). Hispanic achievement: Old views and new perspectives. In H. T. Trueba (Ed.), *Success or failure? Learning and the language minority student* (pp. 15-32). New York: Newbury House.

Waxman, H. C., & Padrón, Y. N. (1995). Improving the quality of classroom instruction for students at risk of failure in urban schools. *Peabody Journal of Education, 70*(2), 44-65.

Waxman, H. C., Wang, M. C., Lindvall, C. M., & Anderson, K. A. (1983, February). *Classroom Observation Schedule technical manual.* Pittsburgh: University of Pittsburgh, Learning Research and Development Center.

Waxman, H. C., Wang, M. C., Lindvall, C. M., & Anderson, K. A. (1983, February). *Teachers' Roles Observation Schedule technical manual.* Pittsburgh: University of Pittsburgh, Learning Research and Development Center.

Wehlage, G., Rutter, R., & Turnbaugh, A. (1987). A program model for at risk high school students. *Educational Leadership, 44*(6), 70-73.

Willig, A. (1985). A meta-analysis of selected studies on the effectiveness of bilingual education. *Review of Educational Research, 55*(3), 269-317.

Zappert, L., & Cruz, B. (1977). *Bilingual education: An appraisal of empirical research.* Berkeley, California: Bay Area Bilingual Education League.

CHAPTER 5

Disproportionate Minority Placement In Special Education Programs: Old Problem, New Explanations

Richard A. Figueroa & Alfredo Artiles

Introduction

The indices of systemic failure in the American public education system have been ubiquitous and persistent: under-achievement, segregation, tracking, inequality, drop-outs, racism, etc. However, there is one index that embodies all of these and has historically defied correction; the anomalous normal distribution of actualized "ability" and "disability" of some minority group children. Hispanic, African American, and Native American children have had a unique distinction in the history of the public education system of the United States: they have had more "disabled" individuals in special education and very few exceptional students in programs for the gifted.

This chapter examines the phenomenon of ethnic over-representation in special education classes with the primary focus on Hispanic children. The first section of this chapter reviews the historical and legal implications regarding the phenomenon of disproportionate racial and ethnic prevalence rates in mild mental disabilities such as "educable mentally retarded" (EMR) and "learning disabled" (LD) in public schools. The second section examines research literature which supports the hypothesis that the over-representation of minorities labeled as having mild mental disabilities is due to a socially constructed phenomenon, not medical facts.

93

The Disproportionate Representation Debate:
Background and Contexts

The distribution of low mental abilities in minority immigrants has been a constant finding of prominent researchers in American psychology (Garth, 1920, 1923, 1931; Brigham, 1923; Jensen, 1969; Hernstein & Murray, 1995). Goodenough (1926) provides an example of this genre in her description of Italian immigrants:

The Italian continues to rank low even on the non-verbal tests. .... Noting that squalor... is characteristic of the Italian....section, the researchers speculate that it seems probable, upon the whole, that inferior environment is an effect at least as much as it is a cause of inferior ability, as the latter is indicated by intelligence tests. (Goodenough, 1926, p. 391)

This genre in psychological research fundamentally set the stage for the diagnosis of mental disabilities among those minority groups who by the 1950s had not succeeded in crossing over to the middle-class socioeconomic level. For those who did succeed in making that crossing (e.g., Italians, Jews, Chinese, Japanese), the danger of finding inflated levels of mental disabilities or extreme academic under-achievement diminished (Figueroa, 1990), even in the face of internment, dislocation, and government-produced poverty. Cultural capital, once achieved, is far more robust than money. The history of Cuban Americans' successes in the United States, after their disenfranchisement and exodus from Cuba, is a testament to this.

Those groups who by the 1950s still remained without property and without cultural capital, however, found their children overpopulating EMR classes because of low IQs (below 85 until 1961, and below 70 subsequently). Preeminently, it was African American, Hispanic and Native American children who were disproportionately placed in special education classes. Interestingly, Sputnik played a considerable role in the increase of referrals for psycho-educational "diagnoses." As Sleeter (1994) noted, the call for educational reform in the United States after the Russian technological surprise raised educational standards for those who were already being taught relatively well, and raised the prevalence levels of mental disabilities for those minority group children who were in segregated, unequal, tracked, and in remedial programs (Carter, 1970; *Brown v. Board of Education,* 1954; Erikson, 1954).

In the 1960s, researchers began to document the pervasive practice of placing disproportionately large numbers of Mexican American and African American students in EMR classes (Palomares & Johnson, 1966; Mercer, 1973; Carter & Segura, 1979). In the 1970s, the federal courts were asked to examine this unique phenomenon in California's public schools.

The Defining Court Cases: Diana and Larry P.

Two cases in California virtually framed the major issues surrounding the phenomenon of disproportionate minority representation in special education classes. Their influence extended to Public Law 94-142 (and now the Individuals with Disabilities Act, IDEA), as well as to the inquiry regarding minority over-representation in the 1980s as discussed in a report by the National Academy of Science (Heller, Holtzman, & Messick, 1982).

In *Diana v. California Board of Education* (1970), nine Mexican American families filed a class action suit in the Ninth Circuit, Judge Robert Peckham presiding, contending that the misdiagnosis and misplacement in EMR classes caused irreparable harm to the children. The *Diana* complaint noted that the children spoke predominantly Spanish and were diagnosed with an English IQ test. The children had spent three years in EMR classes even though their nonverbal IQs were never below the cut-off of 80 and their verbal IQs produced ludicrous scores (e.g., 30). In addition, the tests and the EMR curriculum ignored all aspects of the children's language and culture, and the EMR classes in their county (Monterey), and throughout all of California, were over-represented with Mexican American children, There were 36 points in the plaintiffs' complaint of which the most salient laid the foundation for subsequent debates surrounding the issue of over-representation: test bias, disproportionate placements, and educational harm.

The statewide data on over-representation was so compelling (Chandler & Platkos, 1969) that California opted to settle the suit. The settlement stipulated the following: the children had to be tested in Spanish and in English, they could be tested using nonverbal measures of intelligence, all Mexican American children in California had to be retested using nonverbal IQ tests, school districts had to report on both their retesting efforts and on how they would transition children from EMR classes to the general education program, a Mexican American test of IQ would be developed, and districts had to determine if their EMR classes were over-represented with Mexican American pupils. Between 1970 and 1974, a protracted argument developed over what would constitute over-representation "to a significant degree." Lawyers for California argued that the E-formula (a standard deviation of a proportion) ordered by the Court to determine significant over-representation constituted a quota. Their preference was a 15% variance around the proportion of Mexican American children in the district. In effect, in a district where 30% of the children were Mexican American, the EMR population of Mexican American pupils would not constitute over-representation if it was below 45%.

Ultimately, the E-formula won. Lawyers for the plaintiffs countered that the E-formula was not inflexible and that it did not penalize small districts. In point of fact, however, the E-formula has a unique predilection. Table 1 demonstrates the unique distribution of leniency generated by the E-formula.

Table 1 shows that regardless of district size, the critical element in the latitude of non-significant variance is the ethnic proportion of Mexican American students in the district. Those districts that had a 50% representation of Mexican American students in their total enrollment were allowed the greatest variance in absolute numbers. The formula, in effect, generates a normal distribution of "variances" based on ethnic representation.

Concerns by the California State Department of Education that the E-formula was a quota persisted. In a series of stipulations, however, Judge Peckham made it clear that the E-formula functioned more as a warning sign than as a quota.

> Before any punitive or remedial sanctions will be imposed upon any district by the court, however, the Stipulation provides for a review hearing at which an opportunity can be given to the district in question to present any unique factors which might affect the appropriateness or the nature of such sanctions. (Memorandum and Order, 1974, pg. 3-4)

However, administrators in the California State Department of Education, Division of Special Education, continued a

Table 1. Distribution of Maximum-allowed Numbers of Chicano Children in EMR Classes for Districts that Vary in Size. EMR Incidence, and Chicano Representation as Generated by the E Formula

$$E = A + \sqrt{\frac{A(100-A)}{N}}$$

EMR Incidence	District Size	5%	30%	50%	70%	95%
2%	100,000	109.8*(+9,8)**	620.4(+20.4)	1022.4(+22.4)	1420.4(+20.4)	1909.78(+9.8)
	10,000	13.08(+3.08)	66.49(+6.48)	107.08(+7.08)	146.48(+6.48)	193(+3)
1%	100,000	56.9(+6.9)	314.5(+14.5)	515.8(+15.8)	714.5(+14.5)	956.9(+6.9)
	10,000	7.18(+2.18)	34.58(+4.58)	55(+5)	74.58(+4.58)	97.18(+2.18)

* = E

** = Absolute number of Chicano students allowed after EMR representation has reached parity with the district percentage of Chicano students.

campaign to portray the *Diana* agreement as a quota. In a critical position paper distributed to school psychologists, the Department reasserted this portrayal and touched on an unspoken belief about Hispanic and African American children in California's public schools.
The *Diana* case was temporarily resolved by a consent decree which required a local school district to apply a standard deviation formula to make comparisons with a theoretical expectancy and the actual number of Chicano pupils who are, or have been, assigned to EMR classes. This resolution of the *Diana* case on the basis of a quota system as a criterion fro (sic) service may be ethically questionable, if not illegal. The data thus far seem to indicate a greater need for special (EMR) class help among Hispanic and Black pupils. A "quota system" presents a dilemma to many individuals that cannot be ignored; to place or not to place - - the decision is always difficult. (Hanson, 1977, pg. 5)
Nowhere in the documents from Judge Peckham's court was there mention of using a quota system as a criterion for service to individual children. Furthermore, the use of a standard deviation formula, together with a review process for districts that could still remain with significant disparities, can best be described as stringent safeguards to protect individuals from misplacement and potential irreparable harm.
Mr. Hanson's paper is particularly interesting from another point. Though he objected to comparisons between expected and actual rates of EMR prevalence, he does not hesitate to suggest that there are more EMR children in African American and Hispanic populations, or that the over-representations may be empirically defensible. The former is fundamentally a racist position, the latter did not exist.
In testimony given in Judge Peckham's court, Mr. Hanson made his position explicitly clear:
The Court: You really think that there were....that many mildly mentally retarded people among the Spanish surname people?
The Witness: Absolutely.
The Court: You do? And you think that there were that many among the blacks?
The Witness: Absolutely. (*Larry P.*, 1979, pg. 28)

The real reason why California, after agreeing to an out-of-court settlement in *Diana*, continued to oppose and characterize *Diana* as a quota was that the *Larry P. v. Riles* case was also in Judge Peckham's court and the Department did not want solutions such as the E-formula to find their way to *Larry P.* The facts surrounding this case were nearly identical to *Diana* except for two critical points. *Larry P.* involved African American children being over-represented in California's EMR classes, and it argued that IQ tests were culturally (rather than linguistically) biased. Unlike in *Diana*, California was not willing to settle in *Larry P.* and the case went to trial in 1977. In 1979 Judge Peckham ruled that: IQ tests were biased against African American children; EMR placement constituted a "dead end" educational program; and, the California State Department of Education intended to do harm to African American children.

As to the question of over-representation, several critical points were noted by Judge Peckham which were derived from the empirical evidence, from the 10,000 pages of testimony taken between 1977 and 1978, from the corpus of applicable state and federal laws, and from extant court decisions. The over-representation rates could not have happened by chance even if one were to concede an incidence rate of educable mental retardation in African American children 50% percent higher than in non-Hispanic white children. Accordingly, "there is no question that a "color-related" factor contributed to the over-enrollment." (*Larry P.*, 1979, pg. 23). The use of "racially and culturally biased" IQ tests (*Larry P.*, 1979, pg. 101) was directly implicated in this over-representation, potentially as the primary determinant in this matter. Finally, the over-representation of African American children in EMR classes violated their "right to equal protection of the laws. Many African American children have been isolated, stigmatized, and provided inadequate education on the basis of unwarranted and impermissible assumptions." (*Larry P.*, 1979, pg. 101).

These two court cases, *Diana* and *Larry P.*, were litigated in California. However, they were actually the precursors for a series of similar challenges to the assessments, diagnoses, and practices in special education that were seen as responsible for the over-representation of minority children. In Chicago (*PASE v. Hannon*), New York (*Jose P. v. N.Y.*), Florida (*OCR Consent Decree*), and other states, similar court cases pursued the same sort of solution as *Diana* and *Larry P.*, an assessment system capable of not confounding cultural, linguistic, or background factors with a disability. Due to the legal challenges, a direct nexus was established between the problem of ethnic over-representation in some special education classes, the educational harm inflicted on children misplaced in EMR classes, racism and the discriminatory impact of psychometric tests, particularly measures of intelligence.

Over-Representation and The Congressional Reports

Since 1975 and the passage of P.L. 94-142, the U.S. Office of Education has annually reported to Congress on the implementation of this federal law and its subsequent reiteration, the Individuals with Disabilities Act (IDEA). The eighteen reports to Congress have one unique characteristic that is germane to the topic discussed here. In spite of the fact that over-representation directly influenced the nondiscriminatory assessment reforms promulgated under P.L. 94-142, the reports over the last two decades seldom devote any informed attention to nondiscriminatory assessment. Further, until the fourteenth report (United States Department of Education, 1992), the issue of ethnic children in special education seldom received any real scrutiny. The two exceptions are the fifth and fourteenth reports..

The fifth report (United States Department of Education, 1983) includes a section on "Efforts to Prevent Erroneous Classification." Using the data from the 1980 Elementary and Secondary Schools Civil Rights Survey, it notes that over-representation exists with African American and Native American pupils. This is a conclusion which does not coincide with a study by the National Academy of Sciences using the same data (Finn, 1982). The eleventh report (United States Department of Education, 1989) briefly raises an important issue about minority children in special education. Of the 209,442 children who left special education in the 1986-87 school year, 25.1% dropped out. That report notes that "research has documented significantly higher drop out rates for males, youth from low income families, minorities and youth in urban areas..." (pg. 72). However, two pages later it states that drop out rates were not significant across ethnic groups.

The fourteenth report (United States Department of Education, 1992) is perhaps the most intriguing. It focuses on the status of migrant, Native Pacific Basin and Native Hawaiian students in special education. In the section on migrant students the U.S. Office of Special Education devotes three and a half pages to "Language and Culture" (pg. G-17). The report asserts that cultural and linguistic differences impede both the delivery of special education services and the validity of diagnoses.

Most of the recommendations in this report for assessing migrant children (using interpreters, translating tests, and tests normed in Spanish) are standard practice in assessing all children from bilingual backgrounds and abilities. These are also contrary to professional standards (American Educational Research Association, American Psychological Association, National Council on Measurement, 1985) or without any empirical validation (Valdes & Figueroa, 1994).

In the section on Native Pacific Basin and Native Hawaiian students, the fourteenth report to Congress included information not previously analyzed in other reports, the proportions, by disabilities, of ethnic children in special education. Unlike most measures of over-representation, the statistics in Table 2 examine the total number of students in special education in a given ethnic group and breaks this down by the proportions in each of the categories of disabilities served by special education. These data are for the 1986-87 school year (from Table G.7, Report Number 14), for migrant Students (from Table G.1, Report Number 14) and for LEP students (from Table F.1, in report number 15 (United States Department of Education (1993))

As Table 2 shows, there are two broad types of disabilities, those with large incidence rates and large differences in the percent of students in each category of disability across ethnic groups, and those with low incidence rates and small differences in the percent in each category across ethnic groups. The former include Specific Learning Disabilities (SLD), Speech and Language Impairments (SLI), Mental Retardation (MR), and Serious Emotional Disturbances (SED). In the SLD category two thirds of all migrant pupils in special education were diagnosed as having SLD, whereas only one half of Asian American students in special education were so diagnosed. On the other hand, in the SLI category, 46% of Asian American students were diagnosed as SLI and only 13% of migrant pupils were in this category. In the MR category, approximately 18% of migrant pupils who were in special education in 1986-87 were in this category, yet only 6% of

TABLE 2. Proportions, by Disability, of Ethnic Children in Special Education, 1986-87 (Report 14), 1988 (For LEP in Report 15).

DIS-ABIL	NATV AMER	ASIAN AMER	HISPN AMER	MIGRT	AFRIC AMER	HWAIN-AMER	FILI-PINO	PACF ISLN	LEP	ANGO-AMER	TOT
SLD	56.86	32.59	59.61	63.8	47.54	56.82	45.55	58.45	53.8	44.61	48.36
SLI	25.49	46.08	21.39	13.4	25.12	26.6	30.96	21.04	26.9	32.67	30.70
MR	5.88	8.32	7.8	13.6	8.62	6.39	10.95	9.53	17.6	5.65	7.4
SED	5.88	3.10	5.35	2.9	6.65	2.94	2.81	3.60	1.7	6.89	4.67
H.I.	0	1.85	.65	.09	1.72	1.73	2.77	2.34	--	1.24	1.65
S.M.D	0	1.25	1.01	--	1.72	.86	1.59	.9	--	1.44	1.3
O.I.	0	2.63	1.08	.8	1.72	.69	1.72	1.44	--	1.91	1.78
O.H.I	0	1.69	.29	1.2	1.48	1.04	.46	.18	--	1.31	.70
V.I.	0	1.69	.43	.6	.74	0	.76	.36	--	.51	.48
D-B	0	1.09	.14	--	.25	0	0	0	--	0	.04
Autism	0	1.26	.29	--	.25	.17	.21	0	--	.35	.20

U.S. Department of Education (1992, 1993). To Assure the Free Appropriate Public Education of All Children With Disabilities: Fourteenth and Fifteenth Reports to Congress on the Implementation of The Individuals With Disabilities Act. Washington, D.C.: U.S. Government Printing Office.

Native American children were so diagnosed. In the Severe Emotionally Disturbed category, Limited English Proficient children had only 2% of its special education population in this category whereas nearly 7% of non-Hispanic white children were diagnosed with this disability.

Most migrant children are Hispanic and so are most LEP pupils. Yet, the Hispanic subsets of "migrant" and "LEP" show unique patterns of disability rates: larger prevalence of Severe Emotional Disturbance, lower rates of Mental Retardation, similar rates of Speech and Language Impairments with LEP students, and more Specific Learning Disabilities than LEP children. Compared to non-Hispanic white pupils, however, Hispanic students are more susceptible to Specific Learning Disabilities, and less likely to have Speech and Language Impairments.

Across Table 2, migrant pupils have more SLD, Asian students show the most SLI, LEP children have more MR, and non-Hispanic white pupils demonstrate more SED. Though the proportions in the more medical categories are fairly close, an interesting pattern emerges for Asian children. They have the highest rates for Orthopedic Impairments, Other Health Impairments, Visual Impairments, Deaf-Blindness, and Autism. Finally, a disturbing fact also emerges from Table 2. Native American and Hawaiian children in some of the severe physical categories of disabilities are either not getting any special education services or they are not being accurately counted and included in these Congressional reports.

Overall, the data in Table 2 are hard to interpret from any epidemiological perspective. The variation in the total number of children in the categories of mild disabilities when examined across ethnic groups echoes back to the in original complaints and issues of test bias and false positives raised in *Diana* and *Larry P.* except that in this instance the scenario is a national one. We propose that the data in Table 2 compels an explanation of special education (certainly for the mild disabilities) that is based on a social construction explanation. Even report number fourteen seems to acknowledge this: "Current research suggests that it is very difficult to distinguish between the impact of a disability on the student's learning and the failure of a·student to understand the majority language and culture" (U.S. Dept. of Education, 1992, pg. G-17).

The Social Construction Issue

A critical assumption of the gravamen against over-representation in special education classes has always been that such over-representation is not based on a real, medical prevalence rate but rather on some artificial, capricious, perhaps racist, social phenomena. The opposite position is fundamentally faced with having to argue either lower genetic aptitude in racial-ethnic minorities or profound environmental insults comparable to extreme third world conditions in hygiene, medical care, malnutrition, and toxicity. However, the question of whether there are more disabilities in certain minority group children is not unique. In fact, it is a subtext to a larger question about the veracity of prevalence rates in general in the United States.

Redefining Mental Retardation
    One of the more dramatic examples of the social construction of ability and disability occurred in 1961. At that time, the American Association on Mental Deficiency (AAMD) decided that the diagnosis of mental retardation needed to be changed (Heber, 1961). Rather than rely on single measures of intelligence to diagnose mental retardation, the AAMD resurrected the oldest, historical yardstick of mental competence, how an individual took care of himself or herself in society. In 1973, it operationalized this two-prong definition. Instead of relying on an IQ cut-off of one standard deviation below the mean, the association decided that mental retardation would involve an IQ under two standard deviations below 100 together with substandard performance in adaptive behavior (using measures that assess an individual's ability to meet the *culturally* imposed demands for independence and social functioning). Virtually overnight, thousands of individuals in the United States technically ceased to be mentally retarded. Typically, these were individuals with no discernible medical problems or symptomatology.
    It also became much harder to catch mental retardation. As Mercer (1973) empirically demonstrated, the number of persons who would fail both IQ (<70) and adaptive behavior was small. Interestingly, the majority of those who were "cured" by this two-prong definition of mental retardation (Mercer, 1973) were African American and Hispanic citizens.

Mercer's studies in the 1960s were influential in the broad recognition that many children in EMR classes were really "The Six-Hour Retarded Child." The President's Commission on Mental Retardation (1969) formally described this child as: "..retarded from 9 to 3, five days a week, solely on the basis of an IQ score, without regard to his adaptive behavior which may be exceptionally adaptive to the situation and community in which he lives." Considering that the President's Commission on Mental Retardation (1969, 1970) was a unique advocacy group for the Mentally Retarded, the recognition that contextual factors rather than true individual differences could be implicated in the misdiagnosis of Mental Retardation with minority children was and is a major admission of the social construction phenomena that has plagued special education assessment, diagnosis and programs.

Switching Disabilities. During the time when P.L. 94-142, *Diana* and *Larry P.* were occurring, Tucker (1980) examined the longitudinal changes in the representation rates across eight years (1970-1977) for the learning disability and EMR categories in more than fifty school districts in the Southwest. One of his specific questions was "To what extent are African American, Anglo, and Mexican-American students labeled LD as opposed to EMR? Or, to what extent has there been an increase in LD proportional to a decrease in EMR?" (Tucker, 1980, pg. 102). One finding of this study was that as the EMR category dwindled, the LD category grew enormously. Also, the racial-ethnic over-representation in the EMR category was taken over and magnified in the LD category. When he combined the LD and EMR pupil percentages by ethnic group, the old problem of over-representation emerged. He observed:

> The traditional accusation of racial discrimination cannot be refuted on the basis of these data. In fact, since 1970 the disproportion of minority students in LD and EMR classes (combined) has remained virtually the same for Mexican Americans relative to Anglos but has steadily increased for blacks. (Tucker, 1977, pg. 104).

As noted by Tucker (1977), his findings were accentuated by the unique irony of the origins of the LD label. Professor Samuel Kirk, on April 6, 1963, literally invented the name during a conference presentation as part of a speech denouncing the use of labels in special education. Kirk talked about those children who had learning problems but who were not handicapped. That night, the special educators at that conference created the Association for Children with Learning Disabilities and reified Professor Kirk's observation about underachievers into a category of a mental disability, probably one of the most successful social constructions in the field of education.

A Strategy for Equity. In 1982, the problem of ethnic over-representation in special education classrooms was taken up by the National Academy of Sciences (Heller, Holtzman, & Messick, 1982). In five sections of the report and six separately authored chapters, *Placing Children in Special Education: A Strategy for Equity* fundamentally portrays a tense debate between those who believe in the viability of the EMR category of disability (and the concomitant validity of the psychometric technology used to diagnose it) and those who worry about the attenuating impact of culture and language on tests and the diagnosis of mild mental retardation. In our judgment the latter win on three grounds.

First, in the empirical analysis of the 1978-79 national OCR school survey, Finn (1982) presents a series of anomalous interactions related to ethnic status and school contexts. In school districts where there are no bilingual programs, more Hispanic children are diagnosed as EMR. Southern states had the greatest and least amounts of over-representation. In school districts where many children were referred and placed in EMR classes, the ethnic levels of over-representation were the highest. Also, as the percentage of minority, school-district enrollment increased, over-representation tended to decrease. In some school districts with large Hispanic enrollments, their EMR over-representation was high. In school districts with high African American enrollments, Hispanic over-representation was negligible. For Native American, Alaskan, and African American children, attending a middle to high SES school district lowered the probability of their over-representation in EMR classes.

Second, the text is replete with the acknowledgments that historically the definition of mild retardation has often changed. Even in contemporary times, different societies deal with the EMR entity as either being non-existent or requiring special status as a disability. On this point, the report acknowledges the arbitrariness of the category although it inherently seems to justify it on the basis of posited intellectual prerequisites in a future, cognitively-demanding society. Supposedly this society would preclude some supposedly limited individuals from employment and competence. The futurist argument has been used consistently since the 1930s. Arthur Jensen did not hesitate to conjure it up in 1967 (Jensen, 1967). The National Academy Report repeats it in the 1980s.

> Although its genesis may dig deeply into biological as well as social roots, the phenomenon of mild mental retardation is primarily a cultural construct. Its very nature has changed dramatically over time, and its contemporary definitions are highly influenced by differences among societies. Within the United States in the past 100 years, arbitrary shifts in diagnostic criteria has moved children in and out of the mildly retarded populations. Moreover, as society becomes increasingly complex in its technological demands, new classifications of "defectiveness" will undoubtedly arise. (Heller, Holtzman, & Messick, 1982, p. 168)

Third, the major recommendation made by the report inherently recognizes the role that the instructional context might play in the creation of false positives. The National Academy recommended that before a child is "diagnosed," his or her current classroom had to be "diagnosed" *first*. Specifically, diagnosticians were urged to determine the following: whether there was evidence that the curriculum used was valid for the type of child under consideration, whether the teacher was effectively applying the curriculum, whether early modifications of the educational program had been tried, and whether there was evidence that the student was actually not learning. In actual fact, the entire report repeatedly worries about differential impacts in instructional and curricular variations across the country. It is one of the great tensions in the report, the acknowledgment that the educational system might be responsible for the over-representation and the reluctant, almost hidden, recognition that it might also hold the key to resolving the question of ethnic/racial disproportionality in classes for children with no discernible symptomatology other than poor scholastic and test performance.

Interaction of Language and Culture. In the early 1980s, the federal government funded two Handicapped Minority Research

Institutes, one in Texas (Garcia, 1985; Ortiz, 1986; Wilkinson & Ortiz, 1986; Ortiz & Polyzoi, 1986, 1987; Ortiz & Yates, 1987; Swedo, 1987; Willig & Swedo, 1987) and the other in California (Rueda, Cardoza, Mercer, & Carpenter, 1984; Rueda, Figueroa, Mercado, & Cardoza, 1984). Both studied the assessment and instructional processes in special education with Hispanic pupils already placed in special education. The California Institute also investigated variations from the existing practices to see what would be the impact from using Spanish language tests and testing. The Texas Institute studied impacts from doing a different type of pedagogy.

The data from this research augured badly for Hispanic children who were referred for special education assessment. If their parents were born in Mexico or Latin America, they had a greater likelihood of being diagnosed as "disabled." Hispanic students were typically referred to special education because of low achievement (GPA's in the C and D levels), poor reading, and "poor oral skills." If they were in the processes of acquiring English, their articulation errors, limited vocabulary, and poor comprehension in English all became evidence of a Speech and Language Disability. A high percentage of these pupils went to programs for the Communication Handicapped. If they were tested only in English they had a higher probability of qualifying as Learning Disabled. If they were given certain tests of intelligence (e.g., the *Kaufman Assessment Battery of Children*) they were more likely to be diagnosed as Learning Disabled. If they were re-evaluated after being in special education for some time, their IQs had decreased and often they were placed in even more restricted special education programs. Limited English proficient students changed categories of disability more often than English speakers.

Diagnostic tests in Spanish were no better than English diagnostic tests because bilingual pupils are not validly assessed when they are compared to monolingual students be these Spanish or English speakers (Valdes & Figueroa, 1994). Diagnostic tests when given to children who had *never* been referred to special education mistakenly determined that 53% of them qualified as Learning Disabled. The same diagnostic tests, when given to Hispanic children in EMR classes, determined that 46% of them also qualified as Learning Disabled (Rueda, Figueroa, Mercado, & Cardoza, 1984).

Special education classrooms for Hispanic children typically produced low levels of task engagement. Once a bilingual child entered special education, bilingual support services ended. In the California study, 44% of those place in special education had unofficially been placed in a special education program as a "modification of their regular program." The classes that were effective in this regard were atypical of what normally happens in special education instruction: they had culturally/linguistically comprehensible subject matter, lots of peer interaction, engagement of feelings of pride and success and a more holistic orientation to literacy development and subject matter.

"Handicapping the Handicapped." In 1986, Hugh Mehan, a sociologist-anthropologist, published an extremely important book titled *Handicapping the Handicapped*. It is one of the least read texts in special education and at the same time one of the most important. Mehan's ethnography of the special education system in the Oceanside School District in California unpacks the extant practices in special education in a manner that traditional experimental designs are incapable of doing. Using decision-making theory as the conceptual basis for his extended observations of the main players in special education in a school district, Mehan and his colleagues concluded that unlike the rational decision-making processes outlined in the federal law, educators in that district (and there is no reason to believe otherwise for every other school district) bartered, bargained and generally failed to carry out the rational, problem solving procedures prescribed by the federal law.

Among the most important areas of inquiry, Mehan et al. (1986) videotaped the diagnostic process. He visually recorded how school psychologists and the IEP (Individual Educational Plan) meetings "do" diagnoses. He found that testing was carried on and on until the diagnostic profile of the suspected disability appeared. Some children took more than twenty diagnostic tests in this quest. Also, contrary to the tenets of standardization and objectivity in testing, he found that testers and their test subjects produced a distinct social reality of cuing based on the quality of their social interactions.

At the IEP meeting, the decision was usually presented in the official case study reports of those who held primary status in those meetings, the diagnosticians. Parents and general education teachers listened, were not expected to ask questions, and where generally left out of the decision making process in what Mehan called "The Discourse of Persuasion." Mehan's study unveils the special education process for what it actually is: a social phenomenon posing as a medical reality.

The Deconstruction of Special Education. In 1991, Thomas Skrtic (1991) examined much of the special education empirical literature to try and determine the effectiveness of the system. He asked three questions from this literature. First, Are mild handicaps real? For many children,

> because of the number of definitional and measurement problems, as well as problems related to the will or the capacity of teachers and schools to accommodate student diversity, many students identified as mildly handicapped are not truly disabled in a pathological sense.....particularly....for students identified as learning disabled. (Skrtic, 1991, pg. 154-155)

Second, is diagnosis objective and useful? His answer: "...there are no instructionally relevant reasons for making the disabled-nondisabled distinction" (Skrtic, 1991, pg. 155) and "effective instructional and management procedures will be substantially the same for non-handicapped and most mildly handicapped students" (Kaufman, Gerber, & Semmel, 1988, pg. 8).

Finally, he asks: Is special education effective and rational? His answer is no. Further, he quotes one of the main camps in special education as follows:

> ...given the weak effects of special education instructional practices and the social and psychological costs of labeling, the current system of special education is, at best, no more justifiable than simply permitting students to remain unidentified in regular classrooms and, at worst, far less justifiable than regular classroom placement in conjunction with appropriate in-class support services. (Skrtic, 1991, pg. 156-157)

Admissions and Anomalies in the Reports to Congress. Since 1975, when the regulations for 94-142 codified the categories of disabilities that qualify for special education services, the annual incidence figures reported by the U.S. Office of Education have suggested that there are two broad types of disabilities: those with clear medical etiology and symptomatology and those without. The former's incidence figures have always been small in numbers and easily explained when longitudinal fluctuations or changes appeared (e.g., severe head injury among adolescents involved in auto accidents). The incidence figures for those disabilities with no discernible biological symptoms have been very large, and they have also been difficult to explain, thereby prompting socio-causal explanations.

In the Eighteenth report to Congress (U.S. Department of Education, 1996), for example, data for the 1994-95 academic year showed that across the fifty states and the District of Columbia the rate of pupil participation in special education classes varied between a low of 5.37 percent in Idaho to 11.9 percent in Massachusetts (pg. A-34). Most of this variation was directly attributable to the invisible disabilities, particularly Learning Disabilities.

Also, the longitudinal trend in incidence rates clearly shows two different, general types of "disabilities." For those with clear medical symptoms, the incidence rates across grades (K-12) are consistently small and similar until the twelfth grade when drop-out or other special programs and services begin. The Learning Disabled population, however, nearly triples in the second grade (91,900), reaches high volume in the sixth grade (267,989), and then dwindles to 91,454 when the students reach 18 years of age. The Speech or Language Impaired reaches its high mark at the first grade (202,405) and then steadily declines to three percent of its high mark by the twelfth grade (6,336). The Mentally Retarded category (which includes a small percent of children with clear biological symptoms and nosology (e.g., Down's Syndrome) and a majority with no such symptoms) grows steadily throughout the elementary and high school grades until it reaches its zenith at the ninth grade (49,875). Then, it drops so dramatically by the age of 18, that drop out factors and the "Six Hour Retarded" syndrome seem likely. A similar pattern appears for the Emotionally Disturbed (49,641 to 15,091).

The Critical Literature. The literature on the social construction of disabilities is controversial. The mainstream special education literature is more extensive, generally not supportive of the social construction hypothesis and occasionally provides compelling arguments to support its position (e.g., Fuchs & Fuchs, 1994). The studies presented here, however, are a small sample from a substantial genre that spans over fifty years and that provides an intellectual landscape against which to consider the over-representation of ethnic children in special education (e.g., Manuel, 1935; Mercer, 1973; Ysseldyke, Algozzine, Shinn, & McGue, 1982; Coles, 1987; Cummins, 1984; Rueda, Figueroa, Cardoza, & Carpenter, 1984; Rueda, Mercer, Cardoza, & Carpenter, 1984; Poplin, 1988; Taylor, 1991; Valdes & Figueroa, 1994; Skrtic, 1995; Poplin & Cousin, 1996). We maintain that, in many ways, over-representation is the most egregious aspect of the social construction phenomena. The issue of stigma is seldom discussed when a child is misplaced in special education. The prejudice that is visited on disabled youngsters by their non-disabled peers is essentially inherited by the misplaced, non-disabled minority child. Over-representation also carries with it a group effect, a social construction that says "they have more children with limited ability," fundamentally, a stereotype that affects the members of groups that in American education have historically been denied an equal educational opportunity.

Conclusion

It is a fact that there is over-representation of minorities in special education programs. This chapter advances the proposition that over-representation is a socially constructed phenomenon. The typical solutions to the problem of over-representation have generally focused on the assessment-diagnostic processes. Some have attempted to make the testing more complex (Mercer, 1979). Others have instituted an elaborate pre-referral process. Both solutions work under the principle of "do more." This is typically very costly. It may also be ineffective. The New York Consent Decree under *Jose P.* provides the most compelling example of how "do more" only leads to potential bankruptcy and not to the diminution of over-representation (Dillon, 1997).

What practical factors can school personnel use to safeguard against disproportionate minority placement in special education? In our next chapter we attempt to answer this question. We suggest a combination of enriched pedagogy and paradigmatic reform. The model for such an undertaking? The program for "gifted" and "talented" children.

References

Brigham, C. C. (1923). *A study of American intelligence.* Princeton: Princeton University Press.

Brown v. Board of Education. 347 U.S. 483 (1954).

Carter, T. (1970). *Mexican Americans in school: A decade of neglect.* N.Y.: College Entrance Examination Board.

Carter, T. & Segura, R.D. (1979). *Mexican Americans in school: A decade of change.* N.Y.: College Entrance Examination Board.

Chandler, J. & Platkos, J. (1969). *Spanish speaking pupils classified as EMR.* Sacramento: California State Department of Education.

Cummins, J. (1984). *Bilingualism and special education: Issues in assessment and pedagogy.* San Diego, CA: College - Hill.

Diana v. California Board of Education, No. C-70-37. (N.D. Calif. 1970).

Dillon, S. (1997). Special education soaks up New York's resources. *The New York Times,* April 6, 1997.

Erikson, E.H. (1950). *Childhood and society.* New York: Norton.

Figueroa, R.A. (1990). Assessment of linguistic minority group children. In C.R. Reynolds and R.W. Kamphaus (Eds.), *Handbook of psychological and educational assessment of children: Vol. 1. Intelligence and achievement.* New York: Guilford.

Finn, J.D. (1982). Patterns in special education placement as revealed by OCR surveys. In K. A. Heller, W. H. Holtzman, & S. Messick (Eds.), *Placing children in special education: A strategy for equity.* Washington, D.C.: National Academy Press.

Fuchs, D. , & Fuchs, L.S. (1994). Inclusive schools movement and the radicalization of special education reform. *Exceptional Children, 60,* 294-309.

Garcia, S.B. (1985, Fall). Characteristics of limited English proficient Hispanic students served in programs for the learning disabled: Implications for policy, practice and research (Part I). *Bilingual Special Education Newsletter,* 1-5. Austin: University of Texas, Department of Special Education, Handicapped Minority Research Institute

Garth, T. R. (1920). Racial differences in mental fatigue. *Journal of Applied Psychology, 4*, 235-244.

Garth, T.R. (1923). A comparison of the intelligence of Mexican and full blood Indian children. *Psychological Review, 30*, 388-401.

Garth, T.R. (1931). *Race psychology: A study of racial mental differences.* New York: MacGraw Hill.

Goodenough, F.L. (1926). Racial differences in the intelligence of school children. *Journal of Experimental Psychology, 9*, 388-397.

Hanson, F. (1977). Presentation to California school psychologists. Sacramento, CA: California State Department of Education.

Heber, R. (1961). A manual on terminology and classification in mental retardation. *American Journal of Mental Deficiency*, Monograph Supplement.

Heller, K.A., Holtzman, W.H., & Messick, S. (1982). *Placing children in special education: A strategy for equity.* Washington, D.C.: National Academy Press.

Hernstein, R.J. & Murray, C. (1994). *The bell curve: Intelligence and class structure in American life.* N.Y.: Free Press.

Jensen, A.R. (1969). How much can we boost IQ and scholastic achievement? Harvard Educational Review, 39, 1-123.

Kaufman, J.M., Gerber, M.M., & Semmel, M.I. (1988). Arguable assumptions underlying the regular education initiative. *Journal of Learning Disabilities, 21*, 6-11

Larry P. v. Riles. 343 F. Supp. 1306 (N.D. Cal. 1972) *aff'r* 502 F. 2d 963 (9th Cir. 1974); 495 F Supp. 296 (N.D. Cal. 1979); appeal docketed, No. 80-4027 (9th Cir., Jan. 17, 1980).

Manuel, H.T. (1935). Spanish and English editions of the Stanford Binet in relation to the abilities of Mexican children. University of Texas Bulletin (no. 3532). Austin, TX: University of Texas.

Mehan, H. (1986). *Handicapping the handicapped: Decision making in students' educational careers.* Stanford, CA: Stanford University Press.

Mehan, H., Hertweck, H., & Meihls, J. L. (1986). *Handicapping the handicapped.* Palo Alto, CA: Stanford University Press.

Memorandum and Order (1974). *Diana v. California Board of Education*, No. C-70-37. (N.D. Calif. 1970).

Mercer, J.R. (1973). *Labeling the mentally retarded.* Berkeley, CA: University of California Press.

Mercer, J.R. (1979). *The system of multicultural pluralistic assessment.* New York: Psychological Corporation.

Ortiz, A.A. (1986, Spring). Characteristics of limited English-proficient Hispanic students served in programs for the learning disabled: Implications for policy and practice (Part II). *Bilingual Special Education Newsletter*, p. 1-5. Austin: University of Texas, Department of Special Education, Handicapped Minority Research Institute.

Ortiz, A.A.. & Polyzoi, E. (1986). *Characteristics of limited English-proficient Hispanic students served in programs for the learning disabled: Implications for policy and practice.* Austin, TX: University of Texas (ERIC Document Reproduction Services No. ED 2676-597).

Ortiz, A.A.. & Polyzoi, E. (1987). *Language assessment of Hispanic learning disabled and speech and language handicapped students: Research in progress.* Austin: University of Texas, Department of Special Education, Handicapped Minority Research Institute.

Ortiz, A.A., & Yates, J. (1987). *Characteristics of learning disabled, mentally retarded and speech-language handicapped Hispanic students at initial evaluation and re-evaluation.* Unpublished manuscript. Austin: University of Texas, Department of Special Education, Handicapped Minority Research Institute.

Palomares, U.H. & Johnson, L.C. (1966). Evaluation of Mexican American pupils for EMR classes. *California Education, 3,* 27-29.

Poplin, M. (1988). The reductionist fallacy in learning disabilities: Replicating the past by reducing the present. *Journal of Learning Disabilities, 21,* 389-400.

Poplin, M. & Cousin, P.T. (1996). *Alternative views of learning disabilities.* Austin, TX: Pro ED.

President's Commission on Mental Retardation (1969). MR 69, Washington, D.C.: Government Printing Office.

President's Commission on Mental Retardation (1970). MR 70, Washington, D.C.: Government Printing Office.

Rueda, R. (1989). Defining mild disabilities with language-minority students. *Exceptional Children, 56,* 121-129.

Rueda, R., Cardoza, D., Mercer, J.R., & Carpenter, L. (1984). *An examination of special education decision making with*

Hispanic first-time referrals in large urban school districts. Los Alomitos, CA: Southwest Regional Laboratory.

Rueda, R., Figueroa, R.A., Mercado, P., & Cardoza, D. (1984). *Performance of Hispanic educable mentally retarded, learning disabled, and nonclassified students on the WISC-RM, SOMPA, and S-KABC (Final Report - Short-term Study One).* Los Alomitos, CA: Southwestern Regional Laboratory for Educational Research and Development.

Skrtic, T. (1991). The special education paradox: Equity as the way to excellence. *Harvard Educational Review, 61,* 148-206.

Skrtic, T. (1995). *Disability and democracy.* New York: Teachers College Press.

Sleeter, C. E. (1995). Radical structuralist perspectives on the creation and use of Learning Disabilities. In T. M. Skrtic (Ed.), *Disability and democracy: Reconstructing special education for postmodernity.* New York: Teachers College Press (p. 153-165).

Swedo, J. (1987). Effective teaching strategies for handicapped limited English proficient students. *Bilingual Special Education Newsletter.* Austin, Texas: University of Texas at Austin, 1-5

Taylor, D. (1991). *Learning denied.* Portsmouth, NH: Heinemann.

Tucker, J.A. (1980). Ethnic proportions in classes for the learning disabled: Issues in nonbiased assessment. *Journal of Special Education,* 14, 93-105.

United States Department of Education (1983. 1989, 1992, 1993, 1996). Fifth, Eleventh, Fourteenth, Fifteenth, and Eighteenth annual reports to Congress on the implementation of The Education of the Handicapped Act. Washington D.C.: Government Printing Office.

Valdes, G. & Figueroa, R.A. (1994). *Bilingualism and testing: A special case of bias.* Norwood, N.J.: Ablex.

Wilkinson, C.Y., & Ortiz, A.A. (1986). *Characteristics of limited English-proficient and English proficient learning disabled Hispanic students at initial assessment and re-evaluation.* Austin: University of Texas, Department of Special Education, Handicapped Minority Research Institute.

Willig, A.C., & Swedo, J. (1987). *Improving teaching strategies for exceptional Hispanic limited English proficient students: An exploratory study of task engagement and teaching strategies*. Paper presented at the annual meeting of the American Educational Research Association, Washington, D.C.

Yseldyke, J.E., Algozzine, B., Shinn, M., Mc Gue, M. (1982). Similarities and differences between low achievers and students classified learning disabled. *Journal of Special Education*, 16, 73-85.

CHAPTER 6

Minority Underrepresentation in Gifted Programs: Old Problems, New Perspectives

Richard A. Figueroa & Nadeen T. Ruiz

Introduction

In the last chapter we concentrated on the overrepresentation of Hispanic students in special education classes. We concluded by asking: What practical factors can school personnel use to safeguard against disproportionate minority placement in special education? In this chapter, we focus on the underrepresentation of Hispanic children at the other end of the "normal curve," the gifted and talented. Here we begin by asking: What practical factors can school personnel use to safeguard against disproportionate minority underrepresentation in programs for the gifted and talented? As we intimated previously, the answer to both questions is elegant, but not simple. It is in an educational contextualism that is capable of actuating academic achievement among Hispanic boys and girls irrespective of "learning disabilities," "average ability," "at-risk status," "bilingualism," or "giftedness."

With respect to the latter, we have come to this conclusion because of several intractable, longitudinal problems that have plagued gifted education in relation to Hispanic children and youth. First, there is the issue of disproportionate underrepresentation. For more than seventy years, this phenomenon has defied the best efforts of educators and researchers. Then, there is the question of identifying superior academic performance in children who have varying levels of bilingualism and bicultural-

119

ism in their backgrounds. Assessment procedures have not succeeded in removing the subtractive impact of these variables on achievement scores and other indices of ability. Also, attempts at making gifted programs more culturally receptive and appropriate have not produced generalizeable models that can be widely used throughout the country.

On top of these challenges, there also exists a critical body of work which suggests that gifted education is a problem both in terms of its negative impact on all other programs and in terms of its status as a separate opportunity for a chosen few. Whereas special education has joined the national reform emphases to fully include in the general education program the majority of students with disabilities, gifted education has no such initiative. In fact, some of the literature on the gifted seems more reactionary and balkanized than innovative or inclusive (Purcell, 1995; Silverman, 1995).

Our "solution" to these problems is based on an emerging body of work which suggests that for the Hispanic student (as well as for the at-risk student) the best course of action is in providing a gifted classroom. Remediation has not worked. Neither has Reductionism (Poplin, 1988a). Current research suggests that enrichment for all students may be the best direction to take. Clearly, this is in line with the national emphases on higher standards. What we propose here, however, is that enrichment should begin with a pedagogy that can actuate the upper range of children's academic achievement, particularly Hispanic children who have been kept out of gifted programs and whose demographic presence will greatly affect the future of public education.

Hispanic Children and Educational Programs for the Gifted

Prior to 1978, the primary eligibility criterion for admission into a program for gifted children was having a high intelligence quotient (IQ). The range of IQ scores that determined eligibility varied from state to state, ranging between 150 and 130. This standard basically excluded those below the 99.94 or 97.73 percentile of measured intelligence as determined by an IQ test. After 1978, the criterion was broadened. Specifically,

> gifted and talented children means children....who are identified at the preschool, elementary, or secondary level as possessing demonstrated or potential abilities

that give evidence of high performance capabilities in areas such as intellectual, creative, specific academic, or leadership ability, or in the performing and visual arts, and who by reason thereof, require services, or activities not ordinarily provided by the school. (Section 902 of the *Gifted and Talented Children's Act of 1978,* Public Law 95-561, 1978).
More recently, the *Jacob Javits Gifted and Talented Students Education Act of 1988* (Public Law 100-297), defined giftedness along similar lines: high intelligence, creativity, artistic ability, leadership, or specific academic talent that require unique school services for their full development.

Why Minorities are Underrepresented in Gifted Education
    Currently, the criteria for identifying gifted students is echoed in textbooks and takes various overlapping forms. Renzulli (1978) offered one version that has retained considerable staying power: high intellectual ability, task commitment or persistence, and creativity. However, these changes in eligibility criteria have not altered two facts, IQ still remains the most consistently used measure for determining eligibility, and Hispanic and minority children do not get identified as gifted in numbers that are anywhere near demographic proportionality.
    Historically, the underrepresentation of Hispanic students in gifted and talented programs has been well documented. In 1933, Reynolds reported to the U.S. Department of the Interior that the IQs of "Spanish-speaking" children throughout the Southwest typically mirrored that of a large sample (N=1,240) of Mexican children tested in the Los Angeles Unified School District. These data presented a negatively skewed distribution of IQ that at the gifted range "identified" only 2.48 Mexican American children (out of the 1,240) as gifted when in fact a normal curve distribution would have identified 28.15 children as gifted. In effect, only 8.8% of those that should have been identified as gifted (under typical normal curve conditions) were actually designated as gifted. By 1987, this situation had improved in the Los Angeles Unified School District. Hispanic students made up 56% of the public school population. Their representation rate in the gifted and talented program, however, was 29% (Perrine, 1989). With IQ as the main index for determining giftedness, Mexican

American children were, and continue to be, significantly underrepresented in such classrooms.

Research conducted on gifted children between the 1920s and the 1960s typically ignored certain ethnic groups (e.g., Terman & Oden, 1925, 1947). Among these were Mexican American, African American, Italian, and Portuguese children (Adler, 1967). In great part this was due to a research program generally called Race Psychology. It usually found few gifted individuals in these populations. By the 1960s, the paucity of research and the disparate prevalence findings on ethnic giftedness were causing investigators to speculate about the broad parameters involved:

> Some of the factors behind these differences may be the nature of our current intelligence tests, language facility [in English], differences in cultural value systems and background, socioeconomic class, physical and psychological environment, schooling, and perhaps others still not identified. (Adler, 1967, p. 105)

In the 1970s, the U.S. Commission on Civil Rights reported to Congress that: the "distribution of Chicano and Anglo students across ability groups also shows overrepresentation of Mexican Americans in low ability group classes and underrepresentation in high ability group classes" (U.S. Commission on Civil Rights, 1974, p. 22). In the 1990s the same finding holds true (Callahan, Hunsaker, Adams, Moore, & Blend, 1995).

Over the last 30 years, researchers who have studied this problem (Bernal, 1974, 1978; Gregory, Starnes, & Blaylock, 1989; Maker & Schiever, 1989; Barkan & Bernal, 1991; Maker, 1996) often either over-focus on the eligibility criteria and assessment tools used to identify students for entrance into these programs (Bernal & Reyna, 1975; Chambers, Barron, & Sprecher, 1980; Perrine, 1989; Zappia, 1989; Bermudez & Rakow, 1990; Marquez, Bermudez & Rakow, 1992; Johnsen, Ryser, & Dougherty, 1993; Sawyer & Marquez, 1993; Garcia, 1994; Maker, 1994, 1996), or they accept the justification and need for school programs for the "gifted" (they often do so by attempting to create culturally appropriate versions of such programs). In our judgment, neither emphasis has succeeded in improving the national representation rates of Hispanic students in gifted classrooms. As Feldman (1991) acknowledges, this failure has even led to questioning the foundations and practices associated with giftedness and gifted education in the United States.

IQ Test Bias

A large cadre of researchers have focused on how to circumvent or repair the inequities caused by the IQ-dominated criteria used for placing children in programs for the gifted. Bernal (1974, 1978), for example, has concentrated on the bias of IQ tests. His alternatives have included community behavioral descriptors of children to see if talent or exceptional mental ability can be documented. De Avila & Havassy (1974, 1975) have published extensively on the bias in IQ, and recommend using Piagetian tasks to identify a more equitable number of Hispanic children who are gifted and talented. Mercer (1979), after critiquing IQ testing bias, developed a statistically generated measure of IQ called the Estimated Learning Potential. Supposedly, it could identify gifted minority students.

Recent efforts, such as Gardner's Multiple Intelligences constructs (Gardner, 1983, 1993; Maker, Nielson, & Rogers, 1994), have received a great deal of attention. Although Gardner himself acknowledges that the empirical validation of interventions based on the Multiple Intelligence model is at the anecdotal stage (quoted in Collins, 1998). In the identification of minority gifted students, some empirical data also indicate that assessment procedures based on the Multiple Intelligence theory face serious validity problems (Plucker, Callahan, & Tomchin, 1996). Sternberg's efforts at operationalizing "Tacit Knowledge" measures (Sternberg, Wagner, Williams, & Horvath, 1995) with bilingual students may have a better chance at success. His concept of Tacit Intelligence attempts to break from the tradition laid down by Binet. Tacit Intelligence is far more contextual, authentic, and less academic than IQ. However, the stimuli he is considering using in order to elicit Tacit Intelligence from English language learners (vignettes where a student is interpreting for a non-English speaker) may prove too contrived and complex. But all these efforts to test for superior ability face a serious problem with regard to Hispanic children: the issue of bilingualism.

Currently, there are data which strongly indicate that testing bilingual children may involve psychometric bias regardless of whether they are tested in English or in Spanish (Figueroa & Garcia, 1994; Valdes & Figueroa, 1994). The current and future

Standards for Educational and Psychological Testing (American Educational Research Association, American Psychological Association, National Council on Measurement, 1985) clearly acknowledge bias in tests given in English to bilingual individuals. Empirical data exist which document that for bilingual individuals mental tests, particularly tests of intelligence, show bias in prediction (Figueroa, 1990; Valdes & Figueroa, 1994). Ironically, nonverbal tests of intelligence appear to be the most vulnerable to predictive bias (Figueroa & Garcia, 1994), a finding which may explain why the use of these types of measures has never really taken hold in the public schools as a viable method for identifying equitable rates of giftedness and for predicting superior achievement (DeAvila & Havassy, 1974, 1975; Chambers, Barron, & Sprecher, 1980; Tucson Unified School District, 1987; Mills & Tissot, 1995).

For psychometricians, bias in prediction poses serious legal, technical, and conceptual problems. For educational consumers, these issues are at the heart of many problems concerning equal educational opportunity. In cases where tests are used to make high-stakes decisions, or where tests play a pivotal role in individualized programming, educators need to reconsider the human costs associated with using tests that discriminate on the basis of social class (Mercer, 1973; Neisser, Boodoo, Bouchard, Boykin, Brody, Ceci, Halpern, Loehlin, Perloff, Sternberg, & Urbina, 1996), that produce higher rates of disabilities among certain ethnic/linguistic groups (Heller, Holtzman, & Messick, 1982), and keep these groups out of gifted programs (Callahan, Hunsaker, Adams, Moore, & Bland, 1995).

"Culturally Appropriate" Gifted Education Curricula
Another area of professional and published interest has been the creation of gifted education curricula that are "culturally appropriate" (Perrine, 1989; Banda, 1989). Some of these efforts have simplistically focused on using ethnic pupils as cultural carriers in gifted settings. Others have studied the impact of teaching diverse populations of children different ways of processing information and solving problems (Gregory, Starness, & Blaycock, 1989; Maker, Nielson, & Rogers, 1994). Still others involve the addition of culturally loaded goals on top of those that would normally apply to gifted programming. Banda's (1989) work is a good example in this regard. She includes a few

culturally appropriate goals within a series of more traditional ones for gifted education, such as: "Increase students' knowledge and appreciation of their own and others' value system.....Develop students' sense of their individual and ethnic identities and their potential contributions to society....." (p. 31).

There is also another model for including culture. In one of the most recent texts on gifted education and minority populations (Maker & Schriever, 1989), the authors begin with list of "Absolute Aspects of Giftedness" and then proceed with two lists on "Cultural Values Often Characteristic of Hispanics" and "Behavioral Differences" that typify Hispanic gifted students. From these lists other authors (Udall, 1989) in that text propose a "Curriculum for Gifted Hispanic Students" that supposedly accommodates the traditional, fatalistic, familial, cooperative, present-time orientation, limited-stress-on-material-possessions, and "Being" values of Hispanic culture (pg. 43). Two aspects to this approach and these texts are relevant. Irrespective of caveats to the contrary by the authors, the lists are basically stereotypes with little empirical validity (cooperative style being the exception).

Just as important, these types of culture-treatment efforts have never really worked out (e.g., Figueroa & Gallegos, 1978; Figueroa, 1980). Like Aptitude-Treatment interactions (Slavin, 1991), there is little evidence to support the belief that using culture in this manner leads to higher levels of learning or academic achievement. In many ways, these attempts at infusing culture can be considered as historical, albeit flawed, precursors to the current emphases on constructivism. Valid and genuine applications of cultural content, such as using a child's family-cultural knowledge as a scaffold to new learning presently exist, are empirically grounded, and do not rely on either stereotypes or guesses about their use in curriculum and instruction (Moll, Amanti, Neff, & Gonzalez, 1992).

The disappointing part of the efforts to infuse culture into gifted classrooms is that there is no compelling, empirical, or valid evidence with control for the most powerful intervening variables, biculturalism and bilingualism (or language proficiency levels). In fact, the lack of attention to bilingualism has occasionally precluded the delivery of gifted programming to Hispanic children (Barkan & Bernal, 1991; Sawyer & Marquez, 1993). Further, in all of these programs, tacitly, the need and validity of "gifted" education are accepted. Yet, there is another viewpoint on this matter.

Problems of the Gifted Category

What is interesting from a social perspective, is that the perception people have about gifted children takes on moral dimensions. They have, for example, been described as "goodness personified " (Margolin, 1994). Over the last twenty years, they have also become the subject of an advocacy movement. It is argued that gifted education is a civil rights issue (Gallagher, 1998). Gifted children need a gifted education in order to receive their equal educational opportunities. But a strong empirical critique argues otherwise.

Mara Sapon-Shevin (1994) conducted an ethnographic study on the characteristics and social impacts of an elementary school program for gifted students in one small, Midwest rural community of 8000 which she calls "Prairieview." The unique aspect of this study is not just its anthropological, qualitative grounding, but its comprehensive examination of program effects in and out of school on gifted and nongifted students and their families.

She interviewed parents, teachers, administrators, and students who were in various degrees affected by the existence of the gifted program and its rituals. She describes the high status enjoyed by students in this program. Even in a community where issues of race and ethnicity are not prevalent, she documents how questions of socioeconomic equity in participation rates emerge. There are moving descriptions of how parents feel when their child does not qualify. There are conversations with students about how they feel when gifted students get privileges and special treatment. There are emotional and insensitive narratives by students in the gifted program denouncing the costs associated with educating students with disabilities. There are also the historical justifications for providing enriched educational programs to future leaders, scientists, and artists. If they are not educated as gifted students, the nation will suffer.

Shapon-Shevin reaches altogether different conclusions about gifted education. She fails to see any compelling evidence as to why only a small proportion of students should receive enriched educational experiences. She concludes that one of the strongest reasons for a gifted program is not just because high IQ students need special attention, but that there are linear, boring classrooms in the public schools which stifle all students and propel parents to fight, literally, for programs that purport to be enriched. Winters (1997) makes the same point, but frames it in a broader context.

> One major problem that gifted students face is that American schools hold low expectations for students in general and make minimal demands, as compared with, say, schools in many Western European and East Asian countries. In my view, if America's schools were able to be modeled on the more rigorous approaches in such countries, it seems likely that many of America's moderately gifted students, currently bored and languishing, would be appropriately challenged in regular classrooms. (p. 1077)

For Sapon-Shevin and others, gifted education is tracking. It removes children who potentially offer some of the best learning models for their age peers. It reifies and exaggerates the social stratification in society. It compromises the possibilities for democratic institutions and social harmony. It is worth noting that this position finds strong support in the professional and scientific literature (Berliner & Biddle, 1995; Oakes, 1985; Kozol, 1991; Kingston & Lewis, 1990; Margolin, 1994).

A key aspect to the Sapon-Shevon study is the conclusion that gifted children can be taught in a general education classroom using an effective, nonlinear, gifted pedagogy and curriculum. We concur with this assertion and argue that not only is such an educational description possible, it is also what children in both general and special education need. But what theoretical bases would support the idea that the learning needs of many types of children can be met in an optimal learning environment? And what would such programs look like?

Optimal Educational Contexts for Hispanic Students

To consider the possibilities of an educational system that is fully inclusive for gifted and special students such as that proposed by Sapon-Shevin, ideas about human intelligence and human learning have to undergo a paradigm shift. As Vygotsky (1962) and Piaget (Piaget & Inhelder, 1954) have demonstrated, human learning and human intelligence are not exclusively governed by individual mentation or effectively assessed through a decontextualized measure such as IQ. They are also strongly governed by the human social context. In effect, thinking and learning are also social products. They are susceptible to social contexts. They are best measured in optimal social contexts of academic learning.

The Importance of Context
        Context is an extremely powerful moderator and actuator of human behavior and human learning. A substantial body of work on the education of bilingual children (Rosebury, Warren, & Conant, 1992; Cummins, 1996; August & Hakuta, 1997; Faltis & Huddelson, 1997) currently suggests that the conceptual and applied aspects of education need to attend closely to the impact of contexts on learning. Interestingly, there is also some recognition of this paradigmatic shift in the literature on the education of "gifted minority students" (Maker, 1996) and gifted education in general (Coleman, 1995).
        From a contextualist point of view of education, the focus should not be on the hypothesized learning traits of an individual, on learning styles, learning strategies, levels of intelligence or even Multiple Intelligences. It should be on the design of lessons, on the selection of children's literature, on environmental changes that compel children's curiosity, on the technology that engages interests, on teaching strategies, on the home funds of knowledge, on even on how the day is scheduled. But the question is: Is such a paradigm shift demonstrably effective across a wide variety of learners?
        After five years of research and after examining the last twenty years on effective instruction for English Language Learners (ELL), the National Center on Culture and Second Language Learning at the University of California at Santa Cruz identified five key parameters for the effective education of culturally and linguistically diverse students (Tharp, 1997). These are as follows (paraphrased).

- Principle I: Learning is facilitated when an expert and a novice work jointly on a task, discuss their work and create a common context (Moll 1990; Rogoff, 1991; Tharp and Gallimore, 1988).
- Principle II: Academic language, or language that includes reading, writing, listening and speaking

should be part of "all instructional activities" (Tharp, 1997, p. 7) and should build on the native language strengths by "building learning contexts that will evoke children's language strengths" (Tharp, 1997, p. 7).

- Principle III: "Contextualize teaching and curriculum in the experiences and skills of home and community." (Wyatt, 1978-79; Au & Jordan, 1981; Erickson & Mohatt, 1982; Moll, 1992).
- Principle IV: Make school work cognitively complex and challenging rather than reductionist, rote, repetitive, detail-level skills (Tharp, 1997, pg. 8); or, in other words, enriched and more like classrooms for the gifted.
- Principle V: Make teacher-student dialogues, "the process of questioning and sharing ideas" (Tharp, 1997, pg. 8), a main vehicle for learning both basic skills and higher order thinking. "Teachers who use it, like parents in natural teaching, assume that the student has something to say beyond the known answers in the head of the adult. The adult listens carefully, makes guesses about the intended meaning, and adjusts responses to assist the student's efforts" (Tharp, 1997, pg. 8).

There are two critical characteristics embedded in all of these principles: the absence of a Skinnerian, linear model for learning and teaching; and the presence of contextual emphases in all matters related to teaching at-risk learners.

These principles are antithetical to the direct instruction methodology and reductionist pedagogical paradigms that permeate much of general (Shepard, 1991) and special education (e.g., Forness, Kavale, Blum, & Lloyd, 1997). With bilingual learners, the principles are supported by current research for both bilingual and special education programs (Willig, & Swedo, 1987; Goldman & Rueda, 1988; Gutierrez, 1992; Echevarría, & McDonough, 1994; Ruiz & Figueroa, 1995; Thomas and Collier, 1995; Lopez-Reyna, 1996; Ruiz, 1996a, 1996b; Gutierrez & Stone 1997) and there are even programmatic applications (e.g., Ortiz, 1991; Ruiz, Garcia, & Figueroa, 1996), including some for bilingual children in gifted programs (e.g., Gregory, Starness, & Blaycock, 1989; Perrine, 1989).

The latter are particularly important since they operationalize the major assertion of this paper: that a gifted classroom is the answer to the underrepresentation of minority children in educational programs for the gifted and talented and that it is also the answer to the overrepresentation of ethnic children in most special education classrooms. There is a pedagogy currently available that can sustain and advance learners with "disabilities" and learners with "high abilities."

Programs That Work

At least two nationally and internationally recognized literacy programs for Spanish-speaking students with language learning disabilities have based their instructional strategies on these principles: the Optimal Learning Environment (OLE) Project based at California State University Sacramento (Ruiz, García & Figueroa, 1996) and AIM for the Best based at the University of Texas at Austin (Ortiz & Wilkinson, 1991).

The most contextualist and de-psychologized of these is the Optimal Learning Environment (OLE) Project (Ruiz, 1989; Figueroa & Ruiz, 1993; Ruiz & Figueroa, 1995; Ruiz, Rueda, Figueroa, & Boothroyd, 1995; Rueda, R., Ruiz, N.T., & Figueroa, R.A., 1996; Ruiz, Garcia, & Figueroa, 1996). It is also the most permutated, having been applied in special education pull-out programs for Hispanic students, in special education segregated classes for multicultural populations, in Chinese bilingual classes, in classes for deaf students (California and Mexico City), in Migrant Education programs throughout California, and in "gifted," upper-middle class, private schools in Mexico City. The following description of the OLE Project is meant as an example not as the exemplar. The OLE Project incorporates the proposals advanced by many researchers from disparate educational disciplines but with the same, new vision about learning, learning in schools, and a new, more powerful pedagogical context (Tharp & Gallimore, 1987; Skrtic, 1995; Poplin & Cousin, 1996; Faltis & Huddelson, 1997; Smith, 1998; Taylor, 1998).

This Project began with a review of the most effective instructional strategies for literacy development in bilingual, Hispanic children and youth (Ruiz, 1989). These instructional strategies are the heart of the OLE Project (Ruiz, Garcia, & Figueroa, 1996). They work in concert with the following optimal conditions for classroom teaching: (1) students exercise choice in what they read and write, (2) the classroom is centered on what the students bring to the classroom both in terms of language and cultural knowledge, (3) classroom activities are meaning-driven, that is, they focus on whole texts, projects, and investigations, (4) students are active not passive, (5) ideas come before mechanics (spelling, phonics, vocabulary), (6) the work is authentic, that is, it has a real purpose (communication, demonstration, exhibit), (7) the classroom immerses children in language and print, (8) teachers and peers demonstrate to each other how things are done (e.g., the process of writing a story), (9) the correct answer is approximated as in real life, versus demanding that only the correct answer is acceptable, (10) feedback about the work is immediate, (11) the classroom is constructed as a learning community where cooperative work constitutes a major portion of the activities, and (12) teachers and students have high expectations for each other.

The strategies and conditions form an educational context where multiple types of cultural and linguistic interests are accommodated. They also occur in a physical context where a certain type of children's literature predominates. Multiple copies of books with strong story grammar are available in both English and Spanish. The books are chosen specifically because they evoke a strong emotional response from the students and because they reflect their bicultural worlds in and out of school. The OLE classroom is environmentally enriched with technologies (computer, printer, copying machine), and multiple forms of literacy (books, newspapers, audio and visual electronic equipment). The anchor for optimizing this environment, however, are the instructional strategies used and the optimal conditions for classroom teaching. The Project came to realize that both of these actually operationalize the five key parameters for the effective education of culturally and linguistically diverse students that were published by the National Center on Culture and Second Language Learning (Tharp, 1997).

The Project has proven highly reliable in replicating these optimal instructional contexts and in producing unexpected levels of achievement (Ruiz & Figueroa, 1995; Ruiz & Enguidanos, 1997). The pedagogy sustains multiple levels of "abilities" since it does not rely on a linear/hierarchical model of learning (Poplin, 1988b). The original, unique idea was: What would happen if Hispanic learning disabled children were offered a classroom and a pedagogy that was more like the educational experiences given to gifted and talented students? To date, the results have been surprising. Multiple populations of students seem to benefit from the OLE contexts.

Conclusion

Both special education and gifted education can be and have been conceived as the products of ineffective general education classrooms (Heller, Holtzman, & Messick, 1982; Sapon-Shevin, 1994). The over- and underrepresentation issues that apply to Hispanic and minority populations emanate from this failure. In this chapter, we have argued that since the origins of both inequities stem from something peculiar to the general education classroom, the answer may lie precisely in addressing the source of the failure: the pedagogy in many general education classrooms which views human learning as a mechanistic, linear phenomenon. All children deserve a "gifted education," and the additional enrichment experiences that are offered in such a program. We suggest that optimal pedagogy in optimal learning contexts holds the key to the inequities associated with over and under-representation of minorities in gifted programs.

References

Adler, M. (1967). Reported incidence of giftedness among ethnic groups. *Exceptional Children, 34*, 101-105.

American Educational Research Association, American Psychological Association, National Council on Measurement (1985). *Standards for Educational and Psychological Testing.* Washington , D.C.: American Psychological Association.

Au, K. H.,& Jordan, C. (1981). Teaching reading to Hawaiian children: Finding a culturally appropriate solution. In H. Trueba, G.P. Guthrie, & K. H. Au (Eds.), *Culture in the bilingual classroom: Studies in classroom ethnography* (pp. 139-152). Rowley, MA: Newbury House

August, D. & Hakuta, K. (1997). *Improving schooling for language-minority children: A research agenda.* Washington, D.C.: National Academy Press.

Banda, C. (1989). Promoting pluralism and power. In C.J. Maker & S.W. Schiever (Eds.), *Critical issues in gifted education:*

Vol. 2. Defensible programs for cultural and ethnic minorities. Austin, TX: Pro-Ed Publishers. (pp. 27-33)

Barkan, J. H., & Bernal, E.M. (1991). Gifted education for bilingual and limited English proficient students. *The Gifted Child Quarterly, 35,* 144-147.

Berliner, D.C. & Biddle, B.J. (1995). *The manufactured crisis.* New York: Addison-Wesley.

Bermudez, A. B. & Rakow, S. J. (1990). Analyzing teachers' perceptions of identification procedures for gifted and talented Hispanic limited English-proficient students at-risk. *Educational Issues of Language Minority Students, 7,* 21-34.

Bernal, E.M. (1974). Gifted Mexican American children: An ethno-scientific perspective. *California Journal of Educational Research, 25,* 261-273.

Bernal, E.M. (1978). The identification of gifted Chicano children. In A.Y. Baldwin, G. H. Gear, & L. J. Lucito (Eds.), *Educational planning for the gifted: Overcoming, cultural, geographic, and socioeconomic barriers* (p. 14-17). Reston, VA: The Council for Exceptional Children.

Bernal, E.M. & Reyna, J. (1975). Analysis and identification of giftedness in Mexican American children: A pilot study. In B.O. Boston (Ed.), *A resource manual of information on educating the gifted and talented.* Washington, D.C.: Clearinghouse on Handicapped and Gifted Children. The Council for Exceptional Children.

Callahan, C. M., Hunsaker, S. L., Adams, C. M., Moore, S. D., & Blend, L. C. (1995). *Instruments used in identification of gifted and talented students.* Charlottesville, VA: National Research Center on the Gifted and Talented, Monograph 95130.

Chambers, J. A., Barron, F., & Sprecher, J. W. (1980). Identifying gifted Mexican American Students. *Gifted Child Quarterly, 24,* 123-128.

Coleman, L. J. (1995). The power of specialized educational environments in the development of giftedness: The need for research on social context. *Gifted Child Quarterly, 39,* 171-76.

Collins, J. (1998). Seven kinds of smarts. *TIME, 152,* 94-96.

Cummins, J. (1984). *Bilingualism and special education: Issues in assessment and pedagogy.* San Diego: College-Hill.

Cummins, J. (1996). *Negotiating identities: Education for empowerment in a diverse society.* Ontario, CA: California Association of Bilingual Education.

De Avila, E. A. & Havassy, B. (1974). The testing of minority children: A Neo-Piagetian approach. *Today's Education,* 63, 72-75.

De Avila, E. A. & Havassy, B. (1975). Piagetian alternatives to I.Q.: Mexican American Study. In N. Hobbs (Ed.), *Issues in the classification of exceptional children* (Vol. 2)(p. 246-265). San Francisco, CA: Jossey-Bass.

Echevarría, J. & McDonough, R. (1994). Instructional conversations in special education settings: Issues and accommodations. Educational Practice Report, Washington, D.C.: National Center for Research on Cultural Diversity and Second Language Learning.

Erikson, F. & Mohatt, G. (1982). The cultural organization of participation structure in two classrooms of Indian students. In G. Spindler (Ed.), *Doing the ethnography of schooling* (p. 132-174). New York: Holt, Rhinehart & Winston.

Faltis, C. J. & Huddelson, S. J. (1998). *Bilingual education in elementary and secondary school communities.* Boston, MA: Allyn and Bacon.

Feldman, D. H. (1991). Has there been a paradigm shift in gifted education? In N. Colangelo, S. G. Assouline, D. H. Ambronson (Eds.), *Talent Development: Proceedings from the 1991 Henry B. and Jocelyn Wallace National Research Symposium on Talent Development* (p. 89-94). Boston, MA: Trillium Press.

Figueroa, R. A. (1980). Field dependence, ethnicity, and cognitive styles. *Hispanic Journal of the Behavioral Sciences,* 2, 35-42.

Figueroa, R.A. (1990). Assessment of linguistic minority group children. In C.R. Reynolds & R. W. Kamphaus (Eds.), *Handbook of psychological & educational assessment of children.* N.Y.: The Guilford Press (p. 671-696).

Figueroa, R. A. & Gallegos, E. A. (1978). Ethnic differences in school behavior. *Sociology of Education, 51,* 289-298.

Figueroa, R.A. & Garcia, E. (1994). Issues in testing students from culturally and linguistically diverse backgrounds. *Multicultural Education, 2,* 10-23.

Figueroa, R.A. & Ruiz, N.T. (1993). Bilingual pupils and special education. In R. C. Eaves and P. McLaughlin (Eds.)

Recent advances in special education and rehabilitation. N.Y.: Andover.

Forness, S. R., Kavale, K. A., Blum, I. M., & Lloyd, J. W. (1997). What works in special education: Using meta-analysis to guide practice. *Teaching Exceptional Children, 29*, 4-9.

Gallagher, (1998). Education of gifted students: A civil rights issue? In K. L. Frieberg (Ed.), *Educating exceptional children 98/99* (p. 190-193). Guilford, CN: Dushkin/McGraw-Hill.

Garcia, J. H. (1994). Nonstandardized instruments for the assessment of Mexican American children for gifted/talented programs. In Garcia, S. B. (Ed.), *Addressing cultural and linguistic diversity in special education: Issues and trends.* Reston, VA: Council for Exceptional Children (p. 46-57).

Gardner, H. (1983). *Frames of mind: The theory of Multiple Intelligences.* New York: Basic Books.

Gardner, H. (1993). *Multiple Intelligences: The theory in practice.* New York: Basic Books.

Goldman, S. R., & Rueda, R. (1988). Developing writing skills in bilingual exceptional children. *Exceptional Children, 54*, 543-551.

Gregory, D. A., Starness, W. T., & Blaycock, A. W. (1989). Finding and nurturing potential giftedness among Black and Hispanic Students. In A. A. Ortiz & B. A. Ramirez (Eds.), *Schools and the culturally diverse exceptional student: Promising practices and future directions.* Reston, VA: Council for Exceptional Children. (p. 76-85)

Gutierrez, K. D. (1992). A comparison of instructional contexts in writing process classrooms with Latino children. *Education and Urban Society, 24*, 244-262.

Gutierrez, K. D. & Stone, L. D. (1997). A cultural-historical view of learning and learning disabilities: Participating in a community of learners. *Learning Disabilities Research and Practice, 12*, 123-131.

Heller, K. A., Holtzman, W. H., & Messick, S. (1982). *Placing children in special education: A strategy for equity.* Washington, D.C.: National Academy Press.

Johnsen, S. K., Ryser, M. G., & Dougherty, E. (1993). The validity of product portfolios in the identification of gifted students. *Gifted International: A Talent Development Journal. 8,* 40-42.

Kingston, P. W. & Lewis, L. S. (1990). *The high status track.* Albany, NY: State University of New York Press.

Kozol, J. (1991). *Savage inequalities.* New York: Crown Publishers.

Lopez-Reyna, N. A. (1996). The importance of meaningful contexts in bilingual special education: Moving to whole language. *Learning Disabilities Research and Practice, 11,* 120-131.

Maker, C.J. (1994). Authentic assessment of problem solving and giftedness in secondary school students. *The Journal of Secondary Gifted Education.* Fall, 19-29.

Maker, C.J. (1996). Identification of gifted minority students: A national problem, needed changes, and a promising solution. *The Gifted Child Quarterly, 40,* 41-50.

Maker, C.J., Nielson, & Rogers (1994). Giftedness, diversity, and problem-solving. *Teaching Exceptional Children, 27,* 4-19.

Maker, C.J. & Schiever, S. W. (Eds.)(1989). *Critical issues in gifted education: Vol. 2. Defensible programs for cultural and ethnic minorities.* Austin, TX: Pro-Ed Publishers. (pp. 3-18).

Maker, C.J. & Schiever, S. W. (Eds.) (1989). *Critical issues in gifted education: Vol. 2. Defensible programs for cultural and ethnic minorities.* Austin, TX: Pro-Ed Publishers.

Margolin, L. (1994). *Goodness personified: The emergence of gifted children.* New York: Aldine de Gruyter.

Marquez, J. A., Bermudez, A. B., & Rakow, S. J. (1992). Incorporating community perceptions in the identification of gifted and talented Hispanic students. *The Journal of Educational Issues of Language minority students, 10,* 117-127.

Mercer, J. (1973). *Labeling the mentally retarded.* Berkeley, CA: University of California Press.

Mercer, J. (1979). *The System of Multicultural Pluralistic Assessment.* New York: Psychological Corporation.

Mills, C.J. & Tissot, S. L. (1995). Identifying academic potential in students from under-represented populations: Is using the Ravens Progressive Matrices a good idea? *The Gifted Child Quarterly, 39,* 209-217.

Moll, L.C. (Ed.)(1990). *Vygotzky and education. Instructional implications and applications of sociocultural psychology.* New York: Cambridge University Press,

Moll, L.C. (1992). Bilingual classroom studies and community analysis. *Educational Researcher, 21*, 20-24.

Moll, L. C., Amanti, C. , Neff, D. & Gonzalez, N. (1992). Funds of knowledge for teaching: Using a qualitative approach to connect homes with classrooms. *Theory into Practice, 31*, 132-141.

Neiser, U., Boodoo, G., Bouchard, T.J., Boykin, A. W., Brody, N., Ceci, S. J., Halpern, D. F., Loehlin, J. C., Perloff, R., Sternberg, R. J., & Urbina, S. (1996). Intelligence: Knowns and unknowns. [Task Force Report of the American Psychological Association]. *American Psychologist, 51*, 77-101

Oakes, J. (1985). *Keeping Track.* New Haven: Yale University Press.

Ortiz, A. A. (1991). *Aim for the BEST: Assessment and intervention model for the bilingual exceptional student.* Arlington, VA: Development Associates, Inc.

Ortiz, A. A. & Wilkinson, C. Y. (1991). *Aim for the BEST: Assessment and intervention model for the bilingual exceptional student. A technical report for the innovative approach research project.* Arlington, VA: Development Associates, Inc.

Perrine, J. (1989). The efficacy of situational identification of gifted Hispanics in East Los Angeles through nurturance that capitalizes on their culture. In C.J. Maker & S.W. Schiever (Eds.), *Critical issues in gifted education: Vol. 2. Defensible programs for cultural and ethnic minorities.* Austin, TX: Pro-Ed Publishers. (pp. 3-18).

Piaget, J. & Inhelder, B. (1969). *The psychology of the child.* New York: Orion Press.

Plucker, J. A., Callahan, C. M., & Tomchin, E. M. (1996). Wherefore art thou Multiple Intelligences? Alternative assessments for identifying talent in ethnically diverse and low income students. *The Gifted Child Quarterly, 40*, 81-92.

Poplin, M. (1988a). The reductionist fallacy in learning disabilities: Replicating the past by reducing the present. *Journal of Learning Disabilities, 21*, 389-400.

Poplin, M. (1988b). Holistic/constructivist principles of the teaching-learning process: Implications for the field of learning disabilities. *Journal of Learning Disabilities, 21*, 401-416.

Poplin, M. & Cousin, P. T. (1996). *Alternative views of learning disabilities.* Austin, TX: Pro ED.

Public Law 95-561 (1978). *Gifted and Talented Children's Act of 1978*

Public Law 100-297 (1988). *Jacob Javits Gifted and Talented Students Education Act of 1988*

Purcell, J. H. (1995). Gifted education at a crossroads: the program status study. *The Gifted Child Quarterly, 39*, 57-65.

Ranzulli, J. S. (1978). What makes giftedness: Reexamining a definition. *Phi Delta Kappan, 60*, 180-184.

Reynolds, A. (1933). *The education of Spanish-speaking children in five southwestern states* (Bulletin No. 11). Washington, D.C.: U.S. Department of the Interior.

Rogoff, B. (1991). Social interaction as apprenticeship in thinking: Guidance and participation in spatial planning. In L. B. Resnick, J. M. Levine, & S. Teasley (Eds.), *Perspectives on socially shared cognition.* Washington, D.C.: American Psychological Association.

Rosebury, A., Warren, B., & Conant, F. (1992). *Appropriating scientific discourse: Findings from language minority classrooms.* Santa Cruz, CA: National Center for Research on Cultural Diversity and Second Language Learning.

Rueda, R., Ruiz, N.T., & Figueroa, R.A. (1996). Issues in the implementation of innovative instructional strategies. *Multiple Voices for Ethnically Diverse Exceptional Learners, 1*, 12- 23.

Ruiz, N.T. (1989). An optimal learning environment for Rosemary. *Exceptional Children, 56*, 130-144.

Ruiz, N.T. (1996a). The social construction of ability and disability I: Profile types of Latino children identified as language learning disabled. In M. Poplin & P. T. Cousin (Eds.). *Alternative views of learning disabilities.* Austin, TX: ProEd.

Ruiz, N.T. (1996b). The social construction of ability and disability II: Optimal and at-risk lessons in a bilingual special education classroom. In M. Poplin & P. T. Cousin (Eds). *Alternative views of learning disabilities.* Austin, TX: ProEd.

Ruiz, N.T. & Enguidanos, T. (1997). Authenticity and advocacy in assessment: Bilingual students in special education. *Primary Voices, 5*, 35-45.

Ruiz, N.T. & Figueroa, R. A. (1995). Learning handicapped classrooms with Latino students. *Education and Urban Society, 27*, 463-483.

Ruiz, N.T., Figueroa, R.A., Rueda, R.,& Beaumont, C. (1992). History and status of bilingual special education for Hispanic handicapped students. In R. V. Padilla & A. H. Benavides (Eds.), *Critical Perspectives on Bilingual Education Research. Tempe*, AZ: Bilingual Press.

Ruiz, N.T., Garcia, E., & Figueroa, R.A. (1996). *The OLE curriculum guide: Creating Optimal Learning Environments for students from diverse backgrounds in special education and general education*. Sacramento, CA: California Department of Education.

Ruiz, N.T., Rueda, R., Figueroa, R.A., & Boothroyd, M. (1996). Bilingual special education teachers' shifting paradigms: Complex responses to educational reform. In M. Poplin and P. T. Cousin (Eds.), *Alternative views of learning disabilities*. Austin, TX: ProEd.

Ruiz, R. (1989). Considerations in the education of gifted Hispanic students. In C.J. Maker & S.W. Schiever (Eds.), *Critical issues in gifted education: Vol. 2. Defensible programs for cultural and ethnic minorities*. Austin, TX: Pro-Ed Publishers. (pp. 60-62)

Sapon-Shevin, M. (1994). *Playing favorites: Gifted education and the disruption of community*. New York: State University Press.

Sawyer, C. B. & Marquez, J. A. (1993). Discrimination against LEP students in gifted and talented classes. *The Journal of Educational Issues of Language Minority Students, 12*, 143-149.

Shepard, L. A. (1991). Psychometricians' beliefs about learning. *Educational Researcher, 20*, 12-16.

Silverman, L. K. (1995). Gifted and talented students. In E. L. Meyen & T. M. Skrtic (Eds.), *Special education and student disability*. Denver, CO: Love Publishing Company. (pp. 377-414)

Skrtic, T. (1995). *Disability and democracy*. New York: Teachers College Press.

Slavin, R. (1991). *Educational psychology*. Englewood Cliffs, NJ: Prentice Hall

Smith, F. (1998). *The book of learning and forgetting*. New York: Teachers College Press.

Sternberg, R., Wagner, R. K., Williams, W. M. & Horvath, J. A. (1995). Testing common sense. *American Psychologist, 50*, 912-927.

Taylor, D. (1998). *Beginning to read and the spin doctors of science: Political campaign to change America's mind about how children learn to read.* Urbana, IL: National Council of Teachers of English.

Terman, L. & Oden, M. (1925). *Mental and physical traits of a thousand gifted children. V. 1. Genetic studies of genius.* Stanford. CA: Stanford University Press.

Terman, L. & Oden, M. (1947). *The gifted child grows up.* Stanford, CA: Stanford University Press.

Tharp, R. (1997). *From at-risk to excellence: Research, theory, and principles for practice.* Santa Cruz, CA: Center for research on education, diversity and excellence.

Tharp, R. G. & Gallimore, R. (1988). *Rousing minds to life: Teaching, learning, and schooling in social context.* New York: Cambridge University Press,

Thomas, W. P. & Collier, V. P. (1995). *Language Minority Student Achievement and Program Effectiveness.* Washington, D.C.: National Clearinghouse for Bilingual Education.

Tucson Unified School District (1987). Report: GATE review committee. Tucson, AZ: GATE Program.

Udall, A. J. (1989). Curriculum for gifted Hispanic students. In C.J. Maker & S.W. Schiever (Eds.), *Critical issues in gifted education: Vol. 2. Defensible programs for cultural and ethnic minorities* (pp. 39-54) Austin, TX: Pro-Ed Publishers.

United States Commission on Civil Rights (1974). *Mexican American Education Study: Report VI: Toward quality education for Mexican Americans.* Washington, D.C.: U.S. Government Printing Office.

Valdes, G. & Figueroa, R.A. (1994). *Bilingualism and testing: A special case of bias.* Norwood, N. J.: Ablex.

Vygotzky, L. S. (1962). *Thought and language.* Cambridge, MA: M.I.T. Press.

Willig, A. C. & Swedo, J. (1987). Improving teaching strategies for exceptional Hispanic Limited English Proficient students: An exemplary study of task engagement and teaching strategies. Paper presented at the Annual Meeting of the American Educational Research Association, Washington, D.C.

Winters, E. (1997). Exceptionally high intelligence and schooling. *American Psychologist, 52,* 1070-1081.

Wyatt, J. D. (1978-79). Native involvement in curriculum development: The native teacher as cultural broker. *Interchange, 9,* 17-28.

Zappia, I. (1989). Identification of gifted Hispanic students: A multidimensional approach. In C.J. Maker & S.W. Schiever (Eds.), *Critical issues in gifted education: Vol. 2. Defensible programs for cultural and ethnic minorities* (pp.19-26). Austin, TX: Pro-Ed Publishers.

CHAPTER 7

Legal Issues Affecting the Educational Outcomes of Hispanics in Public Schools

Eugene E. Garcia

Introduction

Today, one in three children nationwide is from an ethnic or racial minority group, one in seven speaks a language other than English at home, and one in fifteen is born outside the United States The linguistic and cultural diversity of America's school population has increased dramatically during the past decade, and is expected to increase even more in the future. In California for example, Hispanics will be the majority ethnic population by the middle of the new century (Figure 1) while the majority of the California K-12 population will be Hispanic by the year 2005 (Figure 2). The concept of "minority" group as a title for Hispanics will become obsolete.

Figure 1. California Population Projections 1990-2040

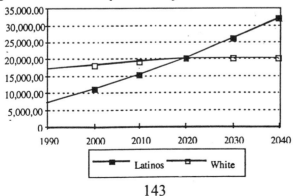

144   *Legal Issues Affecting the Educational*

Educating children from Hispanic immigrant and ethnic minority groups is a major concern of school systems across the country. For many of these children, American education is not a successful experience. While one-tenth of non-Hispanic White students leave school without a high school diploma, one-third of Hispanics and two-thirds of immigrant students drop out of school before graduating (National Research Council, 1997).

Figure 2. California K-12 Enrollment by Ethnicity

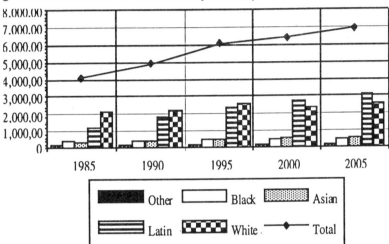

Source: California Department of Finance, Demographic Research Unit [9/90]. 1985 Actual: 1990-2005 are projections.

Confronted with this dismal reality, administrators, teachers, parents and policy makers (executive, legislative, and judicial branches) have urged each other to do something different--change teaching methods, adopt new curricula, allocate more funding and hold educational institutions accountable. Such actions at the federal and state level have and will continue to affect Hispanic students in general and language minority Hispanic students in particular. The present discussion is my attempt to put into writing these intersecting but distinct voices as they relate to policy declarations in order to help further our understanding of how such declarations attempt to enhance the education of Hispanic students. For there is no doubt that the historical pattern of the education of these populations in the United States is a continuous story of under achievement. It need not be that way in the future. Educational institutions today must address issues of both equity and excellence. Our educational endeavors aimed at under achieving students have been to provide equal educational opportunity. The challenge today is for those opportunities to produce excellence in academic outcomes. This is how our three decade effort in serving these students must change: from compensatory education to educational excellence.

Who Are These Students?

The vast majority of teachers and administrators are non-Hispanic white and speak English as their native and only language, which is in contrast to the racial, ethnic, and linguistic diversity found among students. Many teachers are experiencing the daunting personal and professional challenge of adapting in adulthood to a degree of diversity that did not exist during their childhood.

The average teacher and administrator in his 30s and 40s grew up in the 1950s and 1960s (Valencia, 1991). People who were raised in the postwar period, before desegregation, were likely to have attended school with those of their own ethnic group. Not until young adulthood did they encounter the Civil Rights Movement and other expressions of ethnic presence on a national level. Nor did they experience the swift increases in diversity that have occurred recently. They and their parents grew up expecting a much different world than the one they now face. The parents and teachers of today's teachers grew up in the 1930s and the 1940s, following at the end of a period of massive immigration from Europe. Today's senior teacher entered school at a time when the United States had a much larger proportion of foreign-born persons than today. But this diversity was perhaps not as evident because of segregated ethnic enclaves in housing and schooling and less widespread mass communications. And over the course of their lifetime, people who are now in their 70s experienced decreasing diversity. The melting pot ideology matched their own observations; the children of immigrants abandoned their native language and culture as they were urged to become 100% Americans.

However, the 30 year period straddling the mid-century mark was an anomaly in our history. Until the 1930s, the story of the United States was a tale of immigration. The grandparents of today's teacher, who grew up in the early 1900s, and many of whom were immigrants themselves, experienced increasing ethnic and linguistic diversity during their formative years. To these Americans, the immigration movement that brought our ancestors to this country is a closed chapter, part of our national past. But from the perspective of the entire spectrum of American history, immigration has been the norm rather than the exception. Two generations of adults have grown up in an unusually low immigration period, an environment which has shaped our perceptions of our country. The new reality is that America in 2000 will resemble America in the 1900s more closely than America in the 1950s. Today's kindergartner will experience increasing diversity over their lifetime, as did their great grandparents generation.

From 1900 to 1910, nearly 9 million immigrants entered the United States thus increasing the entire population by 10%. In the 1980s, about the same number of immigrants came to the United States but they accounted for only a 4% increase in a much larger United States population. In the early decades of this century, and back as far as 1850, as many as one in seven people in the United States were foreign-born. The current rate of one in thirteen is high only in comparison to the low immigration decades of the 1950s and 60s, when one in twenty Americans were foreign-born. By 2020, when today's kindergartners are in the work force, the foreign born population of the United States is again projected to reach one in seven people (National Research Council, 1997).

Because the United States is so closely identified with the English language, many people assume that Anglo-Americans have always formed the majority group in United States society. But the 1990 census reveals that only 13% of Americans claim English ancestry. This group is outnumbered by the 15% whose families originated in Ireland, many of whom did not speak English as a native language. An additional 5% identify their ancestry as "American"; many of these are Americans whose families have been in the United States for nine or ten generations. Thus, at most, about one-third of Americans trace their ancestry to the various cultures and languages of Great Britain.

Today, nearly one in five Americans live in households in which a language other than English is spoken. Half of these households are Spanish-speaking; the next most common are French, German, Italian, and Chinese. Educating students from immigrant families, particularly Hispanic immigrant families, may seem like an entirely new challenge, but it is not; such students have always been in American schools in large numbers. Throughout most of our history, one in four or five non-Hispanic white Americans grew up in an immigrant family.

What Worked in the Past May Not Work Now

One mission of educators is to prepare young people for an occupational life. The economic environment in which today's students will seek employment has changed radically in the past few decades. Manufacturing jobs used to provide a good living for immigrants and ethnic minority group members. Most jobs in the industrial sector did not require a high level of education, or academic competence in English.

But those jobs have disappeared. The new economy will require workers who have more than basic skills; employees must be able to think critically and engage in group decision making, communicate effectively orally and in writing, and be able to adapt to changing conditions by learning new skills. A larger proportion of jobs in the future will require the kind of educational preparation that has traditionally been provided to only the top students.

The American economy is now intertwined with the global market place; workers who can interact easily with people of different cultural and linguistic backgrounds will be prized (Garcia, 1994). Even the domestic workplace that today's students will enter is changing as employees and customers are becoming more diverse. Business leaders are well aware that most of their new employees will be minorities and women. Observers of American business trends comment that many companies have gone beyond debating whether they need to change; they are now actively managing diversity. If one of the purposes of education is to train young people for productive work lives, then schools will need to prepare all students for employment in a more ethnically, culturally, and linguistically diverse occupational environment than in the past.

One Size Does Not Fit All Students

Students from immigrant families are often defined by the characteristics they share--a lack of English fluency. But such a definition masks their diversity, and underestimates the challenge facing schools. Schools serve students who are new immigrants, ignorant of American life beyond what they have seen in movies, as well as African Americans, Mexican Americans, Asian Americans, Native Americans and European American students whose families have lived here for generations. Students representing dozens of native languages may attend a single school; in some school districts more than 125 languages are spoken by students. In many schools, a majority of the students come from immigrant or ethnic minority families. Some schools face a mobility problem; student turnover is high and the ethnic mix shifts radically from year to year.

Academic preparation can vary from student to student. Some students visit their home country frequently, while others lack that opportunity. Some immigrant students have had excellent schooling in their home country before coming to the United States; others had their schooling interrupted by war, while others never attended school. Still others are illiterate in their own language, and some have languages that were only oral until recently; others come from cultures with long literary traditions.

The complexity of the task for schools can be illustrated by three students in a recent immigrant family. Each of these students have very different needs. The Escalonas immigrated from Colombia and the parents work together on an electronics assembly line. The Escalonas are both college graduates, and taught high school math in their homeland and have three children.

- Maria Escalona-- 8th grade
  She had excellent schooling through the 7th grade in Colombia. The math and the science curriculum in her school was more advanced than in the United States system. She studied English in school for three years, but lacks substantive English proficiency in academic areas.
- Raul Escalona-- 5th grade
  He had good prior schooling, but had not yet begun to study English. Because he is only 10, his academic mastery of Spanish is incomplete.
- Teresita Escalona-- kindergarten
  She attended pre-school in Colombia, and knows the Spanish alphabet as well as songs, stories, numbers, shapes and colors. She knows no English.

The differences among these students – their age and entry into the American school, the quality of their prior schooling, their own and their parents/family/community native language and number of native language compatriots in their class, their parents' education and English language skills, and their family history and current circumstances – will affect their academic success much more than their common lack of English.

Federal Policies and Hispanic Education

The preceding discussion attempted to lay a foundation for understanding who the Hispanic language minority student is and how that student has been served. This discussion turns now to educational policy: first, federal executive, legislative and court articulations, and, second, state articulations and recent initiatives.

Federal Legislative Initiatives

The United States Congress set a minimum standard for the education of language minority students in public educational institutions in its passage of Title VI of the Civil Rights Act of 1964 prohibiting discrimination by educational institutions on the basis of race, color, sex or national origin and by the subsequent Equal Educational Opportunity Act of 1974 (EEOA). The EEOA was an effort by congress to define specifically what constitutes a denial of constitutionally guaranteed equal educational opportunity. The EEOA provides in part:

> No state shall deny equal educational opportunities to an individual on account of his or her race, color, sex, or national origin, by the failure by an educational agency to take appropriate action to overcome language barriers that impede equal participation by students in its instructional programs. (20 U.S.C. ss 1703 (f))

This statute does not mandate specific education treatment; but it does require public educational agencies to sustain programs to meet the language needs of their students.

The Congress of the United States on six occasions (1968, 1974, 1978, 1984, and 1987) has passed specific legislation related to the education of language minority students. The Bilingual Education Act (BEA) of 1968 was intended as a demonstration program designed to meet the educational needs of low-income limited English speaking children. Grants were awarded to local educational agencies, institutions of higher education, or regional research facilities to: (a) develop and operate bilingual education programs, native history and culture programs, early childhood education programs, adult education programs, and programs to train bilingual aides; (b) make efforts to attract and retain as teachers, individuals from non-English-speaking backgrounds; and (c) establish cooperation between the home and the school.

Five major re-authorizations of the BEA have occurred since 1968-in 1974, 1978, 1984,1987 and a major re-authorization in 1994. As a consequence of the 1974 Amendments (Public Law 93-380), a bilingual education program was defined for the first time as "instruction given in, and study of English and to the extent necessary to allow a child to progress effectively through the education system, the native language" (Schneider, 1976). The goal of bilingual education continued to be a transition to English rather than maintenance of the native language. Children no longer had to be low-income to participate. New programs were funded, including a graduate fellowship program for study in the field of training teachers for bilingual educational programs, and a program for the development, assessment, and dissemination of classroom materials.

In the Bilingual Education Act of 1978 (Public Law 95-561), program eligibility was expanded to include students with limited English academic proficiency as well as students with limited English-speaking ability. Parents were given a greater role in program planning and operation. Teachers were required to be proficient in both English and then native language of the children in the program. Grant recipients were required to demonstrate how they would continue the program when federal funds were withdrawn.

The Bilingual Education Act of 1984 created new program options including special alternative instructional programs that did not require use of the child's native language. These program alternatives were expanded in 1987. State and local agency program staff were required to collect data, identify the population served and describe program effectiveness.

New National Educational Policy in 1994. From this broader context, specific changes in policy with regard to these students developed in the re-authorization of 1994. Typical rationales for changes in national policy are often related to crisis intervention:

There is a problem and it must be addressed quickly, usually with more political and philosophical rhetoric than action. The past national policy for serving linguistically and culturally diverse students and their families was driven to a large extent by the "crisis" rationale. Accordingly, crisis policies in this arena have been short sighted, inflexible, minimally cohesive and integrated; they are not always informed by a strong knowledge base-- conceptual, empirical, or one related to the wisdom of practice. Past articulations of Title I and Title VII of the Elementary and Secondary Education Act (ESEA), both prime examples of the crisis intervention approach related to providing services to Hispanic language minority students, have suffered from these disadvantages.

New policies emerging under the 1994 re-authorization of ESEA, while recognizing the acute need to serve this student population, also recognized the following in developing new policy:

1. The new knowledge base, both conceptual and empirical, must be central to any proposed changes.
2. Consultation with the field is critical so as to capitalize on the wisdom of current policy, administration, curriculum, and instructional practice.
3. Policies and programs must be cohesive, in order to effectively integrate services that are to be provided-- this cohesiveness reflecting the partnership between national, state and local educational policies and programs.
4. The demographic and budgetary realities that are present today and will be operative throughout this decade, continuing to influence new directions, must be acknowledged.

New policy directions, primarily those related to Title I and Title VII will be implemented in line with the presuppositions mentioned above. (See *The Teachers College Record*, Spring, 1995, for a comprehensive description of the policy foundations for this re-authorization.)

Effective Educational Practices and Legislative Implications
The foundation established by recent findings has documented effective educational practices related to linguistically and culturally diverse students in selected sites throughout the United

States. These descriptive studies identified specific schools and classrooms serving language minority students that were academically successful. The case study approach adopted by these studies included examinations of preschool, elementary, and high school classrooms. Teachers, principals, parents and students were interviewed and specific classroom observations were conducted that assessed the "dynamics" of the instructional process.

The results of these studies provide important insights with regard to general instructional organization, literacy development, academic achievement in content areas (like math and science), and the views of the students, teachers, administrators and parents. Interviews with classroom teachers, principals and parents revealed interesting set of perspectives regarding the education of the students in these schools.

In summary, effective curriculum, instructional strategies, and teaching staffs reflect the understanding that academic learning has its roots in sharing expertise and experiences through multiple avenues of communication. Effective curricula provide abundant and diverse opportunities for speaking, listening, reading, and writing, along with scaffolding in order to help guide students through the learning process. Further, effective schools for diverse students encourage them to take risks, construct meaning, and seek reinterpretation of knowledge within compatible social contexts. Under this knowledge driven curriculum, skills are tools for acquiring knowledge, not ends in themselves. The curriculum recognizes that any attempt to address the needs of these students in a deficit or "subtractive" mode is counter productive. Instead, this knowledge base recognizes, conceptually, that educators must be "additive" in their approach to these students, that is, adding to the rich intellectual, linguistic, academic, and cultural attributes and skills they bring to the classroom. Moreover, programs for these students are integrated and comprehensive. They are not segregated and consider English development and academic content mastery equally important. Separate educational goals are not articulated for these students-- they are the same as for all students. Yet, federal efforts to assist local school districts, particularly in programs that may be perceived by parents as inappropriate for their students(s), inform parents of the program's nature and goals and parents voluntarily agree to their student(s) participation.

Wisdom of Practice. Too often in the heat of legislation and the political process, policy development is highly centralized in the domains of various interest groups and professional policy makers. Therefore, new national policy initiatives were crafted in consultation with diverse constituencies. For linguistically and culturally diverse communities, the usual players were consulted. These included the National Association for Bilingual Education, the Mexican American Legal Defense Fund, which has made specific legislative recommendations of major proportion, and other educational groups, which have made recommendations related to their own interests and expertise.

This new legislation was also organized by broader efforts of school reform. Of particular significance was the call by Carnegie Foundation for the Advancement of Teaching in it's synthetic report, *The Basic School: A Community for Learning* (Boyer, 1995). That work acknowledged the notion that there are key components of an effective school that need to be brought together in an integrated and cohesive manner. A good teacher alone, in a good classroom guaranteeing effective teaching/learning is not enough. Good schools are effective teaching/learning communities which undermine the significance of the early schooling years and place a high priority on language and a knowledge with cohesiveness. *The Basic School* is an idea based on best practice, a comprehensive plan for educational renewal that has as its goal the improvement of learning for every child. This same idea is at the core of new federal education policy.

The work of the Stanford Working Group was of particular significance. This group, funded by the Carnegie Corporation of New York, consulted widely with many individuals representing a broad spectrum of theoretical, practical, and policy significant expertise. In published reports and in various forums, they put forward a comprehensive analysis and articulated precise recommendations for policy and legislation related to linguistically and culturally diverse populations. Thus, new policy proposals were shaped in consultation with others; to do otherwise would be to negate the importance of shared wisdom from various established perspectives. Moreover, any proposed changes, if they are to be effective, must be embraced by those individuals and organizations presently on the field.

Cohesiveness. The proposed policy selections have also attempted to view the provisions of the services to students in a comprehensive and integrated manner. Through the introduction of new legislation in goals 2000, the United States Department of Education has set the stage for the state by state development mention of standards. Then with the passage of IASA the re-authorization of the Elementary and Secondary Educational Act (ESEA), an alignment of the goals and standards initiative with specific goals and standard initiatives with specific resource allocation policies was accomplished. This alignment recognizes the integration of federal, state, and local government efforts must occur in order to enhance effectiveness and efficiency. Moreover, the federal role must allow flexibility at the state and local levels while requiring that all children achieve at the highest levels.

Title VII re-authorization, services to limited English proficiency students as a component of the ESEA, is also highly congruent with the alignment principle. As such, Title VII is not seen as yet another intervention aimed at meeting an educational crisis in American education. Instead it is a key component of the integrated effort to effectively address the educational needs of students. Specifically, Title VII will continue to provide for leadership and national, state and local capacity building with regards to educational services, professional development and research related to linguistic and culturally diverse populations. However, other programs, particularly Title I, are important and will more directly increase the services needed by all students living in poverty, including those with limited English proficiency.

Demographics and Budget Realities. Over the last decade, large increases in the number of LEP students in our schools have occurred. In the last 6 years, that increase is near 70%, approxi-mately 1 million students. There is no reason to believe this trend will subside. However, it is important to recognize that the national presence and the diversity of this population is substan-tial. In the last decade ten states have been added to the count of those states with more than 2% of their students population as limited English proficiency. Today, 20 states can be counted in such a column, half of these states have student populations that vary between 5 and 25%. Moreover, the diversity of non-English language students served was itself quite diverse. Presently over

180 language groups are represented in programs funded under Title VII.

Unfortunately, the fiscal resources that can be consolidated to meet the growing and diverse demands of this population is not likely to be increased in any significant way. National, state, and local funding for these populations has not grown in proportion to their increase. Critics of bilingual education like Linda Chavez and Congressman Bill Light of New York have indicated that bilingual education cost taxpayers anywhere form $5.5 to $15 billion dollars yearly. How they arrive at those figures is a mystery, since federal funding for bilingual education programs in the last decade has ranged between $125 to $200 million yearly. A four percent increase in these federal funds was requested by the Clinton administration in 1996. No major increases in this program area will likely be requested in the near future. Although, new legislation in the IASA regarding the disposition of Title I funds to high poverty areas should bring more resources to Hispanic language minority students, such funding will still be limited. This means that present resources must be utilized more efficiently.

Specific Changes in Title VII. The Title VII legislation of 1994 was part of a cohesive policy direction from the U.S. Department of Education. Title VII will continue to serve the mission of leadership and capacity building with regards to educational services, professional development, and research related to linguistically and culturally diverse populations. However, series for language minority students will be packaged in a comprehensive manner, one that recognizes the significance of Goals 2000, Title 1, and other ESEA programs, and state, and local education efforts. The needs of linguistically and culturally diverse children are not only recognized, but are directly re-sponded to in new federal legislation. Title 1 legislation, for example, will be opened up in a deliberate manner to serve as a major source of federal educational programming for language minority students.

Within this framework, several changes are present in Title VII. Direct assistant to local and state educational agencies has been the core federal services to LEP children in our nation's schools. Under the new legislation, existing programs would be replaced by new programs: development and enhancement grants, comprehensive school grants, and comprehensive district grants. This new configuration recognizes the complexity of educational responses for language minority students as well as the necessity for locally designed and integrated programs. State review of proposals will reinforce the implementation of state plans for these students.

Other changes under research, evaluation, and dissemination are responsive to input from the field. Research activities will be developed by the Office of Bilingual Education and Minority Language Affairs with required consultation from the field and enhanced coordination with other Department of Education research activities. Program evaluation requirements are simplified to be more "user friendly" and directed at program improvement, assessment of student English and academic outcomes and dissemination. To showcase the success of existing Title VII programs, there will be added emphasis on Academic Excellence Programs-programs with proven effectiveness that disseminate that demonstrate their expertise locally, regionally, and nationally. The work of Multi-functional Resource Centers and the Evaluation Assistance Centers will be merged with new Department of Education comprehensive technical assistance and professional development efforts.

After twenty years of efforts to develop a teaching force prepared to meet the needs of LEP students, this area remains a major challenge. Professional development programs place renewed emphasis and resources on professional development, including a new career-ladder program. In addition to these continuing efforts to prepare teachers, opportunities for professional development through doctoral fellowships remain in place. To continue the development of a strong research and theoretical base, opportunities for postdoctoral studies were created.

These changes are framed by a commitment to the value of bilingualism and the belief that all children can achieve to high standards. The new policy will strengthen services from federal resources for language minority students not only through Title VII, but also through Title I and related federal K-12 education funding, thus opening the possibility of several million additional dollars in funding to meet the great need for services to linguistically and culturally diverse students, particularly the large number of Hispanic students.

<u>English Only</u>. At this writing, the U.S. House of Representatives has passed H.R. 123, the "English Language Empowerment Act of 1996," by a 259-169 vote. But the Senate has not acted on similar legislation. This legislation would permit states to craft "English Only" laws which could restrict the use of languages other than English in the provision of any form of governmental services including education. It would also restrict the federal government in the same way and would prohibit elections from being conducted in languages other than English. Such a national legislative provision would have important effects on the use of Spanish in bilingual education programs which serve Hispanic students.

Future action on this federal legislation seems to be related to a recent supreme court decision regarding a case in Arizona which failed to act before adjournment and so the bill died. On March 4, 1997, the U.S. Supreme Court declined to rule on the constitutionality of Arizona's English Only amendment -- in effect, dismissing the case after eight years of litigation without ruling on its merits. Article 28 of Arizona's constitution -- also known as Proposition 106, adopted by voters in 1988 -- requires all levels of state and local government to "act in English and no other language." Two lower federal courts have overruled the measure as a violation of the First Amendment right to freedom of speech for state employees and elected officials. The Supreme Court threw out those decisions on procedural grounds.

For now the practical impact will be negligible. A 1989 opinion by Arizona's attorney general minimized the restrictive impact of Article 28, arguing that it would not prohibit employees from using languages other than English "to facilitate the delivery of government services." A separate challenge to Article 28, *Ruiz v. Symington*, is under consideration by the Arizona Supreme Court and the measure has already been ruled unconstitutional by a lower state judge. So, until that case is resolved, the English Only amendment will not be enforced. Any decision by the Arizona Supreme Court could, of course, be appealed to the U.S. Supreme Court – further delaying a final disposition of the case.

Federal Court Cases
The 1974 United States Supreme Court decision in *Lau v. Nichols* (414 U.S. 563) is the landmark statement of the rights of

language minority students indicating that limited English proficient students must be provided with language support: [T]here is no equality of treatment merely by providing students with English instruction. Students without the ability to understand English are effectively foreclosed from any meaningful discourse. Basic English skills are at the very core of what these public schools teach. Imposition of a requirement that, before a child can effectively participate in the education program he must already have acquired those basic skills is to make a mockery of public education. We know that those who do not understand English are certain to find their classroom experiences wholly incomprehensible and in no way meaningful.

This articulation of the rights of language minority students prevails today. The following is a brief discussion of the progression of this and related court action.

Lau v. Nichols (1974). There is a clear starting point for the development of court-related policy regarding language-minority students: the 1974 United States Supreme Court decision *Lau v. Nichols.* The court suit was filed on March 25, 1970, and involved 12 American-born and foreign-born Chinese students. Prior to the suit, in 1966, at the request of parents, an ESL pullout program was initiated by the district, and in a 1967 school census, the district identified 2,456 limited-English-speaking Chinese students. By 1970, the district had identified 2,856 such students. Of this number, more than half (1,790) received no special instruction. In addition, over 2,600 of these students were taught by teachers who could not themselves speak Chinese. The district had made initial attempts to serve this population. The district was both formally conscious of the problem and had attempted to address it. On May 26, 1970, the Federal District Court found that the school district had no legal obligation to provide the special services, but encouraged the district as an educational policy to attempt to address the problem as an educational (as opposed to the legal) obligation to these students. On January 8, 1972, the Ninth Circuit District Court of Appeals upheld this lower court ruling. The plaintiffs appealed to the U.S. Supreme Court.

The Supreme Court's majority opinion overruled the appeals court and favored the pupils and parents. The opinion relied on statutory (legislative) grounds in granting relief, and avoided any reference to constitutional determination, although plaintiffs had argued that the equal protection clause (of the Fourteenth Amendment) of the United States Constitution was relevant to the case. Pupils' right to special education services flowed from the district's obligations under the Title VII of the 1964 Civil Rights Act and the HEW qualifying regulation articulated in its May 25, 1970 memorandum. The plaintiffs did not request an explicit remedy, such as a bilingual or ESL program, nor did the Court address this issue. Thus *Lau* does not stand for the proposition that children must receive a particular educational service (such as bilingual/bicultural instruction or ESL) but instead that some form of effective educational programming must be available to "open the instruction" to language-minority students.

After *Lau*, the domain of the language-minority education lawsuits belonged almost exclusively to Hispanics litigants. Although some cases were litigated to ensure compliance with the *Lau* requirements of some special assistance, most subsequent cases were about the issues left unanswered in *Lau*: Who are these students?, and What form of additional educational services must be provided?

Aspira of New York, Inc. v. Board of Education (1975). In *Aspira* (1975), a suit was brought by a community action group on behalf of all Hispanic children in the New York School District whose English language deficiency prevented effective participation in an English schooling context and who could effectively participate in a Spanish language curriculum (Roos, 1984). The district court hearing this case adopted a language dominance procedure to identify those students eligible for non-English, Spanish-language instructional programs. The procedure called for parallel examinations to obtain language proficiency estimates on Spanish and English standardized achievement tests. All students scoring below the 20th percentile on an English language test were given the same (or a parallel) achievement test in Spanish. Students who scored higher on the Spanish achievement test and Spanish language proficiency test were to be placed in a Spanish-language program. These procedures assumed adequate reliability and validity for the language and achievement tests administered. Such an assumption was and still is highly questionable. However, the court argued that it acted in "reasonable manner," admitting that in the absence of better assessment procedures it was forced to follow previous (Lau) precedents.

A subsequent case, *Otero v. Mesa County School District No. 51* (1977), concluded that a clear relationship between low academic achievement and the English language deficiency of students must be clearly demonstrated before a court could mandate special language services for language-minority students. This court suggested that in the absence of the clear relationship low academic achievement could be attributed to other variables (e. g., socioeconomic background). Therefore, merely showing that Spanish is the home language was insufficient to require a school district to provide special language assistance. Instead, a link between non-English proficiency and low school achievement needed to be established. Recall that in *Lau*, the district had conducted its own census and had begun a special language program for some of the students identified as in need. Therefore, the legal obligation related to providing special educational programs for language-minority students is based on the link between lack of English proficiency and the lack of school achievement under English-language instruction.

Castaneda v. Pickard (1981). After the population of students requiring special language services is identified, what types of services must districts provide to language-minority students? In Arizona, a suit was filed against a local school district by a nonprofit corporation, suing on behalf of the children of a community of 5,000 persons, most of whom were of Mexican-American or Yaqui ancestry (*Guadalupe v. Tempe School District No. 3*, 1978). Plaintiffs organized their lawsuit around the claim that the district was acting discriminatory in failing to provide these children with appropriate educational programs in as much as the district curriculum failed to recognize their special educational needs. The curriculum did not reflect the historical contributions of people of appellants' descent to the State of Arizona and to the United States. The plaintiffs requested a maintenance bilingual program that would ensure competence at graduation in the children's native language and English, with biculturalism reflected throughout the curriculum.

The district court entered judgment in favor of the school district, and the plaintiffs appealed to the Ninth Circuit, which put the dispute to rest by affirming the lower court's order. In their opinion, it is noted that "in answer to interrogatories of the appellees and in argument before the district court, [plaintiffs] admitted they did not complain of the school district's efforts to cure existing language deficiencies." The court concluded, in its constitutional holding, "that the Constitution neither requires nor prohibits the bilingual and bicultural education sought by appellants. Such matters are for the people to decide." In assessing the choices made by Congress in the Civil Rights Act of 1964 and the Equal Educational Opportunity Act of 1974, the court concluded that in previous litigation, courts also have not required districts to provide what the plaintiffs sought, even as a condition to receipt of federal funds. As long as the district responds appropriately to the needs of limited-English-proficiency (LEP) children, effectively remediating their English language deficiency, no federal statute has been violated. Essentially, the court failed to find any statutory or constitutional violation committed by the district.

However, in a key Fifth Circuit decision of *Castaneda v. Pickard* (1981), the court interpreted Section 1703(f) of the Equal Education Opportunity Act of (1974) as substantiating the holding of *Lau* that schools cannot ignore the special language needs of students. Moreover, this court then pondered whether the statutory requirement that districts take "appropriate action" suggested a more precise obligation than the Civil Rights Act requirement that districts do something. The plaintiffs predictably urged on the court a construction of "appropriate action" that would necessitate at least bilingual transitional programs. The court concluded, however, the Section 1703(f) did not embody a congressional mandate that any particular form of remedy be uniformly adopted. If Congress wished to intrude so extraordinarily on the local districts' traditional curricular discretion, it must speak more explicitly. This conclusion, the court argued, was buttressed by the congressional use of "appropriate action" in the statute, instead of "bilingual education" or any other educational terminology.

However, the court concluded that the Congress did require districts to adopt an appropriate program, and that, by creating a cause of action in federal court to enforce Section 1703(f), if left to federal judges the task of determining whether a given program is appropriate. The court noted that Congress had not provided guidance in that statute or its brief legislative history on what it intended by selecting "appropriateness" as the operative standard.

Continuing with clear reluctance and hesitancy, the court described a mode of analysis for a Section 1703(f) case:

1. The court will determine whether a district's program is "informed by an educational theory recognized as sound by some experts in the field or, at least, deemed a legitimate experimental strategy." The court explicitly declined to be an arbiter among competing theorists. The appropriate question is whether some justification exists, not the relative merits of competing alternatives.

2. The court will determine whether the district is implementing its program in a reasonably effective manner (e.g., adequate funding, qualified staffing).

3. The court will determine whether the program, after operating long enough to be a legitimate trial, produces results that indicate the language barriers are being overcome. A plan that is initially appropriate may have to be revised if expectations of it are not met if the district's circumstances significantly change in such a way that the original plan is no longer sufficient.

After *Castaneda* it became legally possible to substantiate a violation of Section 1703(f), following from *Lau*, on three grounds: (a) The program providing special language services to eligible language-minority students is not based on sound educational theory; (b) the program is not being implemented in an effective manner; and (c) the program, after a period of "reasonable implementation," does not produce results demonstrating that language barriers are being overcome.

It is obvious that these criteria allow a local school district to continue to implement a program with some educational theoretical support for a "reasonable" time before it will make judgments upon its "positive" or "negative" effects. However, the Castaneda court, again reluctantly but firmly, spoke to the issue of program implementation. Particularly, the court indicated that the district must provide adequate resources, including trained instructional personnel, materials, and other relevant support that would insure effective program implementation. Therefore, a district that chooses a particular program model for addressing the needs of its language-minority students must demonstrate that its staffing and materials are adequate for such a program. Implicit in these standards is the requirement that districts staff their programs with language minority education specialists, typically defined by state-approved credentials or professional course work (similar to devices utilized to judge professional expertise in other areas of professional education).

Keyes v. School District No. 1, Denver (1983). The *Keyes* court decision was originally initiated in 1969 by a class of minority parents on behalf of their minor children attending the Denver public schools, to desegregate the public schools and to provide equal educational opportunities for all children. In granting the preliminary injunction the trial court found that during the previous decade the school board had willfully under-taken to maintain and intensify racial segregation (*Keyes v. School District No. 1*, Denver, Colorado, 1969). The court ordered boundary changes to desegregate the Denver public schools. Years of litigation ensued with multiple appeals to the Court of Appeals and the Supreme Court. In 1973, the district court concluded that the Denver public school system was an unlawful dual system in violation of the United States Constitution and ordered the dismantling of the dual system (*Keyes v. School District No. 1, Denver, Colorado*, 1973). In 1974, during the de-velopment of a desegregation plan, intervention was sought by the Congress of Hispanic Educators (CHE) on behalf of themselves as educators and on behalf of their own minor children who attended the Denver schools. CHE was interested in ensuring that the desegregation plan ordered by the court included that educational treatment of language-minority students to overcome the deficits created by numerous years of attendance in segregated and inferior schools. A sequence of additional proceedings and negotiations followed with final comprehensive court hearings commencing in May 1982.

In December 1983, Judge Richard Matsch issued a 31-page opinion, which is the most lengthy and complete language-programming discussion to date in a judicial decision. Judge Matsch, applying the Castaneda standards, found that Denver had failed to direct adequate resources to its language program, the question of teacher skills being a major concern.

Gomez v. Illinois (1987). The Seventh Circuit Court of Appeals, which includes Wisconsin, Illinois and Indiana, ruled on the obligations of the states under the Equal Educational Opportunities Act of 1974 (EEOA). The Court applied the tripartite test established in Castaneda and extended to state education agencies, as well as to local education agencies, the obligation to ensure that the needs of the students of limited English proficiency be met.

Enforcement of Federal and State Regulations.

The Office of Civil Rights (OCR) of the U.S. Department of Education is charged with monitoring school districts' compliance with the Civil Rights Act of 1964. The OCR does not prescribe a specific educational program that will provide adequate learning opportunity for language minority students. Rather, each school district is at liberty to choose any proven approach, or any approach that promises to be successful, that it considers most appropriate to its own needs, conditions, and resources. The OCR, however, requires that all programs carry out basic functions by which schools will:

- properly identify students who need language services;
- develop programs that are effective in promoting learning;
- provide adequate teachers, educational materials and physical space;
- adequately evaluate students' progress; evaluate the whole program on an ongoing basis and implement changes when and where they are found to be needed.

OCR will explore the following fundamental responsibilities of school districts:

1. To take affirmative steps and employ adequate resources to ensure that students acquire proficiency in the language of instruction;
2. To refrain from placing students in classes for the mentally retarded on the basis of criteria which essentially measure English language skills, or to deny access to college preparatory courses as a result of school's failure to impart necessary English language skills;
3. To employ no grouping or tracking systems which impede national origin students' educational development, or that operate as dead-end or permanent

tracks, but to stimulate learning and the mastery of English as quickly as possible;

4. To ensure that parents with limited English proficiency receive information about school activities in a language that they understand.

State Initiatives

Through state legislation, twelve states mandate special educational services for language minority students, twelve states permit these services and one state prohibits them. Twenty-six states have no legislation which directly addresses language minority students.

State program policy for language minority students can be characterized as follows:

1. Implementing instructional programs which allow or require instruction in a language other than English (17 states).
2. Establishing special qualifications for the certification of professional instructional staff (15 states).
3. Providing school districts supplementary funds in support of educational programs (15 states).
4. Mandating a cultural component (15 states).
5. Requiring parental consent for enrollment of students (11 states). Eight states (Arizona, California, Colorado, Illinois, Indiana, Massachusetts, Rhode Island, and Texas) impose all of the above requirements concurrently.

Such a pattern suggests continued attention by states to issues related to language minority students [see Garcia (1994) for details]. Of particular interest is a subset of states which when taken together are home to almost two-thirds of this nation's language minority students: California, Florida, Illinois, New York, New Jersey and Texas. In these states, bilingual credentialing and ESL or some other related credential/endorsement is available. However, in only three of the six states is such credentialing mandated. Therefore, even in states which are highly "impacted" by language minority students, there is not the direct concern for the specific mandating of professional standards. Valencia (1991) has suggested that with the segregation of language minority students, particularly Chicano students in the

Southwest, state school systems are not equally affected by these students. These students tend to be concentrated in a few school districts within the state, and even though their academic presence is felt strongly by these individual districts, Hispanic language minority students do not exert this same pressure statewide.

English Only State Initiative.

A new California state initiative is the most recent effort for state action to restrict the use of a language other than English in the delivery of educational services to non-English speaking children. As indicated in Figures 1 and 2, the population of Hispanic and Hispanic students continues to grow in this state. Some 1.5 million K-12 students in the state (25% of the states K-12 population) have been identified as Limited English Proficient, with 80% of these students identified as Hispanics. The new ballot measure identified as "English for all Children" would,

1. Require that all children be placed in English language classrooms, and that English language learners be educated through a prescribed methodology identified as "Structured English Immersion."
2. Prescribe methodology would be provided as a temporary transition period not normally to exceed one year.
3. Allow instruction in the child's native language only in situations in which a waiver is granted, done so in writing and done so yearly by parents requiring a school visit by a parent, AND,
4. Prohibit native language instruction only if the student already had mastered English, and was over 10 years of age and such instruction was approved by the principal and the teacher.

In addition, this "English Only" initiative would allow native language instruction only through an exclusionary and complicated process: 20 or more parents at each grade level at each school would have to request waivers; they would then have to annually request and personally come to the school to negotiate written consent to continue native language instruction. Moreover, teachers administrators and school board members would be held personally liable for fees and damages by the child's parents and guardians. These provisions, taken together, are the most restrictive measures proposed yet for serving language minority students either nationally or within any state, via legislation or the courts. The California electorate will be voting on this measure in June of 1998. It is anticipated that the results of this election will have substantive effects on the future on bilingual education and its practice within and outside the state of California.

Rights of Language Minority Students

The previous discussion has highlighted the increasing number of court opinions and related state initiatives influencing the educational services for to language-minority pupils. The court opinions in particular have generated some understanding of a language-minority pupil's legal standing as it relates to the educational treatment received. At a national level, this legal standing stems from court opinions specifically interpreting Section 1703(f) of the 1974 U.S. Equal Educational Opportunity Act. The courts have consistently refused to invoke a corollary to the Fourteenth Amendment to the U.S. Constitution in respect to educational treatment. Even so it is evident that litigation has increased (and is likely to continue) and has been an avenue of educational program reform that has produced significant changes in educational programs for language-minority students. However, like almost all litigation, it has been a long (range of 4-13 years in court prior to an operational decision) and often highly complicated and resource-consuming enterprise.

Nevertheless, several important conclusions regarding the responsibilities of educational agencies have been established. The following, in a question-and-answer format, sets out some of these responsibilities. These are adapted from Roos (1984) and Garcia (1991) which are still legally valid today. They represent a practical guide for understanding the legal status of Hispanic language-minority students and the legal liability of the educational agencies that serve them.

Question: Is there a legally acceptable procedure for identifying language-minority students in need of special instructional treatment?

Answer: Yes. The legal obligation is to identify all students who have problems speaking, understanding, reading, or writing English owing to a home language background other than English. In order to do this, a two-phase approach is common and acceptable. First, the parents are asked , through a home language survey or on a registration form, whether a language other than English is utilized in the child's home. If the answer is affirmative, the second phase is triggered. In the second phase, students identified through the home language survey are given an oral language proficiency test and an assessment of their reading and writing skills.

Question: Once the students are identified, are there any minimal standards for the educational program provided to them?
Answer: Yes. First, a number of courts have recognized that special training is necessary to equip a teacher to provide meaningful assistance to limited-English-proficiency students. The teacher (and it is clear that it must be a teacher, not an aide) must have training in second-language acquisition techniques in order to teach English as a second language.

Second, the time spent on assisting these students must be sufficient to assure that they acquire English skills quickly enough to assure that their disadvantages in the English language classroom does not harden into a permanent educational disadvantage.

Question: Must students be provided with instruction in the student's native language as well as English?
Answer: At the present time, the federal obligation has not been construed to compel such a program. As a practical matter, however, the federal mandate is such that a district would be well advised to offer such a program whenever it is possible.

The federal mandate is not fully satisfied by an ESL program. The mandate requires English language help plus programs to assure that students not be substantively handicapped by any delay in learning English. To do this requires either (a) a bilingual program that keeps the students up in their course work while learning English or (b) a specially designed compensatory program to address the educational loss suffered by any delay in providing understandable substantive instruction. Given these alternatives, the legally "safe" posture is to offer native language instruction whenever it can be done. Finally, it is legally necessary to provide the material resources necessary for the instructional components. The program must be reasonably designed to succeed. Without adequate resources, this requirement cannot be met.

Question: What minimal standards must be met if a bilingual program is to be offered?

Answer: The heart of a basic bilingual program is a teacher who can speak the language of the students as well as address the students' limited English proficiency. Thus, a district offering a bilingual program must take affirmative steps to match teachers with these characteristics. These might include allocating teachers with language skills to bilingual classrooms, and affirmative recruitment of bilingual teachers. Additionally, it requires the district to establish a formal system to assess teachers to insure that they have the prerequisite skills. Finally, where there are insufficient teachers, there must be a system to insure that teachers with most (but not all) of the skills are in bilingual classrooms, that those teachers are on a track to obtain the necessary skills and that bilingual aides are hired whenever the teacher lacks the necessary language skills.

Question: Must there be standards for removal of a student from a program? What might these be?

Answer: There must be definite standards. These generally mirror the standards for determining whether a student is in need of special language services in the first place. Thus, objective evidence that the student can compete with English-speaking peers without a lingering language disability is necessary.

Several common practices are unlawful. First, the establishment of an arbitrary cap on the amount of time a student can remain in a program fails to meet the requirement that all language-minority students be assisted. Second, it is common to have programs terminate at a certain grade level, for example, sixth grade. While programs may change to accommodate different realities, it is unlawful to deny a student access to a program merely because of grade level.

Question: Must a district develop a design to monitor the success of its program?

Answer: Yes. The district is obligated to monitor the program and to make reasonable adjustments when the evidence would suggest that the program is not successful.

Monitoring is necessarily a two-part process. First, it is necessary to monitor the progress of students in the program to assure (a) that they are making reasonable progress toward learning and (b) that the program is providing the students with substantive instruction comparable to that given to English-proficient pupils. Second, any assessment of the program must include a system to monitor the progress of student after they leave the program. The primary purpose of the program is to assure that the LEP students ultimately are able to compete on an equal footing with their English-speaking peers. This cannot be determined in the absence of such a post-reclassification monitoring system.

Question: May a district deny services to a student because there are few students in the district who speak her or his language?

Answer: No. The 1974 Equal Educational Opportunity Act and subsequent court decisions make it clear that every student is entitled to a program that is reasonably designed to overcome any handicaps occasioned by a language deficit. Numbers may, obviously, be considered to determine how to address the student's needs. They are not a proper consideration in determining whether a program should be provided.

Although reluctant, United States courts have played a significant role in shaping language-minority educational policy. They have spoken to issues of student identification, program implementation, resource allocation, professional staffing, and program effectiveness. Moreover, they have obligated both local and state educational agencies to language-minority education responsibilities. Most significantly, they have offered to language-minority students and their families a forum in which minority status is not disadvantageous. It has been a highly ritualized forum, extremely time and resource-consuming, and always reluctant. But is has been a responsive institution and will likely continue to be utilized as a mechanism to air and resolve the challenges of educating language minority students.

References

Aspira of New York, Inc. v. Board of Education, 394 F. Supp. 1161 (S. D. N. Y 1975).

Bilingual Education Act (PL 93-380, 21 Aug. 1974), 88, United States Statutes at Large, p. 503-513.

Bilingual Education Amendment of 1978 (PL 95-591, 1 No. 1978), 92, U.S.L.

Boyer, E.L. (1995). The basic school: A community for learning. Princeton, N.J.: Carnegie Foundation for the Advancement of Teaching.

Castaneda v. Pickard (1981). 648 F. 2d 989, 1007 5th Cir. 1981; 103 S. ct. 3321.

Civil Rights Act of 1964, 88-352, (1964). Chicago: Commerce Clearinghouse.

Elementary and Secondary Education Act of 1965, Title II, Pub. L. 89-10, Stat. 27(1965).

English Language Empowerment Act of 1996. H.R. 123, 104th Congress (1995).

Equal Educational Opportunities and Transportation of Students Act of 1974, 294(f).20 U.S.L.

Garcia, E. (1994). The impact of linguistic and cultural diversity in American schools: A need for new policy. In M. C. Wang and M. C. Reynolds (Eds.), *Making a difference for students at risk*. Thousand Oaks, CA: Corwin Press, 156-182.

Garcia, E. (1991). *The education of linguistically and culturally diverse students: Effective instructional practices*. Santa Cruz, CA: National Center for Research on Cultural Diversity and Second Language Learning.

Gomez v. Illinois State Board of Education, 811 F.2d, 1030 7th Cir. (1987).

Guadalupe Organization, Inc. v. Tempe Elementary School District No. 3, 587 F. 2d 1022 (1978).

Keyes v. School District No. 1, Denver, Colorado, 423 U.S. 1066 (1983).

Keyes v. School District No. 1, Denver, Colorado, 423 U.S. 189.198 (1987).

Keyes v. School District No. 1, Denver, Colorado, 380 F. Supp. 673 (1969).

Lau v. Nichols. (1974). United States Supreme Court, 414 US 563.

National Research Council. (1997). *The new Americans: Economic, demographic, and fiscal effects of immigration*. Washington, DC: National Academy Press.

Otero v. Mesa County School District #51, 568 F. 2d 1312 (1977).

172

Roos, P. (1984, July). *Legal guidelines for bilingual administrators*. Invited address, Society of Research in Child Development, Austin, Texas.

Schneider, S. G. (1976). *Revolution, reaction or reform: The 1974 bilingual education act*. New York: Las Americas.

The Teachers College Record (1995). New Policy in the U.S. department of education. *Teachers College Record, 27* (1), 1-14

Valencia, R. (1991). *Chicano school failure and success*. New York: The Falser Press.

SECTION III.

Higher Education and Hispanic Students:
Access, Choice, and Outcomes

CHAPTER 8

Access, Choice, and Outcomes:
A Profile of Hispanic Students in Higher Education

Amaury Nora, Laura I. Rendon, & Gloria Cuadraz

Introduction

As the 1990s come to a close, access has become one of the most controversial issues in higher education. In the 1960s, 70s, and 80s, Hispanics and other minorities could rejoice in the fact that college was becoming more accessible. From the creation of community colleges to the validation of Affirmative Action (the access policy that permits the use of race as a criterion when reviewing admissibility of college applicants), underrepresented groups were encouraged to take advantage of higher education opportunities. But in 1998, Affirmative Action is under siege and access to college for Hispanics is in peril. If educational policy makers want to preserve access for Hispanics, they must understand the complexity of the issues and the context in which access is being debated. This chapter presents a profile of Hispanic students in higher education, describes their barriers to college access, and identifies the factors which enhance access.

Hispanics in Higher Education

There is good and bad news about Hispanic access to college. Table 1 portrays the good news. Between 1976 and 1995, the sheer number of Hispanics enrolled in college tripled. In 1976, Hispanics constituted 383,800 (3.5%) of the college populations.

175

By 1995, 1,093,800 (7.7%) of Hispanics were enrolled in college (*Chronicle of Higher Education Almanac*, 1997).

Table 1. Enrollment by Racial and Ethnic Group, 1976-1995

	1976	Percent	1995	Percent
American Indian	76,100	0.7	131,300	0.9
Asian	197,900	1.8	797,400	5.6
African American	1,033,000	9.4	1,473,700	10.3
Hispanic	383,800	3.5	1,093,800	7.7
Non-Hispanic white	9,076,100	82.6	10,311,200	72.3
Foreign	218,700	2.0	454,400	3.2
Total	**10,985,600**	**100**	**14,261,800**	**100**

Source: *Chronicle of Higher Education Almanac*, August 29, 1997

Despite what appears to be a promising scenario of college participation, access to higher education is still a critical issue for Hispanics. Some would argue that the United States already has universal access and that the nation's higher education system is based on choice. In other words, there is some kind of institution that students can attend regardless of academic credentials. However, Hispanics are not evenly distributed among non-selective, selective, and highly selective, institutions. In fact, Hispanics are clustered in non-selective colleges and universities, especially community colleges. While 47% of all minority students enrolled in college are found in two-year colleges, Hispanics make up more than a third (36%) of total community college enrollments (President's Advisory Commission, 1996).

The issue of choice is significant, as Americans know that greater wealth is found in "A" list institutions, as well as in graduate and professional schools. However, if Hispanics who graduate from high school are not eligible to attend selective or highly selective colleges, then their only "choice" is a community college. In these cases, choice becomes an illusion, as being given a choice is quite different from being able to make a choice. *Real choice* is having the luxury to select from a range of highly selective and non-selective institutions, as opposed to being shunted to certain kinds of institutions. Real choice is delimited when students are not informed about necessary educational backgrounds needed to be college-eligible and when information about admissions requirements in different kinds of institutions is not provided. Rendon (1997) elaborates,

> At issue is how to provide access opportunities for under-represented groups not only in lower and middle tier institutions, but in selective colleges and universities. At issue is how to increase the numbers of college-eligible minority students who qualify to enroll in selective institutions and graduate and professional schools. (p. 4)

Another significant point is that one must cautiously examine reports that college access gaps between Non-Hispanic whites and minorities have narrowed. Rendon (1997) notes that college-going rates are often computed using the high school graduation class and do not account for dropout behavior at earlier stages, nor do they consider the extent that high school graduates are college-eligible. In other words, if out of 1000 first graders only 100 make it to twelfth grade and of those only 50 graduate, then reporting a 50% graduation rate for Hispanics is misleading or presents a very narrow view of Hispanic academic progress. Moreover, only 10 of those 50 students may have the necessary qualifications to enroll in selective institutions.

Geiser (1996) accentuates this important point with an example of the University of California (UC) system. Geiser notes that UC is doing a reasonably good job attracting and enrolling minority and majority students who become "college-eligible" (i.e., took the required college-prep courses, earned a high GPA and a high score on a college admissions test). However, the pool of African American and Hispanic college-eligible students is very small due to differential rates of high school graduation and completion of the college preparatory curriculum (Rendon, 1997).

A full discussion of access must also include successful college completion. For example, the community college open door policy has increased access to college, but it is well known that student retention at two-year colleges is lower than at four-year institutions. The first-year college retention rate in two-year colleges is 56%, and in four-year institutions, it is 73.2%. In addition, transfer rates between two- and four-year colleges hover around 23% and are lower in some urban centers. While the non-Hispanic white and Asian American transfer rate is about 23%, the comparable rate for Hispanics and African Americans is only 12%

(Center for the Study of Community Colleges, 1995). The low transfer rate greatly limits the number of Hispanics who eventually earn bachelor's degrees and go on to pursue graduate degrees. On the plus side, Hispanics registered the largest increase (10.7%) in the number of bachelor's degrees earned in 1994 among the four ethnic minority groups (Hispanics, African Americans, Asians, and American Indians). But despite this increase, Hispanics remain under-represented in degree attainment as compared to their college enrollment. In 1994, Hispanics earned only 6% of all associate degrees, 4.3% of all bachelor's degrees, 3.1% of all master's degrees and 4.2% of all first professional degrees. At the same time, Hispanics represented 7.9% of all four-year undergraduate students, 3.7% of all graduate students, and 4.4% of professional students (Carter and Wilson, 1997).

Access to doctoral study, as well as to graduate work leading to professional degrees such as law and medicine, especially at highly selective institutions, is a particularly critical issue for Hispanics. These degrees provide a specialized academic wealth that allows them to become a part of "American intelligentsia" (Rendon, 1997). According to President Clinton's Advisory Commission on Educational Excellence for Hispanic Americans (1996), in 1994, of the 43,261 Ph.D.s awarded across all fields, only 946 were awarded to Hispanics (2.18%). In contrast, 1,344 (3.1%) Ph.D.s were awarded to African Americans, 132 (.31 %) to American Indians/Alaska Natives, 1,943 (4.49%) to Asian Americans and 26,137 (60.42%) to Non-Hispanic whites. Interestingly, foreign national or alien students earned more Ph.D.s than all minority students combined. At the doctoral level, there are entire fields and disciplines in which Hispanics and other minorities have never received a doctoral degree.

In summary, Hispanics have made small but important gains in college participation and completion rates. However, one needs to look beyond sheer numbers to present a more complete and accurate picture of Hispanic representation and achievement. Indeed, the picture could be brighter and more promising if barriers to college access were reduced or eliminated altogether.

Barriers to College Access

To fully understand access to higher education, one must focus on (1) the political/legal barriers that shape the retreat from access and (2) the longitudinal nature of access, given that barriers to college begin early in a student's life.

Political/Legal Barriers

Access for Hispanics and other members of racial and ethnic groups has been seriously threatened by the most recent, litigious assaults on Affirmative Action: the *Hopwood* case (1996) out of the University of Texas Law School and the passage of Proposition 209 (1996) in California. From a macro point of view both cases represent the extent to which race or "the color line" will continue to be the driving force in admissions policies or access to higher education. Both cases illustrate America's reaffirmation to disparity and stratification with respect to resources in an economic and political base increasingly dependent on technology and an educated workforce. The two cases also focus on the use of the legal apparatus to sustain or pursue objectives in line with the agenda and interests of those who wish to maintain an inequality in our educational system. They represent the extent to which racial animosity, when coupled with competing class-based interests (i.e., admissions), create a collision both among and within America's racial and ethnic populations. Finally, both cases exemplify the inadequacy of social policy (with regard to access to higher education) to respond to constituencies with increasingly diverse and complex set of needs. Thus, it is not enough, or sufficient, merely to aggregate groups with respect to an ethnic category, for example, without taking the various class locations present in that group, as a basis from which to formulate policy. As Hurtado and Navia (1997) reiterate, American society must ultimately provide an answer to the question, "higher education for whom?"

The *Hopwood* Case. In 1992, a lawsuit was filed against the University of Texas (UT) by Cheryl Hopwood and Stephanie Haynes, later to be joined by four additional plaintiffs. Stephanie Haynes discontinued her participation in the lawsuit for "personal reasons." The plaintiffs claimed "reverse discrimination" because Hispanics and African Americans with lower Texas Index (TI) scores--a composite of Grade Point Average (GPA) and Law School Admission Test (LSAT)--were granted admission, arguing they were denied entrance because they were non-Hispanic white.

After a series of decisions and appeals that went all the way to the Supreme Court (who decided not to hear the case), the Fifth Circuit Court of Appeals held that the admissions procedures practiced by UT were inappropriate. At issue were two things: different subcommittees were used to evaluate minority candidates and that there were separate zones of scores for minority candidates from non-Hispanic white candidates. Almost overnight, Texas institutions of higher education, with deliberate speed, abandoned the use of race or national origin in university and college procedures. Hence, a system of rectification that took years to establish was effectively dismantled within days of the decision.

Yet closer investigation of the case revealed that Hopwood had, in fact, not attended schools that were "academically competitive," having completed the majority of her work for the baccalaureate at a community college, later graduating from a California State University, with a degree in Accounting. Moreover, Hopwood's application to the Law School was incomplete, filing no letters of recommendation and failing to provide any personal statement to elaborate on her objectives and circumstances. Another overlooked fact of the case is that 109 non-minority residents with numerical scores lower than Hopwood's were offered admission.

The ruling brought to the forefront, once again, the role of standardized test scores as the criteria for determining admission into undergraduate and graduate programs. As argued by Kaufman and Gonzales (1997),

> the tremendous reliance that the UT Law School, as well as most graduate schools and highly competitive undergraduate schools place upon standardized tests scores creates a need for affirmative action. As long as these institutions rely so heavily on test scores, with their insidious and negative effect on minorities, it will be difficult if not impossible to have substantial minority enrollments at these institutions without some affirmative action. (p. 245-246)

Research on minority populations has shown that a far greater predictor of academic success is high school GPA. Kaufman and Gonzales persuasively conclude that "institutions need to lose reliance on standardized test scores if they do not want to use affirmative action to achieve diversity." In an attempt to address this issue, members of the California Latino Eligibility Task Force in September, 1997, presented to the Board of Regents a radical proposal: to eliminate the use of standardized test scores as one criteria for admissions into the University of California. Presently the proposal is under evaluation (UC Latino Eligibility Task Force, 1997).

The impact the *Hopwood* case is having on the access of Hispanics and other minorities to institutions of higher education is striking and alarming. At the University of Texas, only five African American students, eighteen Mexican Americans, and seven American Indian students were extended invitations to enroll in 1997. Conversely, in 1996, sixty-five African Americans were admitted, along with seven Mexican Americans and eleven American Indians (Haworth, 1997). Similarly, the American Association of Medical Colleges showed a drop of 11% in African Americans, American Indians, Chicanos, and Puerto Ricans applying to medical   schools. Further, 6.8% fewer of these minorities were accepted in 1997 than in 1996 (*Arizona Republic*, 1997). In sum, the litigation challenging affirmative action is effectively and detrimentally affecting the access of Hispanic students to institutions of higher education.

Proposition 209. The passage of Proposition 209, also known as the California Civil Rights Initiative (1996), put an end to race- and gender-based affirmative action policy at the University of California, throughout state and local government, and education. The results of the vote were difficult to comprehend, given the diversity of the state's population. The proposition passed with 55% of the overall vote, including 27% of the African American vote, 30% of the Hispanic vote and 45% of the Asian vote. On November 6, 1996, Richard C. Atkinson, President of the University of California, issued a statement in the aftermath of the passage of Proposition 209 to the faculty of the nine-campus public university system.

> Now we must also look to the broader issue of how, in light of Proposition 209, we can best fulfill our responsibilities as a public university in the nation's most ethnically and culturally diverse state. ...California is changing and so must we. What cannot change, however, is the University's historical responsibility to serve Californians of every back-ground and

condition, including greater numbers of disadvantaged young people. I am confident we have the
individual and institutional resolve to keep the
commitment to diversity alive for the next generation
of Californians.

Scheduled to take effect in fall 1998, its passage represents
the biggest challenge to affirmative action since its incipience.
Having survived the historic *Bakke* (1978) decision, which ruled
that universities had the right to pursue diverse student bodies, and
that race was an acceptable criterion for admission, the passage of
Proposition 209 resulted in a swirl of controversy at every level.
Undergraduate and graduate student bodies mobilized across the
state; faculty and administrators found themselves embroiled in
governance issue with the Board of Regents, and citizens on both
sides of the issues await its impact on hiring and admissions
practices.

Despite evidence released by a seven-year investigation of
Berkeley's admission practices by the Office of Civil Rights of the
Department of Education, which revealed that Berkeley "employed no quotas, limited admission to students who met its high
qualification standards and considered race but one 'plus' factor
among many in a truly competitive admission process," the
passage of Proposition 209, and the *Hopwood* ruling effectively
managed to place at stake, as Karabel (1996) has argued, "nothing
less than the future of the American dream – that the United States
should be the land of opportunity for all its citizens."

In a final ruling issued November 1997, the Supreme Court
of the United States refused to hear the case, rendering the
proposition subject to enforcement and implementation. In the
wake of this ruling, other states are expected to follow suit. The
ramifications for Hispanic access are projected to be grave. Not
since the political mobilizations of the late sixties has the Hispanic
community been faced with the need to re-organize, strategize, and
call upon its leaders to prevent the further loss of ground in the
educational arena.

Access Barriers to Higher Education
To discuss access as simply a college entrance issue is to
seriously misrepresent the matter. By the time Hispanics get to
the twelfth grade it is too late to improve college eligibility or to
increase the number of students who are ready for college

(Rendon, 1997). Access is shaped very early in a student's life. Indeed, working-class Hispanics find multiple barriers at every step of their schooling experiences. Below are the barriers to access from the pre-college to the graduate school levels.

Socioeconomic Barriers. Access to college begins in the socioeconomic context of the home environment. According to the report, *Our Nation on the Fault Line: Hispanic American Education,* developed by President Clinton's Advisory Commission on Educational Excellence for Hispanic Americans (1996, September), Hispanics have been the victims of a legacy of neglect and inequitable opportunity in educational attainment. In 1995, the poverty rate among Hispanics surpassed that of African Americans for the first time. Hispanics now constitute nearly 24% of America's poor, a gain of eight percentage points since 1985 (Goldberg, 1997).

A child born in the context of poverty usually has deficiencies in nutrition and health, all of which lower the quality of social, emotional, and educational conditions, which in turn affect a child's self-esteem, language, cognitive abilities, world view, values, personality, and future social relationships. Poverty generally means attending segregated, poorly funded, and under-resourced schools, where students get the least of the best that American public schools have to offer. Poverty means being labeled "remedial" and "at-risk" because many non-Hispanic teachers and administrators do not understand the children's native language, culture, and socioeconomic realities. By age four, Hispanic children tend to have less well-developed school-related skills than do Non-Hispanic white children (i.e., identifying basic colors, recognizing all letters of the alphabet, counting, and writing). Carefully constructed pre-school programs such as Head Start and Parent-Child Development Centers play a critical role academically preparing children from low-income Hispanic communities (President's Advisory Commission, 1996).

K-12 Barriers. Early schooling shapes future educational opportunities. In fact, it could be said that students begin to drop out of college in the early grades. Given existing conditions, Hispanic children begin to trail other groups throughout elementary and middle school. By age nine they fall behind in reading, mathematics, and science proficiency (President's Advisory Commission, 1996).

Moreover, one must also note that there are systemic barriers that work against Hispanic achievement. Born from the tradition of segregation in public schools, inequity in tax-based funding is one of the key issues affecting the academic progress of students throughout the K-12 system (Kozol, 1991). In addition, grade retention and school suspensions affect dropout behavior. Tracking policies often steer Hispanics into general education courses that satisfy only the basic high school requirements. Failure to take college-prep courses has devastating consequences. Not only does this limit access to college, it does not qualify Hispanics for entry-level jobs in high-tech industries.

Hispanic high school graduates are also less likely than Non-Hispanic whites to have completed the "New Standards" curriculum, which includes four years of English and three years of science, social studies, and mathematics. Often, Hispanic children are misdiagnosed as "learning disabled" and placed in remedial/general education tracks because of inappropriate testing and assessment (President's Advisory Commission, 1996). Schools in poor districts operate with outmoded curricula, lack computers, and hire the least trained teachers. In these schools, it is likely that students will not be challenged with high expectations. Rather, they are likely to engage in mundane tasks that do not require critical thinking. Lack of well-designed bilingual and ESL programs means that many Hispanic children fall behind their peers in both native and English language proficiency (Rendon and Hope, 1996).

The failure of schools to provide Hispanics with a marketable education and their inability to increase the number of Hispanics who graduate from high school prepared to enroll in the nations' selective and highly selective colleges and universities is a key reason for poverty among the Hispanic population. While graduation rates have improved, Hispanics have the highest dropout rate of any ethnic/racial group in the nation. The 1990 Census found that even among American-born Hispanics, only 78% finished high school compared to 91% of Non-Hispanic whites and 84% of African Americans (Goldberg, 1997). As noted earlier, high school graduation rates are usually calculated using the twelfth grade class and do not take into account the dropout behavior that occurred in the earlier stages of the educational pipeline.

      College Barriers. If access is related to ability to pay, then students from low socio-economic (SES) backgrounds are differentially affected. Making college affordable is critical to access. Orfield and Ashkinaze (1991) indicate that economic trends during the 1980s and 1990s reduced college affordability. Federal Pell grants, the key source of scholarship aid for low-income students, increased at a much slower level than the cost of college tuition in the 1980s. To exacerbate matters, the share of family income required to pay for college costs has gone up most for those who occupy the bottom tier of the economic ladder. Low-income families have no reserves to draw upon and are reluctant to secure loans that will exacerbate family debt (Rendon, 1997).

      Hispanics who manage to graduate from high school represent a very select group. However, attending poor schools usually means that students are not prepared to handle a college-level curriculum. The first year of college is critical, as dropout rates tend to be higher at this juncture. Given that many Hispanics are the first in their family to attend college, making the transition to college is critical. Jalomo (1995) and Rendon (1997) note that the transition to college is a time of both excitement and loss. It is a time that Hispanics separate from family and friends, break family codes of unity, learn new values, traditions, and conventions of the academy, learn to live in multiple worlds (i.e., barrio, family, work, college), and assume a new identity.

      Students who have experienced invalidation in the past, who have been told they will not succeed, come to college expecting to be just a number and expecting to fail. Often, these students find an invalidating and intimidating college environment, along with a predominantly Non-Hispanic white faculty that has little understanding of minority cultures, a Euro-centered curriculum, racism, and fiercely competitive learning environments. According to a study conducted by Padilla, et al. (1997), many minority students feel culturally or racially isolated given the lack of minority role models or mentors, lack of minority issues or materials in the curriculum and lack of visible minority support programs. Given these conditions, Hispanic students are unlikely to negotiate the transition to college or to get involved in institutional life, which may lead to higher attrition levels from Hispanic students.

Graduate School Barriers. The challenges facing Hispanic students in graduate and professional degree programs are in many ways similar to those found among undergraduates. As Astin (1982) has argued, with advancement at every stage of the educational pipeline, the under-representation of Hispanic students increases. Thus, it is not uncommon for Hispanic graduate students to experience being the "first" or "the only one" in their respective cohorts and/or disciplines.

Research studies on Hispanic graduate students consistently show that the majority come from low socio-economic backgrounds and from parents with low levels of educational attainment (Noboa-Rios, 1982; Gandara, 1995; Gilford and Snyder, 1977). Because the Hispanic category consists of various subgroups (Mexican, Cuban, Puerto Rican, and others), each with different histories in relationship to the United States political economy, researchers have persuasively argued for the need to disaggregate the subgroups in order to better distinguish the specific needs for each group (Solorzano, 1995; Ibarra, 1996). On a national basis, we know that approximately half of those who enter advanced degree programs will complete their degrees; in the case of minority students, the ratio decreases to four out of ten who will complete their degrees (Astin, 1982; Benkin, 1984).

Studies addressing the factors affecting retention of Hispanic graduate students report the lack of mentoring by faculty as one of the key issues impeding graduate careers (Nettles, 1990; Ibarra, 1996; Nora and Cabrera, 1997). Studies found that institutions which support programs and activities that promote networking between Hispanic graduate students positively affect the experiences of Hispanics in graduate programs (Cuadraz, 1993, Nettles, 1990).

There is a great need to document the experiences of Hispanic graduate students from a qualitative standpoint. Hispanic graduate students consistently report barriers with respect to the culture of the academy, areas or topics of scholarly inquiry, negotiations with faculty, and experiences of cultural.and sometimes political isolation at the departmental and campus levels. Cuadraz (1993) and Ibarra's (1996) research on Hispanic graduate students' experiences showed numerous accounts of conflict along the lines of race and gender. Hispanic female graduate students reported issues of sexism and sexual harassment with respect to men from both minority and majority groups. As Ibarra (1996) recommends, "Barriers to accessing graduate programs still exist but can be surmounted with efforts by culturally sensitive faculty. Cultural conflicts within graduate schools could be minimized by faculty, departmental, and disciplinary reassessments of their academic cultures" (p. 70).

In summary, multiple barriers exist, from the pre-school to the graduate school level, which work against access opportunities for Hispanic students. To preserve access, structural and staff changes need to be made throughout the educational continuum. The next section explores the factors that enhance college access.

Factors That Enhance Hispanic Students' College Access and Persistence

Despite the barriers, a number of factors have been identified in the literature that actually make a difference in expanding access for Hispanics. As previously noted, the issue of access ultimately focuses on college completion or degree attainment, but the role of the family should not be minimized with regard to fostering a "culture of possibility." Access to professional and graduate programs can only be achieved through the attainment of a baccalaureate degree. In an extensive review of factors influencing minority students' educational aspirations and attainments, Nora (1993) notes that these factors fall within four major categories: educational goal commitments (or educational aspirations), financial assistance, social integration or experiences, and institutional commitments (or institutional fit). Research by Nora and associates (1994, 1995, 1996, 1997) subsequent to that review has identified other instrumental factors which include: environmental pull factors, perceptions of prejudice and discrimination, academic performance, support and encouragement by parents, and academic and intellectual development while in college.

A Family "Culture of Possibility"

Access may be conditioned in very early developmental stages through *la familia*. Gandara's (1995) research on the family backgrounds of low-income, highly educated Mexican Americans has shown that parents of these individuals fostered a "culture of possibility" with respect to achievement and schooling. In other words, largely through story, particularly stories (or myths) of family history rooted in a better life, Gandara found that Mexican American parents managed to exude a faith in the future, while cultivating high levels of possibility and powerfully influencing the aspirations of their children. She argues, "in so doing, they reinforce in their children a self-belief of efficacy which resulted in intense achievement motivation" (p. 112). The "culture of possibility" resonates with the concept of "endurance labor." By endurance labor, Cuadraz and Pierce (1994) refer to "the relentless drive to persist, in spite of adversity, and many times, because of adversity" (p. 31). Unlike the traditional concept of "cultural capital" which is available to and transmitted by those who have control over linguistic and cultural competence in society (as well as the form of capital that is valued), endurance labor "arises from those who have little control over those regimes of power, but who create, nevertheless, an inner and collective strength to struggle against the very structures that disempower them." Research based on the stories of minority populations, including Hispanics, abounds with examples of students who grew up not only with a "culture of possibility" but with the "endurance labor" enabling them to prevail, despite the barriers or odds against them.

The implications of this phenomenon are clear. Even before Hispanic children reach the front doors of kindergarten, despite social or economically adverse conditions, parents can play a key role in their children's achievement by cultivating a "culture of possibility" – by influencing the aspirations and expectations of their children. By setting the tone for achievement and hope, Hispanic parents can contribute substantially to their children's educational trajectories.

Nieto (1996) advocates that changing schools requires speaking about transformation rather than simply reform. In other words, changes are needed both in structures (i.e., policies and practices such as the curriculum, tracking, and teaching) and in the individual and collective will to educate students (i.e., treating students as powerful learners, setting high expectations, instilling the idea of college as a viable possibility, providing encourage-ment and support).

Educational Aspirations

Nora, Castaneda, and Cabrera (1992) and Cabrera, Nora, and Castaneda (1993) note that educational goal commitments of Hispanic college students are prominent in affecting these students' intentions to re-enroll in their second year in college as well as in their actual persistence behavior. Minority students' desires to earn an undergraduate degree and further pursue a professional or graduate degree reflect a mind set that Hispanic students bring with them upon entering college regarding the importance of college. Contrary to statements made by insensitive and unenlightened individuals (i.e., *The Houston Chronicle*, 1997), Hispanic students have high educational aspirations for themselves as early as elementary school (Rendon and Nora, 1997) and these aspirations remain high in spite of their dispropor-tionate enrollment in two-year institutions (Nora and Rendon, 1990).

Financial Assistance

Studies by Stampen and Cabrera (1988), Cabrera, Stampen, and Hansen (1990), and Cabrera, Nora, and Castaneda (1992), collectively reflect the importance of financial assistance in the persistence process. Not only did Cabrera et al. (1990) find that financial aid creates an equal playing field among recipients (mostly minorities) and non-recipients (largely non-minorities), but Cabrera et al. (1992) uncovered an intangible component associated with financial aid. In this study, the authors differenti-ated between the tangible (or actual awarding of financial aid) and the intangible (attitudes associated with having received financial assistance) components that make up the construct. In all in-stances, both components were found to influence, directly and indirectly, Hispanic students' decisions to remain in college. It is believed that the intangible component is not only a reflection of stress reduction that comes from being able to pay for college-related expenses but that it may also represent a student's commit-ment to their respective institution centering around the notion that the institution provided the financial means to remain in college.

Social Experiences

While much of the research on the influence of social experiences on the persistence of minority students focuses on informal faculty-student contact (e.g., Iverson, Pascarella and

Terenzini, 1984; Pascarella, 1985; Smart and Pascarella, 1986), recent research examines the influence of this factor on the adjustment of students to college and not simply on persistence (Cabrera, Nora, and Castaneda, 1993; Nora and Cabrera, 1996). With the exception of Nora's (1987) research on Hispanics at two-year institutions, the direct influence of social experiences on persistence has been found to be minimal for minorities. This factor makes its presence felt on the student's academic performance and, to a limited extent, on persistence decisions (Nora and Cabrera, 1996).

Commitment to an Institution
     Findings related to the impact of minority students' commitments to their respective institutions on their withdrawal decisions have been mixed, partly due to student samples. In earlier studies by Braddock (1981), Allen (1988), Nora, Castaneda, and Cabrera (1992), and Nora and Cabrera (1993), the influence of a student's commitment to an institution were found to be positively related to a minority student's decision to remain enrolled in college. However, the studies by Allen (1988) and Braddock (1981) dealt exclusively with African American college students and those by Nora and Cabrera (1993) and Nora, Castaneda, and Cabrera (1992) examined the impact of institutional commitment for a commuter student population comprised of 25% minority students, both Hispanic and African American. In a more recent investigation by Nora and Cabrera (1996), the influence of a minority student's commitment to his or her institution was examined separately from those of non-minority students. The results indicated that while commitment was a driving force for non-minority students in their decisions to re-enroll, this factor was not significant in influencing persistence decisions for minorities. While a sense of belonging at an institution largely affects non-minorities, other cognitive and non-cognitive factors are much more propitious in affecting minority students' departure.

Environmental Pull Factors
     Environmental pull factors were examined by Nora and Wedham (1991). In that investigation the authors identified three factors that exerted a pulling-away effect not only on the student's decision to remain enrolled in college, but also on his or her social and academic integration on campus. Those three factors included

family responsibilities such as taking care of a sibling, grandparent, or an entire family, working off-campus immediately after attending classes, and commuting to college. Nora and Wedham established that those students that could not remain on campus, either because they had familial responsibilities or were having to go to work off-campus, were not able to integrate fully socially and academically and ultimately had to leave higher education altogether. These results were further substantiated by Nora, Cabrera, Hagedorn, and Pascarella (1996) where the authors found that minorities who had to leave campus for work were 36% more likely to drop out of college and minority women who had to take care of a family member were 83% more likely to withdraw from college. While the sample consisted of both Hispanic and African American college students, no differences were found between those two groups. In both cases, differences were found only between minorities and non-minorities. Along this vein, commuting to college was also found to affect student decisions to remain enrolled, although there were no differences found between minorities and non-minorities.

Perceptions of Prejudice and Discrimination
    Nora and Cabrera (1996) tested the validity of three assertions regarding minority students, both Hispanic and African American: (1) the influential nature of academic preparedness on withdrawal decisions, (2) the extent to which separation from family and community makes it easier for a successful adjustment to college, and (3) the role that minority perceptions of prejudice and discrimination have on both the adjustment to college and on college-related outcomes such as academic performance and persistence. In that study, the authors found that both Hispanic and African American students were more prone to sense discrimination and prejudice in the classroom and on campus and that those perceptions were subsequently found to affect minority students' adjustments to college. Some of the affected areas include: their academic performance, their academic experiences with faculty, their social experiences on campus, their academic and intellectual development, their commitment to an institution, and indirectly, their decisions to remain in college. Almost every aspect of a Hispanic college student's life was touched by these perceptions of discrimination and intolerance by the institution itself, and the people associated with the institution. In all cases,

the effect was negatively felt. Hispanic students' grade point averages, their interactions with faculty and peers, their development as students were diminished by a sense of prejudice on campus and in their classrooms.

Support and Encouragement by Significant Others
    In their research, Nora and Cabrera (1996) focused on three factors that heavily weighed on Hispanic students' decisions to remain in college or to drop out. Those three factors were: parental encouragement, grade point averages, and the student's sense that he or she was developing academically while in college. The authors also noted that while perceptions of discrimination and prejudice on campus negatively affected the adjustment to college and several college-related outcomes, much of the negative influence was negated by the student's perceptions that his or her family was supportive and provided encouragement while they were enrolled in college.
    Nora and Cabrera (1996) tested the assertion that "successful adjustment to college included severing previous ties with family, friends, and past communities." Their findings indicated that such links to significant others were key for the successful transition of Hispanics to college. Moreover, for both minorities and non-minorities alike, parental encouragement and words of support were found to exert a positive effect on the integration of students to college, on their academic and intellectual development, their academic performance and commitments, and finally, on their decisions to remain enrolled in college. In studies of Hispanic and African American two- and four-year college students (e.g., Nora, 1987;Nora and Rendon, 1990; Cabrera, Nora, and Castaneda, 1992, 1993; Nora and Cabrera, 1996; Nora, Kraemer, and Itzen, 1997), support and encouragement has been found to significantly impact on the determination of minority and non-minority students to persist.
    In a recent qualitative study, Rendon (1995) coins the phrase "validating experiences" in examining the behavior of faculty toward minorities in the classroom. Rendon notes that when Hispanic two-year college students perceive an air of acceptance and faculty behavior that validates their worth in the class, Hispanic students tend to participate more fully in classroom discussions, interact more effectively with faculty, and reconsider their decisions to drop out.

Academic Performance and Intellectual Development

Perhaps the most influential factor impinging on Hispanic students' decisions to persist in college is their academic performance during their first year in college. While grade point average was found to influence decisions by non-minorities to drop out, this factor was three times as influential for Hispanics and African Americans (Nora and Cabrera, 1996). For minorities, both the academic achievement and the perception that cognitive gains had, or had not, been made while attending college were the most determining factors in decisions to persist in college. It is believed that for Hispanic college students their sense of belonging in college and their perception of academic capital (the ability to earn a college degree) is seriously questioned whenever these students experience a lower than expected academic performance. While non-minorities may be able to "shake-off" a bad semester or year, it may be more devastating for Hispanic students. Again, perhaps being in an environment that they already perceive as intolerant of minorities may contribute significantly to their perceptions that they cannot overcome these setbacks thereby overly influencing their decisions to drop out.

Conclusion

The issue of access at all levels of higher education for Hispanic students is shaped by early school social and academic experiences, by environmental and social conditions prior to and during their school age years, and by family. These experiences help shape future aspirations, desires, and post-secondary possibilities, and opportunities. True access to those areas that require a professional or graduate degree, where Hispanics are disproportionately under-represented, cannot be addressed simply by focusing on admissions into undergraduate programs. True access cannot be reduced to policies that merely open doors for a segment of society but do nothing to provide the experiences necessary to remain enrolled until the attainment of a degree. While the issue of affirmative action is currently a "hot and sexy" topic, issues such as curriculum reform, faculty and staff development with regard to diversity issues, retention policies and programs, transfer from two-year to four-year institutions, articulation between K-12 and post-secondary institutions, and financial aid and choice of college have been minimized in important discussions centered around access.

Every effort should be made to stop the dismantling of what took courageous and visionary men and women many years to achieve in the area of affirmative action. However, discussions today must not lose sight of the holistic nature of access not only for Hispanics but for all groups of students. These discussions must also focus on building coalitions across different ethnic groups and should emphasize the goal of achieving a more diverse society, which in turn is reflected by a more diverse enrollment in higher education. With the prevailing attitudes in today's society questioning what constitutes "fairness" and "color-blindness," access-related efforts may be the only means by which affirmative action, equality, and institutional tolerance can be achieved.

References

Allen, D.F. & Nora, A. (1995). An empirical examination of the construct validity of goal commitment in the persistence process. *Research in Higher Education*, 36 (5), 509-533.

Allen, W.R. (1988). Improving back student access and achievement in higher education. *Review of Higher Education, 11*, 403-416.

Appleborne, P. (1996, March 22). 2 Decisions reflect biter conflict surrounding university affirmative action policies. *New York Times*, Sec. A, p. 12, Col. 1.

Astin, A. (1982). *Minorities in American higher education.* San Francisco, CA: Jossey-Bass Publishers.

Benkin, E.M. (1984). *Where have all the doctoral students gone?: A study of doctoral student attrition at UCLA.* Unpublished doctoral dissertation, University of California, Los Angeles.

Braddock, J.H. (1981). Desegregation and Black students. *Urban Education, 15*, 43-418.

Cabrera, A.F. & Nora, A. (1995). College students' perceptions of prejudice and discrimination and their feeling of alienation: A construct validation approach. *The Review of Education/ Pedagogy/Cultural Studies, 16* (3-4), 387-409.

Cabrera, A.F., Nora, A., & Castaneda, M.B. (1993). College persistence: Structural equation modeling test of an integrated model of student retention. *Journal of Higher Education, 64*(2), 123-137.

Cabrera, A.F., Nora, A., Castaneda, M.B., & Hengstler, D. (1992). The convergence between two theories of college persistence. *Journal of Higher Education, 63*(2), 143-164.

Cabrera, A.F., Stampen, J.O., & Hansen, W.L. (1990). Exploring the effects of ability to pay on persistence in college. *Review of Higher Education, 13*(3), 303-336.

Cabrera, A.F., & Nora, A. (1994). College students' perceptions of prejudice and discrimination and their feelings of alienation. *Review of Education, Pedagogy, and Cultural Studies, 16*, 387-409.

California Civil Rights Initiative (1996, November 5). Proposition 209. California Constitution, Article 1 Section 31.

Carter, D.J., & Wilson, R. (1997). *Minorities in higher education: Fifteenth annual status report*. Washington , DC: American Council on Education.

Caplan, L. (1996, December 23). The *Hopwood* effect kicks in on campus. *U.S. News and World Report, 121* (25), 26-28.

Chenoweth, K. (1996, July 11). Texas twister: Highly successful UT Austin graduate opportunity program imperiled. *Black Issues in Higher Education, 13*(10), 27.

The Chronicle of Higher Education Almanac. (1997, August 29). [Special Edition], Volume XLIV, Number 1.

Center for the Study of Community Colleges. (1995). [Transfer rates]. Unpublished data. Los Angeles, CA.

Cuadraz, G. (1993). *Meritocracy (un)challenged: The making of a Chicana/o professoriate and professional class*. Unpublished doctoral dissertation, University of California, Berkeley.

Cuadraz, G. (1996). Experiences of multiple marginality: A case study of Chicana scholarship women. In C. Turner, M. Garcia, A Nora, and L. Rendon (Eds.), *Racial/ethic diversity in higher education - ASHE reader* (pp. 210-222). Lexington: Ginn Press.

Cuadraz, G., & Pierce, J.L. (1994). From scholarship girls to scholarship women: Surviving the contradictions of race and class in academe. *Explorations in Ethnic Studies, 17*(1), 21-44.

Fernandez, D.D. & Menard, V. (1996, November). Unmasking *Hopwood. Hispanic, 9*(11), 57-62.

Fewer minorities going in medical schools. (1997, November). *Arizona Republic*, p. A.12.

Gandara, P. (1995). *Over the ivy walls*. New York: State University of New York Press.

Garcia, M. (1997). *Affirmative action's testament of hope. Strategies for a new era in higher education*. New York: State University of New York Press.

Geiser, S. (1996). California's changing demographics: Implications for UC. Outreach Forum Proceedings. University of California, Irvine: Center for Educational Partnerships.

Gilford, D., & Snyder, J. (1977). *Women and minority Ph.D.'s in the 1970's: A data book*. The National Research Council: Commission on Human Resources.

Goldberg, C. (1997, January 30). Hispanic households struggle as poorest of the poor in U.S. *New York Times*, pp. A1, D8.

Haworth, K. (1997, April 10). Number of minority students admitted to U. of Texas law school plummets. *The Chronicle of Higher Education*.

Hopwood and its effect on affirmative action (1997, March 20). *The Houston Chronicle*, p. A22.

Hopwood v. State of Texas. 78 F.3d 932 (5th Cir. 1996).

Hurtado, S., and Navia, C. (1997). Reconciling college access and the affirmative action debate. In M. Garcia (Ed.), *Affirmative action's testament of hope. Strategies for a new era in higher education*. New York: State University of New York Press.

Hodgkinson, H.L. (1996). *Arizona education -Birth through graduate school*. Report prepared for the Arizona Minority Education Policy Analysis Center, Arizona Commission for Postsecondary Education, Washington, DC: Center for Educational Policy.

Jalomo, R. (1995). *Latino students in transition*. Unpublished doctoral dissertation, Arizona State University, Tempe.

Ibarra, R.A. (1996). *Enhancing the minority presence in graduate education VII: Latino experiences in graduate education: Implications for change*. Washington, DC: Council of Graduate Schools.

Iverson, B.K., Pascarella, E.T., & Terenzini, P.T. (1984). Informal faculty-student contact and commuter college freshmen. *Research in Higher Education, 21*, 123-136.

Karabel, J. (1996, April 3). At a fork in the road of fairness. *Los Angeles Times*, Sec. B, p. 9, Col. 1.

Kaufman, A.H., & Gonzalez, R. (1997). The *Hopwood* case: What it says and what it doesn't. In M. Garcia (Ed.), *Affirmative Action's Testament or Hope. Strategies for a New Era in Higher Education*. New York: State University of New York Press.

Kozol, J. (1991). *Savage inequalities*. New York: Crown Publication, Inc.

Lum, L (1997, April 8). Applications by minorities down sharply. *Houston Chronicle*, p. 1.

Nettles, M. (1990). Success in doctoral programs: Experiences of minority and white students. *American Journal of Education, 98*(4), 494-522.

Nieto, S. (1996). Lessons from students on creating a chance to dream. *Harvard Educational Review, 66* (1), 77-113.

Nohoa-Rios, A. (1982). An analysis of Hispanic doctoral recipients from U.S. Universities, 1900-1973 with special emphasis on Puerto Rican doctorates. *Metas, 2*, 1-106.

Nora, A. (1993). Two-year colleges and minority students' aspirations: Help or hindrance? In J. Smart's (Ed.), *Higher Education: Handbook of Theory and Research*, IX, 212-247.

Nora, A. (1987). Determinants of retention among Chicano college students: A structural model. *Research in Higher Education, 36*, 31-59.

Nora, A., & Cabrera, A.F. (1993). The construct validity of institutional commitment: A confirmatory factor analysis. *Research in Higher Education, 34* (2), 243-262.

Nora, A., & Cabrera, A.F. (1996). The role of perceptions of prejudice and discrimination on the adjustment of minority students to college. *Journal of Higher Education, 67*(2), 119-148.

Nora, A., Cabrera, A.F., Hagedorn, L.S., & Pascarella, E.T. (1996). Differential impacts of academic and social experiences on college-related behavioral outcomes across different ethnic and gender groups at four-year institutions. *Research in Higher Education, 37*(4), 427-452.

Nora, A., Castaneda, M.B., & Cabrera, A.F. (1992). *Student persistence: The testing of a comprehensive structural model of retention*. Paper presented at the annual conference of the Association for the Study of Higher Education, Minneapolis, MN.

Nora, A., & Rendon, L.I. (1990). Determinants of predisposition to transfer among community college students: A structural model. *Research in Higher Education, 31*(3), 235-256.

Nora, A., Kraemer, B., & Itzen, R. (1997, November). *Factors affecting the persistence of Hispanic college students.* Paper presented at the annual meeting of the Association for the Study of Higher Education, Albuquerque, NM.

Nora, A., & Wedham, E. (1991, April). *Off-campus experiences: The pull factors affecting freshman-year attrition on a commuter campus.* Paper presented at the annual meeting of the American Educational Research Association, Chicago: IL.

Orfield, G., & Ashkinzaze, C. (1991). *The closing door: conservative policy and Black opportunity.* The University of Chicago Press: Chicago, IL.

Olivas, M.A. (1996, March 29). The decision is flatly, unequivocally wrong. *The Chronicle of Higher Education, 42*(29), B3(1).

Padilla, R.V., Trevino, J., Gonzalez, K., & Trevino, J. (1997). Developing local models of minority success in colleges. *Journal of College Student Development, 38*(2), 125-135.

Pascarella, E.T. (1985). Students' affective development within the college environment. *Journal of Higher Education, 56,* 640-663.

President's Advisory Commission on Educational Excellence for Hispanic Americans. (1996). *Our nation on the fault line: Hispanic American education.* Washington, DC: U.S. Government Printing Office.

Rendon, L.I. (1994). Validating culturally diverse students: Toward a new model of learning and student development. *Innovative Higher Education, 19*(1), 33-52.

Rendon, L.I. (1996). Life on the Border. *About Campus, 1* (5), 14-18.

Rendon, L.I. (1997, September). *Access in a democracy: Narrowing the opportunity gap.* Paper prepared for the Policy Panel on Access of the National Postsecondary Education Cooperative, Washington, DC.

Rendon, L.I., & Hope, R. (1996). *Educating a new majority.* San Francisco: Jossey-Bass.

Rendon, L.I., & Nora, A. (1997). *Student academic progress: Key data trends.* Report prepared for the National Center for Urban Partnerships, Ford Foundation, New York.

Scanlan, L.C. (1996). *Hopwood v. Texas*: A backward look at affirmative action in education. *New York University Law Review, 71*(6), 1580-1633.

Smart, J.C., & Pascarella, E.T. (1986). Socioeconomic achievement of former college students. *Journal of Higher Education, 57*, 529-549.

Solorzano, D. (1995). The baccalaureate origins of Chicana and Chicano doctorates in the social sciences. *Hispanic Journal of Behavioral Sciences, 17*(10), 3-32.

Stampen, J.O., & Cabrera, A.F. (1988). Is the student aid system achieving its objectives: Evidence on targeting and attrition. *Economics of Education Review, 7*, 29-46.

University of California Latino Eligibility Task Force. (1997). *Latino student eligibility and participation in the University of California, Ya basta!* (Rep. No. 5). Chicano/Latino Policy Project. Berkeley, CA: Institute for the Study of Social Change.

University of California Regents v. Bakke. 438 U.S. 265 (1978).

Wightman, L.F. (1997). The threat to diversity in legal education: An empirical analysis of the consequences of abandoning race as a factor in law school admission decisions. *New York University Law Review, 72*(1), 1-53.

CHAPTER 9

Examining the Recruitment and Enrollment of Eligible Hispanic and African American Students at Selective Public Texas Universities

Marco Portales

Introduction

In considering policy changes to address the paucity of Hispanic and African American students in selective colleges and universities in Texas and throughout the nation, we need to understand how higher education institutions are ranked, how different schools are perceived by the general public, and the function of the organizations that advise students. Examining college ratings, public perceptions, and the practices at high schools will help to clarify the seemingly mystical process that higher education admissions appear to undertake in selecting students. Admissions regulations and the policies that permit either changes or continuation of the status quo are receiving closer scrutiny by students, the public, the courts, legislatures, and college and university officials, especially in the wake of changing demographics and the 1996 *Hopwood* opinion.

Uses and Implications of the College Ranking System

According to the *1998 Higher Education Directory*, Texas has 39 public, state-supported universities, 29 private institutions, and 73 community colleges. Students are accepted, or not, depending on a variety of factors that usually include high school grades, the nature of the challenge of courses completed, Scholastic Aptitude Test (SAT) scores or American College Test (ACT) scores, promise and potential, and the degree to which applicants can demonstrate that they will be academically successful. The great majority of higher education institutions in the United States have open admissions or minimal entrance requirements, which means that most high school graduates will likely be admitted, if they apply. However, in 1999, about 400 American colleges and universities have selective admissions standards, meaning that entering freshmen must meet more demanding criteria in order to gain entry into these colleges than at the open admissions schools. In 1996, about 350 colleges and universities had selective admissions factors, which means that in the space of three years an additional 50 colleges have developed more selective criteria.

Colleges and universities are rated and ranked according to a variety of criteria. The highly popular *Barron's Profiles of American Colleges* (23th Edition, 1999), for instance, uses the following six categories to rank the overall academic quality of higher education institutions: most competitive, highly competitive, very competitive, competitive, less competitive, and non-competitive. How a college or university is rated on such a scale is based on the perceived academic rank, or the recognized value of the school's "stock," or the total quality of life at a higher education institution. Such ratings are based on the quality of the faculty, the academic preparation of the students attracted, the resources provided by the size of the school's endowment, the nature of the alumni and/or the legislative support, and other aspects dealing with the quality of life on colleges and universities.

By and large, colleges and universities are steady, reliable, and usually conservative organizations that change slowly, primarily because most schools take many years to arrive at how their campuses are perceived and rated by the general public. Since higher education institutions are in the business of admitting, retaining, and graduating students successfully, what schools look for in students, and in the quality of the faculty and staff hired to maintain and extend the reputation of a campus often influences patron support, which, in turn, substantially affects how higher education institutions are academically ranked. How all of these elements mesh and work together is for that reason very important, making institutional stock paramount.

The 1996 edition of *Barron's* listed 46 colleges and universities which were ranked in the first or the "most competitive" category. The 1999 edition of *Barron's*, however, lists 54 most competitive institutions of higher learning. This list of the academically most rigorous institutions in the United States include, among others, Amherst College, Cornell, Harvard, Princeton, Tufts, Notre Dame, Wellesley, Yale, and Rice Universities. In the second category of the "highly competitive" campuses, 88 colleges and universities throughout the United States appeared in the 1996 issue of *Barron's*; while the 1999 edition lists 92, or four more institutions. Both lists include Trinity University and Southwestern University, the only two Texas institutions. Besides requiring highly competitive academic standards from the nation's best high school students, almost all elite schools in the "most competitive" and "highly competitive" categories tend to be quite expensive; the private institutions requiring students to pay considerably more than the public ones. According to the May 30, 1997 issue of *The Chronicle of Higher Education*, yearly tuition and fees, without room and board, costs $22,007 at Amherst College, $21,675 at Oberlin $21,901 at Harvard and Radcliffe, and $20,974 at Cornell University.

In Texas, excluding the private and more expensive institutions like Rice, Trinity, and Southwestern University, which generally admit students from the top 2 percent of the high school graduating classes, Texas A&M University at College Station and The University of Texas at Austin are the next two top public state universities who also employ highly selective admissions criteria. These two well-known large public campuses, which usually enroll more than 43,000 students apiece, are ranked in the third or "very competitive" category by *Barron's*, along with 213 other nationally-known colleges and universities in 1996. The 1999 edition, though, lists 253 institutions, or 40 more than three years previously, who recruit their students nationally. Schools in this category include Southern Methodist University, the University of Texas at Dallas, and the University of Dallas in Texas. Other than Berkeley and UCLA, which rank in the previous "highly competitive" echelon, the other nine University of California campuses are also rated "very competitive," as are almost all of the State University of New York campuses, the University of Iowa at Tulsa and at Marquette, Miami University of Ohio and other institutions of this caliber. Historically, issues of *Barron's* tend to show that the general movement of institutions is to become increasingly selective, as year after year these schools remain academically among the most attractive institutions in the country, and, indeed, the world.

At around $8,000 per year for tuition, fees, room and board, Texas Agriculture and Mechanical University (Texas A & M) and The University of Texas at Austin (UT-Austin) are comparatively more affordable than private institutions in the "very competitive" category, making these two schools among the most desirable public universities in the state. Along with offering students what are widely regarded as high quality educations and the sports visibility that NCAA Division I athletics confers, Texas A & M University and UT- Austin yearly attract students almost entirely from the top 10 percent of the state's high school graduating classes. In the past, both universities have had criteria in place which have allowed them to accept students from the top 25% of the state's high school graduates, as based on leadership, student activities and other comparable factors.

Although not recognized in the research literature of higher education, university rankings are increasingly becoming the unaddressed engine which drives much of the reality which higher education faces today. The rankings and the ratings yearly conducted by *The U.S. News and World Report* and The National Research Council on Colleges and Universities are influential, not only in student recruitment but in university and college decision making as well. Indeed, the yearly evaluations of colleges and universities have become so powerful that many higher education decisions are being made by entertaining how various options will affect the academic quality of an institution, which in turn affect the rankings.

Overview of the *Hopwood* Case

Since the *Hopwood v. State of Texas* opinion, which on March 18, 1996 outlawed the consideration of race as a factor in college admissions in the states of Texas, Louisiana and Mississippi, administrators in all three states have been waiting to see what the full impact of this legal change will be. Hispanic and African Americans students, the two minority populations designated by the Texas legislature as under-represented in higher education, have since noticeably declined at the most competitive, the highly competitive, and the very competitive colleges and universities. Due to this loss of minority students, there is a sense among administrators that unless measures are directly taken to increase enrollment of Hispanic and African American students, these students will be increasingly rechanneled toward the next three levels, the competitive, less competitive and non-competitive campuses.

What is distressing is that some state education leaders do not see the redirection of minority students as a matter of concern. There seems to be a sense that this change is merely a natural consequence of *Hopwood*, a reality that time will somehow correct. Other state leaders, on the other hand, believe that the impact of *Hopwood* should be effectively countered, because demographic changes predict that minority populations, especially the Hispanic population, are expected to grow dramatically. For a law that is intended to be "color blind" and "race neutral," the *Hopwood* opinion has strangely kept race as a very operative and functional factor in the exact area that *Hopwood* is designed to downplay, college admissions. Indeed, college admissions policies have seldom, if ever, received more public attention and close scrutiny.

Pressured by mostly minority groups, including the Mexican American Legal Defense Fund (MALDEF), and the National Association for the Advancement of Colored People (NAACP), the 75th Texas State Legislature passed House Bill 588 in the spring of 1997. This law guaranteed admission to the top 10% of graduating seniors at all 1,044 high schools in Texas. The idea motivating this bill was to continue admitting Hispanic and African American students at least equal to the number of students who have previously been attending the more competitive universities before *Hopwood*.

How this law will work remains to be seen. Although the idea appears attractive, I am uncertain whether it will work because the 10% cut-off still produces an exclusive group. Given the growth of the minority population, we should be looking at increasing the proportion of minority students admitted to the selective institutions, not cutting back or merely maintaining the relatively small numbers of such students enrolled in the past. Whereas 10 percent of the graduating class of a largely minority population school might yield more minority eligible students than in the past, the chances that such students can be academically successful does not appear to be promising without additional K-12 academic support services. Indeed, the 76th Texas legislature, which begins meeting in January of 1999, will likely introduce other policy changes, including allowing higher institutions who are directly affected by *Hopwood* to perhaps make their own recruitment adjustments to attract more Hispanic and African American students.

Hopwood, as interpreted by the Attorney General in Texas, has also effectively made it considerably more difficult for minority students to compete successfully for grants and academic scholarships. In the past, scholarships targeted for high achieving minority students kept a good number of the state's top Hispanic and African American students from choosing to attend out-of-state institutions who offered attractive scholarships. A benefit of the *Hopwood* decision is that it has brought about a new awareness regarding the attributes of students who are admitted into each college and university. Before *Hopwood,* it was simply assumed that society was becoming more diversified without paying close attention to the number of applications received, the number of students accepted, and the students who actually had the resources to enroll. When previous freshmen classes were carefully scrutinized, however, admissions records show that most of the students admitted to Texas A & M University and UT-Austin during the last ten to fifteen years have tended to graduate in the top 6-7% of the state's high school classes, with occasional exceptions that admissions policies have allowed.

Demographic Makeup of the Texas High School Population

The 1995 Texas population consisted of 18,665,000 people, made up of 2,189,000 African Americans (11.2%), 412,000 Asian Americans (2.2%), 5,173,000 Hispanics (27.7%), and 10,891,000 Non-Hispanic Whites (58.3%) (Campbell, 1996). Texas graduates approximately 180,000 students per year from its 1,044 public and private high schools. These figures mean that the average high school graduation class in Texas has about 182 students, although some urban schools have more than 500 graduates and some rural schools have as few as 10 to 20. Out of these yearly group of students, 113,045 Texas graduates enrolled in college in 1996, and 112,272 registered in 1995, compared to a similar 112,586 students in 1994.

The 1996 high school graduation population of Texas consisted of: 12,878 African Americans, 29,899 Hispanics, 66,005 non-Hispanic whites, and 4,263 Asian Americans. The previous year, the state's colleges and universities enrolled 12,133 African Americans, 29,464 Hispanics, 66,519 non-Hispanic whites, and 4,166 Asian Americans. In 1994, the state of Texas enrolled 12,770 African American high school graduates, 30,005 Hispanic graduates, 65,650 non-Hispanic white graduates, and 4,113 Asian American graduates.

The majority of graduates who choose to attend college tend to enroll in open admissions colleges and universities, where a high school diploma generally meets entrance requirements. As students consider the admissions criteria of different universities, and look at the range of colleges from the non-competitive to the most competitive institutions, admissions criteria increasingly become more demanding and costs generally become more expensive (although not necessarily, as large public universities are cheaper in comparison to the private colleges). Nonetheless, paying for a year in college, even at a public university, takes considerable financial resources, currently more than $8,000 per year. For minority students and parents, who are generally less aware that certain colleges and universities have different admissions requirements, applying for college can become such a complicated process that many students opt for attending the nearest and cheapest campus. Securing a successful financial package for academically competitive students allows them to attend the more selective higher education institutions Because timing and knowledge are needed to achieve this difficult endeavor, such efforts often do not work out for minority students who usually learn too late about applying to the better schools.

To comprehend how the admissions offices go about the careful business of selecting students, confirming the generally-known college rankings, two facts need to be known. First, each public high school in Texas yearly tends to contribute only a small number of students who apply, are admitted, and actually enroll in the most competitive, the highly competitive, and in the very competitive institutions. Second, the rest or the great majority of the students, or about 90% of high school graduates, tend to apply and enroll in the other 668 competitive, 218 less competitive and in the 143 non-competitive campuses listed in *Barron's* 1996 edition. The 1999 issue lists 591 competitive, 294 less-competitive institutions, and 136 non-competitive colleges and universities. Numerous studies have shown that Hispanic and African American students tend to receive less-challenging K-12 educations for a variety of socioeconomic reasons (as Carrasquillo points out in Chapter 2 of this volume). Hence, only a very small number of minority students from each Texas high school actually qualify for admission to the nation's top institutions, the ones with the highest entrance requirements.

Texas A&M University at College Station and UT-Austin attract students not only from Texas but from the rest of the country and abroad, each campus enrolling entering classes of over 6,000 freshmen students per year. To assure class sizes of more than 6,000 freshmen at each of two of the largest universities in the United States, Texas A & M University and UT-Austin accept more than 10,000 students from the more than 16,000 yearly applicants, for which each university receives a $50 application fee. If the expense of applying, however, is too onerous, the fee can be waived, provided the student makes such a request. Every higher education institution in Texas, like other colleges and universities throughout the country, recruit the best students by successfully carving out a market niche of high schools which recruitment admissions officers then visit year after year.

Like clients who cater to certain businesses, some types of students traditionally tend to attend certain specific campuses, making change difficult, since perceptions in higher education are closely tied to the rankings or to the institutional stock that particular colleges and universities cherish. Based on the rankings of the colleges and the universities and the general perceptions of the citizenry, some higher education institutions are considered more desirable and thus more sought after than others.

Colleges and universities serve and educate the students traditionally recruited into their institutions, making changes in educational policy difficult and almost impossible, since most of the resources have been targeted and are committed to sustaining the practices that are in place. The crux of the problem is that while minority populations are increasing, the resources to prepare and to recruit them into the more selective higher education institutions are not growing proportionally.

While college educations are becoming academically more competitive and considerably more expensive, offering the better quality educations to minority students are becoming increasing harder. Although changes are clearly needed, resources for the changes that are required are currently not being committed, suggesting that legislatures will have to provide support, and/or inform higher education institutions that their resources will need to be reallocated or rechanneled to advance this goal.

Impact of the *Hopwood* Case

Until the 1964 Civil Rights Act passed during the Lyndon B. Johnson administration, American colleges and universities did not pay much attention to African American, Hispanic, and other minority students. Affirmative Action policies forced institutions of higher learning to re-evaluate their admissions policies concerning minority applicants. William Bowen and Derek Bok discuss this history in the first chapter of *The Shape of the River* (1998), a revealing longitudinal study that carefully examines the rich *College and Beyond* database kept by The Andrew W. Mellon Foundation of more than 80,000 undergraduate students from twenty-eight of the most competitive institutions in 1951, 1976, and 1989. Bowen and Bok concluded that Affirmative Action policies at these institutions not only made a difference in the lives of the African American students admitted to these previously almost totally all-white schools, but that such education has actually helped to shape the rising middle class of African Americans which is now becoming more visible.

Some African American communities have had their own public and private institutions, which are generally poorly funded. However; except for "Hispanic Serving Institutions" (HSIs) whose enrollments consist of at least one quarter Hispanic students, Hispanics in the United States have not controlled institutions of higher learning. Since Affirmative Action policies started in 1965, African American, Hispanics and other minority students began to make their way through higher education in increasing numbers, much as the G.I. Bill had opened academic doors to returning veterans following the end of World War II. Hispanics, however, have tended to advance toward higher education largely because of policy changes designed primarily to benefit African American students.

Between 1965 and 1996, considering an applicant's race was generally seen as a justified and reasonable way to encourage a person's further education as well as to compensate for past discriminatory policies and practices (Orfield, 1998). Considering an applicant's race was legally supported and articulated by the *Regents of the University of California v. Bakke* Supreme Court decision in 1978, which said that race could be taken into account as one of several other factors in college admissions decisions. In March of 1996 the Supreme Court decision on *Bakke* was called into question by *Hopwood*, an opinion written by two justices of the Fifth Circuit Court of Appeals in New Orleans.

History of the Hopwood Case
The 1996-1997 academic year was the first time that universities in Texas, Louisiana, and Mississippi were forced to adhere to the *Hopwood* ruling prohibiting the use of race in college admissions decisions. That year, out of Texas's 20,853 total number of African American graduates, 876 applied to Texas A&M, 528 were accepted, but only 230 students actually enrolled in late August. That same year, out of the state's total number of 50,099 Hispanic high school graduates, 2,038 applied, 1,432 were admitted, and 713 were enrolled on the official twelfth day of classes. Such were the total African American and Hispanic student yields in the last year when Texas A & M University was allowed to consider race as one of the school's seventeen admissions factors. At that point, nearly 80 percent of the minority students enrolled at the Texas A & M University campus were also being provided with scholarships or other financial aid, as was more than half of the total student body.

At UT-Austin the story was roughly the same. For the 1996-1997 academic year, 711 African Americans applied for admission, 369 were accepted, and 162 enrolled. Similarly, 2,373 Hispanic students applied, 1509 were admitted, and 792 enrolled. That same year, 2,301 Asian Americans applied, 1445 were accepted, and 815 enrolled. At UT, as at Texas A&M, the majority of applications are from the state's non-Hispanic white students.

At UT-Austin In 1996, 10,376 non-Hispanic white students applied, 6,396 were accepted, and 3,657 enrolled. That year, to compare, 11,499 non-Hispanic white students applied to Texas A&M, 8,279 were admitted, and 5,136 were counted as enrolled in classes on the twelfth day. Since most entering freshmen classes admit a little over 6,000 students per year, this means that about 1,000 students also admitted that year were African American, Hispanic, Asian Americans, and that less than one percent Native Americans were minority students on each campus.

Table 1. Texas College Enrollment by Ethnicity,1992-97.

Year/Group	Texas H.S. Grads.	Applicants	Accepted	Enrolled
1996 - 1997				
African Amer.	20,853	876	528	230
Asian Amer.	5,340	785	510	177
Hispanic	50,099	2,058	1,432	713
Non-Hisp White	95,283	11,499	8,279	5,136
1995 - 1996				
African Amer.	20,521	837	654	285
Asian Amer.	5,575	830	530	172
Hispanic	49,540	2,093	1,711	891
Non-Hisp. White	94,367	11,333	7,732	4,608
1994 - 1995				
African Amer.	19,241	710	561	290
Asian Amer	5,024	892	554	214
Hispanic	47,936	1,877	1,580	837
Non-Hisp. White	90,768	10,820	7,287	4,607
1993 - 1994				
African American	19,068	627	489	237
Asian Amer.	4,401	752	516	239
Hispanic	43,513	1,762	1,506	809
Non-Hisp. White	91,241	10,492	7,774	5,005
1992 - 1993				
African Amer.	20,486	666	470	251
Asian American	4,233	805	596	248
Hispanic	45,257	1,747	1,332	644
Non-Hisp. White	92,021	10,548	7,542	4,757

If we look at the statistics of each school, we will find that the student enrollment numbers for the six previous years are similar, providing the Texas A&M University community with an overall 1996 minority student population of 9.6% Hispanics and 3.7% African American group, whereas UT has generally had a 12.9%

Hispanic enrollment and a 4% African American enrollment. These were the enrollments before *Hopwood*, and, to understand the significance of these numbers, we need to compare them to the enrollment records that Texas A&M, for instance, experienced between 1992 and 1996.

Post-*Hopwood* Effects in Texas

In June, 1996, three months after the *Hopwood* opinion was delivered, applications and acceptances were down for minority students at both Texas A & M University and UT-Austin. Over the last two years both schools had been studying the situation and making policy changes to incorporate the new *Hopwood* reality, while others anxiously awaited the actual new student enrollments for the fall. In July of 1997, Texas A & M University counted 155 African Americans committed to enroll, while the previous year the campus enrolled 285. At this same juncture, 618 Hispanics committed to enroll, as opposed to 891 in 1995. That same July, 4,979 non-Hispanic white students committed to Texas A&M, as opposed to 4,608 in 1995; 235 Asian Americans committed to enroll, as opposed to 172 in 1995; and 27 Native Americans committed to enroll, as opposed to 25 in 1995.

The 1997 and 1998 minority student applications and enrollments show that the widely-predicted negative impact of the *Hopwood* opinion has materialized. Such losses demonstrate that a smaller number of African American and Hispanic students applied, less were accepted, and even fewer enrolled. Less minority students have been attracted to Texas A & M University and UT-Austin because *Hopwood* also reduced funds to many minority students whose admission to these schools depended on receiving scholarships and grants. Since most minority students do not score high enough in their SATs to receive scholarships and grants, both UT-Austin and Texas A & M University are currently studying the situation further to see what other steps are necessary to better serve the population of Texas, as their mission statements decree.

Unable to provide scholarships and grants to most of the minority students accepted after *Hopwood*, the two "very competitive" institutions of Texas A & M University and UT-Austin have been clearly disadvantaged in the state and national competition for the best minority students by the court's opinion and the

Attorney General's interpretation of that opinion. Since out-of-state institutions are still able to offer attractive scholarships that are not prohibited from taking race into account, colleges and universities from the 45 states following the 1978 *Bakke* decision, excluding California and Washington which have rescinded Affirmative Action by voter elections, enjoy an advantage in recruiting minority students.

As this essay goes to press, Texas A & M University has released its Fall 1998 enrollment numbers, and, together with the 1997 statistics, there are less applications and slight gains in enrollments when compared to the number of minority students enrolled before the 1996 *Hopwood* opinion. The applications, acceptances and enrollments are the official 12th day statistics reported by Texas A & M University for the fall of 1997 and 1998:

Table 2. Projected College Enrollment by Ethnic Group[a]

Year/Group	Texas Grads	Applicants	Accept	Enroll
1998 - 1999				
African Amer.	23,689	581	395	198
Asian Amer.	6,203	734	611	259
Hispanic	59,614	1,571	1,224	684
Non-Hisp.White	104,568	10,007	8,875	6,033
1997 - 1998				
African Amer.	22,997	653	420	178
Asian Amer.	6,977	952	691	224
Hispanic	54,641	1,704	1,298	607
Non-Hisp. White	101,319	10,850	8,658	5,015

a - Although I have not been able to secure the total number of high school graduates produced by the state of Texas for 1997 and 1998, the Western Interstate Commission for Higher Education in a report entitled *Knocking at the College Door* (1998) projects these graduation rates for Texas.

Post-Hopwood Prospects

Statistics from the Texas A&M University Admissions Office and the Freshman Admissions Center at UT-Austin, reveal that the educational pipeline which ought to produce more African American and Hispanic students for the selective universities in Texas is in need of repair. Detecting and repairing the actual junctures where minority students tend to become uncompetitive, some dropping out of school, is part of the challenge. The rest of the challenge is to refurbish the entire K-12 pipeline, if the state's two top public universities are to remain in the business of properly sharing their considerable resources with the state's citizenry. Since both schools receive from a quarter to one third of their funding from tax-money allocated by the Texas Legislature, the missions of both institutions require Texas A & M University and UT-Austin to improve their efforts considerably to enroll students from all geographic and socioeconomic sectors of the state's 254 counties.

Aside from 57 high schools in Texas that enrolled more than 20 students apiece at Texas A & M University in September 1997, there were 97 other public and private Texas high schools that did not enroll a single student at that university. With the 1997 law which mandates that the top 10% of all graduating seniors from every Texas high school be guaranteed admission into the state's public universities, even the most experienced educators are uncertain as to how such a law will redistribute students to the universities over the next few years. Although Hispanics and African Americans continue to decline at the states selective universities, the minority population continues to grow, and K-12 educators are not noticeably improving educational outcomes, producing more poorly achieving minority students than in the past.

In 1996, Texas high schools graduated a combined number of 42,777 African American and Hispanic students who entered college, compared to 66,005 non-Hispanic white college bound graduates. The number of minority students who actually apply, are accepted, and enroll at either Texas A & M University or UT-Austin has remained small. At 1.1% of the total African American high school graduates and 1.4% of all the Hispanic Texas graduates at each university, this number has traditionally been minuscule, especially when we compare this percentage to the more than 40% minority population of Texas. Unless more successful proactive measures are instituted, post-*Hopwood* minority student presence at more selective public state universities is likely to stay at the low 1997 and 1998 levels.

Demographic projections indicate that by the year 2008, the majority of the Texas population will consist of minority groups. This increase will be propelled mainly by the growing birth rate of Texans bearing Hispanic surnames (Murdock, 1997). Demographic forecasts like Murdock's have ironically tended to create a kind of racial gridlock, separating Texans into non-Hispanic whites, African Americans, Hispanics and Asian American, thus stopping and reversing the slow progress that was being made before *Hopwood.* For this reason, addressing the educational problems that Texans as well as Californians currently face will require recognition of this situation and a widespread, enlightened desire to do what is necessary to make the educational resources of the state available to a minority population that historically has been not been sufficiently served by the state.

When considering how a K-college system might work, we can either (1) shape and create the future, given where the State of Texas knows we are headed; (2) we can ignore the needs that the future will certainly bring; or, (3) we can decide to fight the trends, the needs and the projections. Demographic realities can be stalled or delayed, but delaying such forces will only exacerbate and create larger, more complex problems in the future. Demographic projections will impact all Americans, whether we choose to prepare ourselves for a future with a larger minority population, or whether we decide to concern ourselves with only current issues and practices.

Hopwood Implications for the K-12 Educational System

Since universities and colleges are not likely to change admissions criteria drastically as such policies have been developed over generations of educators, most of the needed changes will likely take place in the K-12 sector. A May 29, 1997 *Houston Chronicle* editorial defended the universities, claiming that after *Hopwood* "the problem does not lie with Texas' top universities." The scarcity of minority students in the state's best-ranked college and universities, the editorial claimed, "has little to do with Texas universities. It has everything to do with what takes place in the lives of minority students before they reach college age." Since the results of K-12 educations are varied, a great deal depends on a child's parents, as well as the resources, location, and quality of the instruction delivered. Upgrading the quality of all K-12 schools thus appears to be the best way to counter the uneven education that students in different schools, and sometimes even in the same schools, tend to receive. Recognizing where education seems to be going, a June 1997 *The New York Times* editorial, opined that:

> college enrollment figures show there is no such thing as a "race neutral" admissions policy. If universities do not take disadvantage into account, many minority students will face the prospect of resegregation in higher education.

University administrators may interpret these two editorials as saying that since the problem lies in the educational pipeline leading to higher education, then *Hopwood* requires K-12 educators to address the matter. The burden of responsibility for improving the schools would then fall more squarely on the school districts and on the colleges of education. But school districts and colleges of education have been working on improving the quality of education for minority students for over thirty years, and the reality is that we are still looking for an educational system that delivers more and better prepared African American and Hispanic students. Repairing our educational systems and refurbishing the K-12 curricula is an important component of the agenda that I believe will have to be adopted and on which all K-college educators will need to work.

How can the universities complement the colleges of education who prepare teachers, who, in turn, can increase the number of eligible minority students for the more competitive institutions? That, indeed, is the issue, because *Hopwood*, in effect, redistributes minority students away from the top universities, relegating such students to less competitive higher education institutions. Since the scholarships that used to attract minority students to the more competitive campuses in Texas, Louisiana and Mississippi have also been legally eliminated or substantially reduced, there is a question as to which campuses the best minority students will choose. What we are seeing is that some minority students continue to receive scholarships to the more selective colleges and universities, but roughly half to a third of the types of successful students who used to enroll at these campuses will likely enroll in the less competitive campuses for financial reasons.

On February 6, 1998, Texas Higher Education Commissioner Don Brown testified before the Texas Legislature's Higher Education Committee that "overall, enrollment continued in the same direction as it had for the last five or more years in that the percent of Hispanics and African American students had grown, while the percent of Anglo students had declined." Brown added "that while minorities were becoming more and more represented in higher education as a whole, they were less represented in the student bodies at the more selective institutions. He said he felt those schools," mainly Texas A & M University and UT-Austin, nevertheless "were working to correct the situation in a race neutral way, adding that the state goal should not be to negate *Hopwood*, but to reach the point where enrollment was fully representative of the state's population." The problem with this perspective is that if public colleges, universities, and legislators allow minority students to be routed mainly to the less competitive institutions, the more competitive institutions will once again become the provinces of non-Hispanic white students who have historically received better educations.

In the September, 1998 "The State of the System," Texas A & M University Chancellor Barry B. Thompson succinctly characterized the problem that most state leaders apparently have not yet broached:

> The state of the A&M System is that we have people in the right places to provide leadership for the 21st Century. But a battle is going on right now for the very soul of the A&M System. The battle has to do with whether we continue to be true to our land-grant mission we have pursued since 1876, or whether we become totally elitist. My own best judgment and the judgment of thousands of Texans say we should continue as the land-grant system that provides service, research, technology transfer and responses to people's everyday needs.

In California, the two University of California flagship campuses (UC-Berkeley and UC-LA) will now admit only the top 4% of high school students, leaving the other 96% of students to attend the state's other universities. We should hope that both Texas A&M University and UT-Austin will not become so exclusively dedicated to academic excellence that, despite the 10% law, they too will serve only the top 4-5 % of the state's students.

Recommendations

There are a number of steps that institutions of higher learning across the country, especially campuses like Texas A & M University and UT-Austin, could take to increase the number of minority students on their campuses. Since eliminating race as part of the admissions criteria in Texas appears to be a decision that has been supported and endorsed by the courts, the focus of attention now shifts to what the selective colleges and universities will actually do. As previously said, the K-12 educational system is not properly preparing enough minority students so that such students can successfully compete for admission into the better colleges and universities. Instead of widely saying that *Hopwood* has made it very difficult to recruit minorities, the faculties and the administrations of the more selective universities have to take pro-active steps to better educate students for their campuses.

The main solution in the wake of *Hopwood* is to engage the help of colleges and universities to repair the K-12. educational pipeline, creating more minority students with higher quality educations so that they can compete successfully for scholarships and grants to the more competitive colleges and universities. But articulating this goal, and connecting the existing higher education systems with secondary schools to provide resources to improve educational outcomes are two very different tasks. Despite initial efforts in this direction, K-12 schools in the United States have not yet focused their attention on this desired and much needed goal.

On May 16, 1997, the University of California's Outreach Task Force proposed a plan which revolved around the following three-point strategy:

1. *School-Centered Partnerships:* Establish regional partnerships including a limited number of school systems and local colleges and universities (especially community college and California State University campuses) in regions served by UC campuses, to address the full range of culture and practice in a limited number of partner schools to achieve major improvements in student learning. Through this regional partnership concept, educational institutions will align goals and priorities, region by region, and devote resources for maximum results.

2. *Academic Development*: Expand successful current academic development programs to increase the number of disadvantaged students who are eligible and competitively eligible to attend the University.

3. *Informational Outreach*: Aggressively identify and educate families, early and throughout the academic process, to involve them more deeply in their children's planning and preparation for college and to encourage family support for school improvement. This process will be linked with intensive recruitment of disadvantaged students for enrollment at the University of California, keeping in mind the role of parents as key decision makers in the education process.

The attractiveness of this California proposal is that the focus is "grounded at all of the University's campuses and encompassing all regions of the state, and it will build upon already proven efforts" (University of California Task Force, 1997).

The Texas A&M University System and The University of Texas System could undertake a similar program, especially since the 1997 Texas 75th Legislature provided more than $500 million for a "Back to Basics" initiative organized by the state's Higher Education Coalition of colleges and universities. Both of these two large Texas educational systems, in addition to the University of Houston System, the Texas State University System and the Texas Tech System, have campuses throughout major urban and rural parts of the state. Given these strategically located satellite campuses, all five public higher education systems could be engaged to work with school districts in their immediate regions to implement programs designed to equalize and upgrade the quality of the K-12 educational experience for all students.

The focus would be to establish partnerships or mentorship links between the faculties of the higher education campuses and the individual, surrounding schools. In such a plan, professors who teach Biology, Math, or English in the area universities, and the teachers at the local schools, could work together to fashion more challenging curricula for the students. The faculty members and the teachers would need to be institutionally rewarded and encouraged to design and to create programs that would work alongside those of the regular teachers to improve the quality of the educational experience for K-12 students.

Although California has drafted such a plan, their state legislature has not yet allotted funds for such an effort. The vision, the language, and the idea, nonetheless, have been articulated Texas, on the other hand, has already allotted funding for a "Back to Basics" program that could be fleshed out along the lines of the California plan. In addition, the recent $15.4 billion Texas settlement with the tobacco companies affords the 76th Legislature in 1999, the possibility of earmarking funds for the improved education of Texas's growing population. By investing in the necessary education of its people, Texas, California and other states would responsibly meet the needs of the global economy that otherwise will continue to exclude citizens who have not been educated to take care of themselves and their families in the next century.

At UT-Austin, the Ex-Students Association, the school's private, non-profit, official, alumni group, has reportedly set aside $5 million dollars to legally provide scholarships for eligible, needy, capable, students who have struggled against adversity in their educational journeys. Newly-designed Presidential Achievement Scholarships, awarded to educationally and economically disadvantaged students, based on an adversity index or quotient, are now being provided to high merit, highly needy students of all races. *Hopwood*, which legally allows and encourages college recruiters to target different geographic areas of the states, has prompted the use of more innovative approaches. Using the Texas Education Agency's available manner of dividing the State of Texas in different regions, University of Texas admissions officials are now monitoring the almost year-long application process, making necessary adjustments, and meeting the population diversity needs of the state, as their missions require, in considering incoming aspiring candidates.

Since *Hopwood*, policy and legal issues are being examined in light of the growing Hispanic and African American populations which already dominate K-12 education in Texas, and more populous western states such as California and Arizona. Institutional realities tell us that current practices must be improved to better serve the needs of our future citizens. Maintaining academically attractive institutions while simultaneously providing competitive educations for populations that have not been prepared for higher education is a considerable new challenge. However, with careful higher education system planning, states should be able to muster the necessary resources to meet the educational needs of a new citizenry. Only by better educating all students from kindergarten to high school will the number and the eligibility of minority students be increased so they can more successfully compete for admission into the better colleges and universities, offering them more advantageous futures.

References

After Hopwood: the problem does not lie with Texas's top universities. (1997, May 29). *The Houston chronicle*. Editorial. pp. 30.

Anxiety over tuition: a controversy in context. (1997, May 30). *The chronicle of higher education.* pp. A11, A12, A15, A17, A18.

Barron's Educational Series, Inc. (1996). Twentieth Edition. *Barron's profiles of American colleges.* Woodbury, New York.
Barron's Educational Series, Inc. (1999). Twenty-Third Edition. *Barron's profiles of American colleges.* Woodbury, New York.

Bowen, William G. and Derek Bok. *The shape of the river: Long-term consequences of considering race in college and university admissions.* Princeton University Press, 1998.

Brown, Don, Texas Commissioner of Higher Education. (1998, February 6) Testimony before the Texas Legislature's Committee on Higher Education.

Campbell, Paul R. (1996). *Population projections for states by age, sex, race and hispanic origin: 1995 - 2025.* U.S. Bureau of the Census, Population Division, PPL-47. p. 19.

Higher Education Publications, Inc. (1998). *1998 higher education directory.* Falls Church, Virginia: Higher Education Publications.

Hopwood v. State of Texas, 861 F. Supp. 551 (W.D. Tex. 1994), 78 F.3d 932 (5th Cir. 1995), *cert denied*, 116 S. Ct. 2581 (1996).

House Bill 588, Texas House of Representative, 75th Legislative Session, Spring 1997.

Murdock, S.H., Nazrul, H., Michael, M. White, S. & Pecotte, B. (1997). *The Texas challenge: Population change and the future of Texas.* College Station: Texas A&M University Press.

Orfield, Gary. (1998, January 4). Risky times for latinos. *The Houston Chronicle.* p. 1.

222

Regents of the University of California v. Bakke, 438 U.S. 265 (1978).

Segregation anew. (1997, June 1). *The New York Times*. Editorial. p. 16.

Thompson, Barry B. (1998, September). The state of the system. *Texas A&M system newsletter*. p. 4.

University of California Outreach Task Force. (1997, May 16). Draft Report. *Internet*

Western Interstate Commission for Higher Education. (1998). *Knocking at the college door: Projections of high school graduates by state and race/ethnicity, 1996 - 2012*. p. 121.

CHAPTER 10

Hispanics as Academics:
The Difficult Road to Equity

Mildred García & Carolyn J. Thompson

Introduction

One decade ago Reyes and Halcon (1988) authored a groundbreaking article, *Racism in Academia: The Old Wolf Revisited,* which poignantly illustrates the negative stereotypes and obstacles Chicano faculty face. Today little has changed for Hispanic faculty, or other minority faculty in general. Negative stereotypes persist and minority faculty are marginalized in multiple ways (Thompson and Dey, 1998) creating qualitatively different experiences and placing obstacles in the tenure process. Hispanics along with African American, Asian American, and Native Americans remain underrepresented among college and university faculty. In addition, the desirability of these positions is questioned by those whose advanced degrees can provide them access to other, more lucrative, professional careers. Fewer than 10% of academic positions in higher education are held by members of these minority groups, even though they represent roughly 20-25% of the United States population. (Astin, Korn, and Dey, 1991). Moreover, data suggest a decline in their representation among faculty since the 1980s (Bowen and Schuster, 1986). Hence, it seems that recruitment and retention efforts have not been successful in reducing the underrepresentation of minorities in higher education faculty positions.

This chapter continues the discussion Reyes and Halcon began a decade ago on Chicano faculty and expands it to include other Hispanics in professorial ranks. In order to understand the experiences of Hispanic faculty in higher education institutions dominated by the United States majority culture (Harvey, 1996) and the resulting Hispanic marginality, there is a need to focus on Hispanic populations so as to understand the relationship between Hispanic faculty's work condition to their marginality (Thompson and Dey, 1997). This paper does not seek to compare Hispanics to other minority groups, since presenting such similarities will not heighten our understanding of the Hispanic faculty experience as it relates to their marginality. Rather, it presents information regarding Hispanic college access and degree attainment, then addresses the status of Hispanic faculty in United States higher education. We begin with a demographics review of Hispanic educational attainment, and then explore hiring and tenure procedures. We conclude with recommendations to faculty and administrators for recruiting, hiring, and retaining Hispanic faculty.

Hispanic Educational Attainment

By the year 2020, the Hispanic population will be the largest ethnic group in the United States. The 1990 census figures indicate that the Hispanic population is growing five times faster than the total United States population, and that the Hispanic population is generally younger than the majority population (U.S. Bureau of the Census, 1992). These figures represent a conservative estimate since census data do not capture Hispanics in this country without proper documentation. Regardless of the accuracy of the estimates, Hispanics are entering all levels of education in record numbers. With Hispanics being younger than the majority non-Hispanic white population, the potential is greater than ever for educational systems to produce a highly educated Hispanic citizenry to meet rising technological needs of the United States economy. In addition, this same population is the potential source of Hispanics who hold doctoral degrees, and in turn, the future source of tenure-track faculty for four-year colleges and universities.

Educational Progression From High School

Examining the educational progression rates of Hispanics from high school through college gives an indication of how well United States education is producing an educated Hispanic citizenry. They also give an indication of the size of the potential pool of Hispanic applicants for advanced degree attainment necessary for faculty careers and other professions. Table 1 presents the levels of educational attainment for students six years after their senior year of high school as reported by the National Center for Education Statistics (1993). The data reveal that Hispanics, like other under-represented groups, are more likely to have attained only a high school diploma (70%) or completed a two-year license or degree (21%). Hispanics have the highest percentage of individuals who do not attempt an educational degree beyond a high school diploma six years after graduation.[1] Hispanics are only one-third as likely as non-Hispanic whites, and one-quarter as likely as Asian Americans to have acquired a four-year or graduate degree (6.9%, 21.2%, and 29%, respectively). Thus, within six years of high school more than four of every five Hispanics have not earned college degrees.

Table 1. Level of Education Attained by 1986 of 1980 High School Seniors

Race	Diploma		Degree			
	No HS[a]	HS	Licence	Assoc.	B.S/B.A	Grad
Hispanic	1.7	70.2	13.8	7.3	6.8	0.1
African American	1.2	69.4	13.9	5.3	9.9	0.2
Native Amer, Eskimo	<0.05	61.3	18.6	9.3	10.8	<0.05
Asian/Pacific Islander	<0.05	49.6	12.6	8.7	27.3	1.7
White	0.8	60.0	11.5	6.6	20.2	0.9

Source: U.S. Department of Education, NCES (1993).
a- Seniors who had dropped out of high school after the spring 1980 and had not completed high school by 1986.

Examination of levels of educational attainment by socioeconomic status (SES, a NCES composite measure of parental education, family income, father's occupation, and household characteristics) reveal that Hispanics in the upper SES level lag 20% behind their non-Hispanic white counterparts in the attainment of baccalaureate degrees (Table 2). For those in the middle income levels, comparable attainment at the baccalaureate level trails nearly 6% behind non-Hispanic white students and 16% behind Asian Americans.

Table 2. Level of Education Attained by Spring 1986 of 1980 High School Seniors, by SES and Race.

Race & SES[a]	Diploma		Degree			
	No HS[b]	HS	Licence	Assoc	B.S/B.A	Grad
Hispanic						
Lower 25 percent	1.6	73.9	11.8	7.8	4.9	<0.05
Middle 50 percent	1.0	67.0	14.7	6.5	10.7	0.2
Upper 25 percent	0.3	60.0	11.4	9.6	18.0	0.07
African-American						
Lower 25 percent	1.4	73.0	12.7	5.1	7.7	0.1
Middle 50 percent	0.3	67.5	14.7	6.5	10.7	0.3
Upper 25 percent	<0.05	56.3	12.4	5.4	25.5	0.4
Asian/Pacific Islander						
Lower 25 percent	<0.05	53.4	17.3	15.7	12.0	1.6
Middle 50 percent	<0.05	51.1	11.7	11.1	26.1	<0.05
Upper 25 percent	<0.05	42.9	6.5	4.8	40.0	5.9
White						
Lower 25 percent	0.9	75.1	12.2	5.0	6.6	0.3
Middle 50 percent	0.3	62.0	13.0	8.0	16.3	0.4
Upper 25 percent	<0.05	44.9	8.6	6.2	38.2	2.2

Source: U.S. Department of Education, NCES (1993).

a- SES is a composite score measure of parental education, family income, father's occupation, and household characteristics in 1980.

b- Seniors who had dropped out of high school after the spring 1980 and had not completed high school by 1986.

Thus, even when considering the level of higher degree attainment for more affluent Hispanics, greater attention needs to be given to increasing the levels of degree attainment among Hispanics in all SES groups. Moreover, the aggregation of data on Hispanics provide a distorted picture of the true attainment of various ethnic sub-populations since Cubans are more likely to be at the higher SES levels and have higher attainment, while Puerto Ricans and Chicanos tend to be in the lower SES levels and have lower levels of attainment (Goldberg, 1997). These disturbing findings about

Hispanic educational attainment broken down by SES as compared to other groups is an indication of how the United States educational system is failing its Hispanic citizens.

College enrollment. College enrollment over the fifteen year period from 1976-1991 (see Table 3) indicate that growth in Hispanic college enrollment is not keeping pace with their respective growth in the overall United States population. Undergraduate enrollment increased by less than one percent among Hispanic males, and less than two percent for females. At the graduate level, the gains are only 0.3% for males and roughly one percent for females. These enrollment figures are distressing when considering the slower progression and lower retention rates of Hispanics. In order to have a sizable pool of applicants for graduate study from which to mentor Hispanics into faculty roles, college enrollments among Hispanics must see improvements.

Table 3. 1991 Enrollment in Higher Education by Level, Race and Gender

Undergraduate	1976		1986		1991	
Enrollment	Male	Female	Male	Female	Male	Female
Hispanic	2.1	1.7	2.5	2.8	3.0	3.6
African-American	4.6	5.5	3.8	5.6	3.9	6.2
Native American, Eskimo, Aleut	0.4	0.4	0.3	0.4	0.4	0.5
Asian/Pacific Isl.	1.0	0.8	2.0	1.8	2.3	2.3
White	43.7	39.8	37.5	43.2	35.0	42.9
Graduate	1976		1986		1991	
Enrollment	Male	Female	Male	Female	Male	Female
Hispanic	1.2	0.9	1.6	1.9	1.5	2.0
African-American	2.6	3.7	2.0	3.5	2.1	4
Native American, Eskimo, Aleut	0.2	0.2	0.2	0.2	0.2	0.3
Asian/Pacific Isl.	1.2	0.8	2.0	1.4	2.2	1.8
White	47.1	42.1	40.0	47.2	37.7	48.4

Source: U.S. Department of Education, NCES (1993).
a- Includes master's degree enrollment, and does not include first professional degree enrollment.

Doctoral attainment. In 1995, 27,603 doctorates were awarded to United States citizens, and this number has remained relatively unchanged since 1994 (Hendersen, Clark, & Reynolds, 1996). Hispanic who are United States citizens received 916 doctorates, or 3.3% of the total. Of this total number, women represented nearly half of the recipients, indicating substantial gains in the female attainment of doctoral degrees (see Table 4). Between 1976 and 1995, Hispanic women made inroads in the number of PhDs earned annually (96 to 456, respectively), and now represent nearly half of all United States citizen Hispanic doctoral recipients (49.8%, up from 27% in 1976). Although the number of doctorates granted to Hispanics who are United States citizens has increased since 1976, fewer than two percent of the Hispanic population are even enrolled in graduate education.

Table 4. Growth of U.S. Hispanic Doctoral Attainment

	1976	1980	1985	1990	1995	Change: 1976-95
Men	255	261	300	380	460	+205
Women	96	156	261	341	456	+360
Total	351	417	561	721	916	+565

Source: U.S. Department of Education, NCES (1993).

A review of Table 5 indicates that the number of Hispanics receiving doctorates in the sciences is increasing. While the largest numerical increase in doctorate attainment among Hispanics in the past decade have been in social science, education, and life sciences, the largest percentage increases have been in engineering and physical sciences (Henderson, et al., 1996). Although Hispanic representation in these areas remains small, attainment in the physical sciences more than doubled, and almost tripled in engineering.

One indication of how the United States educational system fails Hispanics is the continued focus of higher education on the Eurocentric value of individual attainment, versus the altruistic Hispanic value to improve social conditions in society at large. Not surprisingly, a recent study conducted by the Higher Education Research Institute at UCLA (Astin, Antonio, Cress, & Astin, 1997) reveals that Hispanics, along with African Americans, are more likely than other underrepresented ethnic groups to say that they chose an academic career because it afforded them an opportunity to effect social change. As a result, Hispanic faculty are concentrated in humanities and social science departments where they can focus their teaching and research on issues of social justice and change (The Almanac of Higher Education, 1995). Such degrees offers the opportunities to enter professions that allow them to work as change-agents within Hispanic communities as teachers, psychologists, sociologists and counselors.

Table 5. Areas of U.S. Hispanic Doctoral Attainment Rank, Ordered by Gains.

Degree Area	1975	1980	1985	1990	1995	Change: 1975-95
Social Sciences	59	95	121	171	214	+154
Education	95	145	181	179	232	+137
Life Sciences	40	36	75	104	145	+105
Humanities	65	80	97	112	130	+65
Physical Sci.[a]	28	27	42	85	86	+58
Engineering	16	18	16	39	61	+45
Prof/Other	10	16	29	31	48	+38
Total	602	313	417	561	721	916

a- Includes math & computer sciences
Source: U.S. Department of Education. NCES (1993).

Hispanic Faculty Representation in Higher Education

In 1993 there were 12,076 full-time Hispanic faculty members in higher education (Carter and Wilson, 1997), representing 2.3% of the entire higher education faculty population. As would be expected given their underrepresentation among college undergraduate and graduate participation, the growth pattern for Hispanics in faculty ranks has increased quite slowly over the last two decades (see Table 6). A large percentage of Hispanic faculty are concentrated in public two-year institutions, since many community colleges do not require a doctoral degree for tenure-track faculty positions. As a result, there is a high percentage of Hispanics teaching at community colleges without doctoral degrees (O'Brien, 1993). However, as already illustrated in Table 3, Hispanic enrollment in graduate education is still low, so the availability of Hispanics with masters degrees to teach at community colleges is also low.

Table 6. U.S. Hispanic Full-Time Faculty in Higher Education, by Gender.

Gender	1979	1985	1989	1991	1993	Change 1979-1993
Males	4,871	5,458	6,757	7,347	12,076	+ 7,205
% total pop	(1.1)	(1.2)	(1.3)	(1.4)	(1.3)	
Females	1,908	2,330	3,330	4,077	7,459	+ 5,551
% total pop	(0.4)	(0.05)	(0.06)	(0.08)	(0.09)	
Total Hisp.	6,779	7,788	10,087	11,424	19,535	+12,756

Source: U.S. Department of Education. NCES (1993).

Table 7 offers several interesting observations regarding Hispanic faculty and their representation by academic rank for academic year 1995-96 (Carter and Wilson, 1997). Within the 1995-96 year, the majority of Hispanic faculty (greater than 60%) worked as assistant professors. Chicano and Puerto Rican faculty are much less likely than other Hispanics to hold full professor status. Hispanics who are not Chicano or Puerto Rican have a greater representation at the associate rank. Meanwhile, Puerto Rican faculty have the highest concentration of individuals at the assistant professor level (41.3% and 44.1% for men and women, respectively), which represents the highest concentration at the lowest rank among all other underrepresented ethnic groups.

Moreover, the disparity in faculty promotions is evident with gender and ethnic differences among the Hispanic faculty population. Hispanic men are more likely than women to achieve full professor status (23.7% and 8.5%, respectively), or associate professor status (20.3 and 15.8%, respectively). Chicano men are three times more likely than Chicanas to achieve full professor status (20.4% and 6.7%, respectively), while Puerto Rican men double the percentage of full professor status (14.7%), when compared to Puerto Rican women (7.2%). While Hispanic women have made inroads in their attainment of doctoral degrees and represent nearly half of the recipients from 1985 to 1995 (see Table 4), their promotion among faculty ranks still lags behind that of Hispanic men. Regardless of the disparity by gender and ethnicity, the fact remains that Hispanic faculty represent only a small percentage of United States higher education faculty in general, challenging their experiences to be somewhat disconnected and marginal from those of the dominant culture (Harvey, 1996).

Table 7. Full-Time Undergraduate Hispanic Faculty, by Academic Rank, 1995-96

Ethnic Origin	Full	Assoc.	Assist.	Lecturer	Instructor	Other
Men						
All Hispanics	23.7	20.3	27.5	1.8	25.5	1.2
Chicano	20.4	15.9	22.5	1.1	39.0	1.1
Puerto Rican	14.7	18.3	41.3	6.5	19.2	0.0
Other Hispanics	30.5	26.5	30.3	1.5	9.7	1.6
Women						
All Hispanics	8.5	15.8	38.4	4.4	30.0	2.9
Chicana	6.7	10.5	34.4	3.1	42.8	2.5
Puerto Rican	7.2	19.9	44.1	3.0	24.3	1.5
Other Hispanics	11.3	20.8	41.4	6.6	16.0	3.9

Source: Carter and Wilson, 1997.

Marginality is experienced in several ways by minority faculty, and is often neither observable nor acknowledged by others in the academy. Thompson and Dey (1997) identify four ways that minority faculty are marginalized. First, focusing one's scholarly agenda on challenging social issues, particularly those that are race-related, often results in marginalization within one's discipline. Second, a teaching agenda that also focuses on race-related social issues can result in marginalization within one's department because these issues are not seen as important or embraced by department members. Often it is others' discomfort with social issues that results in distancing themselves from mentoring minority faculty who choose this scholarly focus, or from discussions related to advancing the scholarship and teaching of minority faculty. The next form of marginalization occurs in the larger college community and is based on an institution-preferred agenda for minority faculty. Most often institutions seek race-specific tokens whom they call upon repeatedly for committees or other salient roles. Thus, minority faculty are seldom able to avoid what Finkelstein (1984) refers to as the stress of being a token. Finally, minority faculty often experience marginalization in their ethnic communities due to being in a profession that imposes a work agenda that is misunderstood by many and benefitted by few. Community marginalization frequently occurs because individuals must usually relocate to secure faculty positions, and becoming an insider to their new ethnic community requires time that often competes with their new career roles.

The Hiring Process

Although Hispanics represent only a small percentage of the faculty in higher education, it is important to look beyond demographics and examine the experiences of Hispanics in colleges and universities in the United States. What is the experience of Hispanic faculty when they apply for faculty positions? This section of the chapter presents a discussion of the hiring practices and includes personal accounts of Hispanic faculty within this process. It concentrates on the major hurdles in the process of these faculty members, highlights issues of pedigree (the search for individuals whose degrees are from elite institutions), and the need by those in positions of power to circumvent the hiring process. These personal accounts illustrate additional ways that Hispanics and other minority faculty are marginalized, along with ways that we have already identified.

The Job Description: "What is not written is at times as important as what is written."

Hispanics encounter barriers as they begin to seek college and university faculty positions that hinder their success in obtaining these positions. Even those who eventually achieve success in acquiring faculty appointments report the grueling process they endure. Elitism in higher education remains strong which can result in Hispanics facing the "pedigree issue." Historically, over 50% of Hispanic students begin their studies at a community college before continuing into upper division course-work in the quest to obtain a baccalaureate degree (Carter and Wilson, 1997). Moreover, Hispanic undergraduates are concentrated in less prestigious colleges and universities and only a small percentage

attend elite undergraduate institutions. The common denominator
of a quality institution remains resource-rich research universities
such as Harvard, Columbia, Berkeley or elite private colleges such
as Bryn Mawr or Smith. This attitude is translated into the hiring
process where pedigree becomes an important issue for selection
committees.   Search committees often seek faculty members
whose backgrounds help them reach the desired elitist standard.
This tendency places graduates of less well-known institutions,
including Hispanic applicants, at a distinct disadvantage. Institutional prestige, rather than the knowledge and skills of the
candidate, often become the measure of a candidate's quality and
potential as faculty.

In addition to the pedigree issue, job descriptions are often
written in such a way as to narrow the field. Over time, disciplines
have become increasingly specialized.   At many institutions
faculty teach only certain courses within narrowly defined fields
within specific departments. The narrow restrictions affect the
hiring process.   Furthermore, job descriptions should clearly
define the necessary qualifications. Although this issue affects all
faculty seeking employment, it affects minority faculty in a more
profound way since these faculty tend to spend more time on
service activities such as mentoring students and applying their
research in the community (Ponterotto,1990). Ponterotto (1990)
underscores this point in the following way.

> Necessary qualifications should be defined carefully.
> Does excellence in the field include being able to
> relate to, mentor, and be a role model for minority
> students, or would this just be a nice extra in a
> candidate? For example, which of the following two
> candidates is more qualified for the job of full profes-
> sor: a generally good teacher with seventy-three
> articles published in academic journals, or a gener-
> ally good teacher with thirty-nine articles published
> and an exemplary reputation for mentoring minority
> students and attracting them to the campus? In this
> example, an important question is what constitutes a
> "qualified candidate." (p. 71)

Musil, Garcia, Moses, & Smith (1996), provide an example
of an institution in the Midwest that was seeking an artist with a
concentration in the arts of the Southwest, and who had earned an
M.F.A. – the terminal degree in that discipline. This institution

was seeking to diversify its faculty. Within its own ranks was a Hispanic adjunct faculty member who was an accomplished artist in the area, and consistently had strong student and peer evaluations and over enrolled classes. Although this candidate had a masters degree in the arts, the faculty committee decided that she could not be considered because of her lack of an M.F.A., even though she fit the job description in every other way. This example points to the need of carefully defining what the job really requires, so that qualified candidates are not overlooked for minor reasons.

The Road to Tenure

When a new faculty member enters the halls of the professoriate, he or she is confronted with the infamous role of being the "new faculty member." They are told that they must be good teachers, good researchers, and still provide service to their institution and their community. Except perhaps at community colleges where teaching is valued above both research and service, most four-year institutions proclaim that teaching and research are equally important and service is a close second. Learning to balance teaching, service, and research, as well as acquiring a mentor, are critical to becoming successful in the role of a professor.

Mentoring. As Tierney and Bensimon (1996) stress, mentoring is key to understanding the nuances of what the emphasis will be at a particular institution. Boice (1992) found that few campuses conduct mentoring programs in a comprehensive or systematic way and that mentoring is normally left for new faculty to establish on their own. He also found that minority faculty were even less likely to find mentors spontaneously. Myers and Turner (1995) found that most minority faculty reported that they have had very little to no mentoring in their academic lives. The lack of mentoring programs for minority faculty reinforces their feelings of isolation (Myers and Turner, 1995).

The literature highlights that new hires often suffer through their initial years being lonely and inefficient (Boice, 1992). It is also a time when new faculty are seeking guidelines and attempting to understand the meaning of the university's culture and structure. Lack of mentor programs might add to Hispanic faculties' feeling of disconnectedness. As new Hispanic faculty enter institutions where they may be the only Hispanic, issues of collegiality, classroom management, processes for reappointment and tenure, and political situations can arise. The lack of mentors for new faculty may underscore their feelings of alienation, and not belonging. Moreover, the marginality experienced by Hispanic faculty without adequate mentoring is heightened by their experiences in graduate school where they were seldom mentored (Turner and Thompson, 1996).

Teaching. Those who decide to go into the professoriate understand that teaching is important. In fact, a study conducted by UCLA (Astin et al., 1997) found that minority faculty enter professions where they believe they can make a difference in society. This study might provide an explanation as to why a large percentage of doctorates granted to Hispanics are in education. As reported by Myers and Turner (1995), minority faculty normally excel in teaching. For these faculty, teaching does not only occur in the classroom but continues outside of the classroom. In fact, at predominantly non-Hispanic white institutions, Hispanic faculty are sought out by Hispanic students for academic guidance, often resulting in their spending time with students beyond the required advising load. Pascarella and Terenzini (1991) have noted that student learning and retention are most successful when faculty engagement with students occurs both inside and outside of the classroom. Connection outside of the classroom, which enhances learning for all students, is embraced by minority faculty, in particular Hispanic faculty, in higher proportions (Myers and Turner, 1995). The commitment to mentoring students often hinders the delicate juggling act and balance between teaching, research and service.

The UCLA study (Astin et al., 1997) found that Hispanic faculty appear to spend the most time teaching and that a large majority of minority faculty, except Asian Americans, describe their primary interests as heavily leaning towards teaching. In our experiences, we have found that in addition to greater student contact and connections with students, Hispanic faculty are more likely to employ feminist philosophies and cooperative learning in their teaching. In our opinion, this risk taking which is the mark of good teaching, places Hispanic faculty at risk with student evaluations.

Service. Because predominantly white institutions usually do not have a critical mass of minority faculty, these individuals carry heavy service loads and often bear the added stress of being a token representative on numerous committees (Finkelsterin, 1984). Unfortunately, minority faculty are often appointed to committees that deal with issues of people of color, such as commissions on affirmative action, minority enrollment committees and diversity committees. As portrayed in the video *Shattering of Silences*, minority faculty also become "experts" in areas that relate to their background. Therefore, Hispanics are asked questions regarding the entire Hispanic group, are asked to give presentations on the Hispanic experience in classroom, and are asked to be present at community functions so that the campus can demonstrate minority representation.

Hispanic faculty are also sought out to meet the diversity requirements of university committees. In one example, a Hispanic woman stated that in her first six months on the job, she had been asked to be on five search committees. As a new assistant professor, she felt she could not decline any of the offers as she was fearful of appearing non-cooperative by saying no to her chair, dean, and vice president.

Hispanic faculty are overburdened as tokens with depart-mental, college, university and community committees. It is admirable that institutions are beginning to become sensitive to hearing the voice of diverse constituents on their committees. Yet hiring only a few minorities and then placing the lack of diversity on the shoulders of Hispanic faculty is an unfair burden on junior Hispanic faculty.

Research. For new faculty who enter research, doctoral, or comprehensive institutions, they discover that research and publishing are valued above all else, and are the primary measure for success. What is important to note is that once Hispanic faculty become immersed in their teaching and then bear the heavier burden of service that majority faculty do not have, their research and publications tend to suffer.

In spite of the heavy loads that Hispanic faculty face, many conduct research in areas of social justice or in areas that focus on race, class, and gender. When Hispanics conduct this type of research it is seen as self-serving or biased, although seldom is a majority faculty member questioned when he or she chooses to conduct research on race, class, and gender. On the other hand Hispanics who choose to conduct what is considered mainstream research, many are still funneled into programs and classes that are based on their ethnic background and culture. Thus, even when their research and teaching is mainstream, they are remarginalized based on their race. In our opinion, the scholarly pursuits of Hispanic faculty are not taken at face value. Hispanic scholars, unlike majority scholars, are not given the space to examine and encounter the areas of research they would love to pursue.

In addition to areas of study, and issues of pedigree of where one gets their degree, Hispanics as faculty members face the issue of where one should publish. Many scholars have found venues to publish their work in journals that are not considered by tenure committees as top-rate journals. These journals concentrate on race, class, and gender topics, and are peer reviewed; however, the editorial boards are comprised of reviewers who know their field, are recognized scholars within them, and are racially diverse. Reviewers are the gate keepers of what topics are published, and therefore, who becomes published. What "mainstream" journals need is the addition of reviewers that can review manuscripts from different perspectives. As Padilla (1993), underscores in his letter to a journal contesting the editor's feedback on his manuscript, what is needed are reviewers that not only know and understand the methods that are being employed, but are also conversant in a variety of alternative perspectives.

Throughout the reappointment years, minority faculty look towards what is required to achieve tenure. Because the quantity and production of publications have become the single most important criteria at most universities, Hispanic faculty understand that their attention should be focused in this area. They realize that tenure is the single accomplishment that will launch their academic career, legitimize their career, and communicate to the profession that they are part of the scholarly community.

The Tenure Process

Institutions across the country are widely pronouncing the need for faculty to be involved in teaching, research, and service. In reality, when junior faculty begin the tenure process only research and publications are given serious weight. Hispanic faculty, like other minority faculty, tend to become immersed in teaching, and are called upon more often for service, student mentoring, and community work.

Institutions are beginning to recognize that a diverse faculty brings quality to an institution through their diverse voices and perspectives. This diversity has changed the knowledge base within disciplines and curriculum, and thus, the face of most disciplines. In addition minority faculty bring different perspectives to the classroom, committee structures, and governance. Another important reason for hiring minority faculty is to provide a diversified faculty to a changing student body. Mirroring society is essential if we are to prepare students for the future, and providing role models and mentors for our students is necessary as we shape the future leaders of our country. Unfortunately, at many universities committee service, mentoring students, and involvement in the community counts very little in tenure decisions. What is startling is that one of the main reasons for bringing Hispanic faculty to colleges and universities seems to be one of main reasons for not tenuring Hispanic faculty.

What Hispanic and other minority faculty are realizing is that the standards to obtain tenure have become more stringent. In fact, newly hired faculty are being held to higher standards than many senior faculty tenured years ago. In the past, it was not unusual for individuals to obtain tenure by primarily publishing several articles. Today, junior faculty are being advised to consider publishing a book along with several refereed journal articles. In many cases the standards being used to evaluate minority faculty today would have resulted in the denial of tenure to the same faculty members conferred with decision making power.

Much fanfare has occurred regarding the importance of teaching and service especially since Ernest Boyer's publication, *Scholarship Reconsidered* (1990), which are the very values to which Hispanic faculty subscribe (Astin et at., 1997). In spite of findings in litigated cases that additional accomplishments of majority faculty, other than scholarly publications, are implicitly recognized and rewarded in tenure decisions, this recognition has rarely been offered to minority faculty members (Mindiola, Jr., 1993). If higher education is committed to diversifying the faculty ranks, mechanisms must be developed that will support Hispanic faculty and change entrenched systems that perpetuate the status quo.

Conclusion and Recommendations

Search committees need to be proactive in their pursuit of encouraging Hispanics and other minorities to become a part of the faculty pool of candidates. As in other market driven areas, such as computer science and business, faculty members are proactively recruited because it is recognized that to provide a quality education diverse individuals are needed. For an institution to be viable and vital, Hispanic faculty need to be part of the community of scholars. We need to demonstrate proactively to young Hispanic scholars that our institutions are a good match for their careers. To raise the proportion of Hispanic faculty in higher education institutions, search committees in all disciplines should be as proactive in seeking Hispanic faculty as are the committees looking for faculty members in disciplines where it is difficult to hire.

Restructuring the Hiring Process

Elitism by search committees needs to be confronted. If an institution is truly committed to diversity, they need to carefully examine an individual's talent and achievements regardless of where they obtained their degrees, since a small percentage Hispanics attend the most elite institutions. If we are to rely on only the traditional measures of hiring faculty members, then we are in essence eliminating individuals who can bring specialized talents and expertise to our institutions.

Before a search committee writes the job description, an in-depth discussion should be conducted as to the true requirements for the position. The chair of the department, along with the committee members, should delineate what type of talent is needed for the position. This job description should be shared with those in the department, including junior and minority faculty to ensure that barriers are not artificially being placed in the very beginning of the process. Furthermore, once the applicant pool is selected, the previously outlined job elements should be brought back to the table. Institutions should also consider the possibility of including minority faculty on search committees. If this process is to be used, however, the service this individual is performing must be considered valuable towards reappointment.

Finally, chairs of departments, chairs of search committees or vice presidents of academic affairs may need to take strong, and sometimes controversial, stands on hiring. An example from a northeastern university illustrates this point. A department had obtained permission to hire a Latin American specialist in the political science department. This particular department consisted of an all male faculty and in the recent past had not hired a woman or person of color in the department. When the pool was forwarded to the Provost's office for approval to begin interviewing, it was noted that all of the candidates recommended for interviews were non-Hispanic white and male. The staff member in the Provost's office reviewed the national data that noted that women and people of color had been granted doctorates in the advertised area and, more importantly, that there were Hispanics in the pool. Upon discussion with the dean it was noted that the individuals in the pool were not acceptable to the search committee, although they met the qualifications as listed in the job description. The reason: they were not as qualified as those that were recommended, which meant that those they were recommending had many more years of experience and publications. Upon review by the Provost, discussion with the affirmative action officer, search committee, dean and chair, the Provost closed the search for lack of a good faith effort in conducting the search. Of course, this created controversy with the union, the majority faculty, and the department. The following year, the department once again obtained approval for the position. They approached the search differently, and this time they hired a Hispanic female who has become one of the most productive faculty members in teaching, research, and service among her colleagues.

Restructuring Faculty Roles and Rewards

The American Association of Higher Education and Ernest Boyer began the conversation of the need to re-examining how faculty are rewarded for the work they preform. For Hispanic and other minority faculty this is essential. Faculty whose research is focused on Hispanic communities, mentor their students in research, and conduct applied research directed at the ameliorations of conditions related to Hispanic students' educational attainment should also be rewarded for these scholarly endeavors. In addition, the service that a Hispanic faculty conducts should be examined and valued if it contributes to student learning, community development, and/or enhances the mission of the institution. Many Hispanic faculty are facing the societal issues that our community, nation, and global society are confronting. This type of work should not only be encouraged but rewarded in the reappointment and tenure process.

Establishing Mentor Programs

Once new faculty members are hired, institutions need to implement comprehensive and holistic mentor programs for them. Boice (1992) states that new faculty need multiple mentors, and the chairperson, dean, and faculty colleagues can all play a role in ensuring that Hispanic faculty excel in the institution they have chosen. At Montclair State University, for example, a one-year new faculty program has been developed. New faculty understand that part of their contract includes meeting every other week for a two-hour period to engage in this program. The director of the program carefully matches new faculty members with established faculty members from outside of their department and college. These faculty colleagues join the new faculty every other week in discussions that include topics such as reappointment and tenure, teaching issues, grant attainment, collegiality, campus culture, technology, departmental politics, research and publications, and networking. Equally important is the fact the new faculty and the Montclair faculty meet as pairs once a week to discuss mutually agreeable issues. Issues that are important to the entire cohort are continued in the joint sessions. Chairpersons and deans are also invited to the new faculty program to discuss with the faculty their departments' mission, goals, and expectations..

The program at Montclair ensures that the new faculty members understand its new mission as a teaching university, and that new faculty members connect with others to make their entrance into a new environment as smoothly and efficiently as possible. Evaluations of the program point to the meeting of such goals. There have been other developments which have also strengthened this program. For example, by the end of the first semester, these faculty members have bonded and friendships have emerged, providing support networks outside of one's own department and college.

In addition to this program, Montclair conducts a chairs' orientation for new chairpersons and a retreat for all existing chairs. One of the main components of these sessions is delineating the role that chairpersons must take in order to assist new faculty in their new environment. A goal of the chairpersons orientation and retreats, is the understanding that new faculty are an important resource and that the chair plays a mentoring, supportive role in the success of each new person hired in the department.

These examples provide ways for individuals at colleges and universities to review their processes in order to establish programs that match the institution's culture and mission. Scholars have noted that these programs help all faculty, in particular Hispanic and other minority faculty. It assists them in grasping the history and tradition of their new institutional setting, acquiring the facility in dealing with organizational procedures and structures necessary for survival, exploring and becoming comfortable with their role as members of the academic profession, and finding their niche as to the best way of contributing as a member of a scholarly community (Tierney & Bensimon, 1996, Boice, 1993).

Providing Clear Expectations for Reappointment and Tenure

As Tierney and Bensimon (1996) note in *Promotion and Tenure*, junior faculty are often told: "You have to publish but I can't tell you how much. You have to teach, but I can't tell what good teaching is; and you need to serve on committees, but I can't tell you how many." Unfortunately the operational definition of what is required to obtain tenure remains a mystery. Almost all universities and colleges use the criteria of research, teaching, and service to evaluate candidates for tenure. What standards are applied to those three criteria, however, varies widely across institutions and academic disciplines. More scientific fields, for example, value peer-reviewed journal articles and grants. In other fields, such as history, a university press book might meet the research criterion. The number of publications considered adequate, as well as which journals are acceptable, remains undefined. Although tenure criteria are written down for prospective tenure candidates to peruse, the operational standards required to meet the standard generally refer to requiring a certain level of performance in qualitative terms, such as "excellent journals" or "very good research".

What is needed in each department are clear expectations and operational outcome measures of what is required to obtain tenure. Hispanic faculty members entering into these institutions can then focus their expectations and work towards producing what is required. If institutions are clear as to what is needed, Hispanic and minority faculty would understand the requirements and then work towards meeting them. Chairpersons could subsequently guide faculty each year as to their progress in each area and cite areas of needed improvement. This would result in Hispanic faculty understanding where they stand in their tenure progress, thus reducing the anxiety and stress attributable to unknown expectations.

Chairpersons also must be held accountable for their additional role as academic leaders for their departments. In addition to clearly defining expectations for all new faculty members, chairpersons have multiple roles. For example, they should be held primarily responsible for establishing mechanisms for enhancing collegiality of all faculty including Hispanic faculty. They should also be protecting Hispanic and other minorities from excessive service commitments. Furthermore, a collegial relationship should emerge whereby junior faculty can discuss with their department chair the unrealistic expectations of the service request.

Moreover, faculty development opportunities should emanate from the department. Chairpersons should be sponsoring, collaborating with central administration, and/or providing workshops that assist new faculty in meeting their goals. Grant funding opportunities, curricular discussions, and scholarly discussions should be made available through the department. Chairs must also take responsibility assisting Hispanic and other new faculty to learn how personnel files for reappointment and tenure are prepared.

As we begin the twentieth-first century, there is an increasing urgency to pause and evaluate the ways in which Hispanic and minority faculty are provided access to our colleges and universities. The new millennium will no doubt be distinguished by significant demographic and global changes, both domestically and globally. The standards by which Hispanic faculty are recruited, hired, and retained remain unchanged and locked into a time warp that imbues the status quo. Together, faculty and administrators must seize the opportunity to dramatically change a system that expels difference and creativity. If our system of higher education is to survive and provide all students the education needed to survive in a new world, change must be implemented in order to bring into the community of scholars diversity of thought, ideas, and goals.

Endnotes

1. Some students who reported having only acquired a high school diploma may be among the college-going population working toward a baccalaureate degree.

References

Almanac of Higher Education 1989-1995 (1995). Chicago: University of Chicago Press.

Austin, H. S., Antonio, A. L., Cress, C. M., & Astin, A. W. (1997). *Race and ethnicity in the American professoriate, 1995-1996.* Los Angeles, CA.: University of California, Los Angeles, Higher Education Research Institute.

Astin, A. W., Korn, W. S., & Dey, E. L. (1991). *The American college teacher: National norms for the 1989-90 HERIfaculty survey.* Los Angeles: Higher Education Research Institute, UCLA.

Boice, R. (1992). *The new faculty member.* San Francisco, CA.: Jossey-Bass

Bowen, H. & Schuster, J. (1986). *American professors: A national resource imperiled.* New York, NY: Oxford University Press.

Boyer, E.L. (1990). *Scholarship reconsidered: Priorities of the professoriate.* Princeton, N.J.: Carnegie Foundation for the Advancement of Teaching.

Carter, D. J. & Wilson, R. (1997). *Minorities in higher education: Fifteenth annual status report.* Washington, DC: American Council on Education.

Chavez, R. C. & Padilla, R. V. (1995), Introduction, in Raymond V. Padilla and Rudolofo Chavez Chavez (Eds.) *The Leaning ivory tower: Latino professors in American universities.* New York: State University of New York Press.

Finkelstein, M. J., (1984). *The American academic profession.* Columbus, OH.: Ohio State University.

Goldberg, C. (1997). "Hispanic households struggle as poorest of the poor in the U.S. *New York Times,* January 30, 1997, p.1.

Harvey, W. B. (1996). Faculty responsibility and tolerance. In C. Turner, M. Garcia, A. Nora, & L. Rendon (Eds.), *Racial and ethnic diversity in higher education,* ASHE Reader Series, Needham Heights, MA.: Simon & Schuster Custom Publishing.

Henderson, P. H., Clarke, J. E. & Reynolds, M. A. (1996). *Summary Report 1995. Doctorate recipients from United States universities.* Washington, DC: National Academy Press.

Mindiola, T., Jr. (1995). Getting tenure at the U, in Raymond V. Padilla and Rudolofo Chavez Chavez (Eds.), *The Leaning Ivory Tower: Latino professors in American universities.* New York, NY: State University of New York Press.

Musil, C., García, M., Moses, Y., & Smith D. (1995) *Diversity in higher education: A work in progress.* Washington, D.C.: Association of American Colleges and Universities.

Myers, S. Jr., & Turner, C. S. V. (1995). *Midwestern higher education commission minority faculty development project,* Technical Report. Minneapolis, MN: Midwestern Higher Education Commission.

National Center for Education Statistics. (1993). *Projections of education statistics to 2003.* Washington, DC: U.S. Department of Education, Office of Educational Research and Improvement.

O'Brien, E. (1993). Latinos in higher education, *ACE research briefs,* 4(4). Washington, DC: American Council on Education.

Padilla, R.V. & Chavez, R.(Eds) (1993). *The leaning ivory tower: Latino professors in American universities.* Albany, NY: State University of New York Press.

Pascarella, E. T. & Terenzini, P. T. (1991). *How college affects students.* San Francisco: Jossey-Bass Publishers.

Ponterotto, J.G. (1990). Racial/ethnic minority and women administrators and faculty in higher education: A status report. *New Directions for Student Services, 52,* 61 -72.

Reyes, M. & Halcon , J. J. (1988). Racism in academia: The old wolf revisited. *Harvard Educational Review, 58* (3), 299-314.

Romero, M. (1997). Life of academia from the view of Chicana faculty. *Women and Work: Race, Ethnicity and Class,* 4(2).

Ruffins, P. (1997). The fall of the house of tenure, *Black Issues in Higher Education,* 4(17), 19-26.

Smith, D. G., Wolf, L., & Busenberg, B. E. (1996). *Achieving faculty diversity: Debunking the myths.* Washington, D.C.: American Association of Colleges and Universities.

Thompson, C. J. & Dey, E. L. (1997). Pushed to the margins: Sources of stress for African American college and university faculty. *The Journal of Higher Education,* 69(3), 323-345.

Tierney, W. & Bensimon, E. M. (1996). *Promotion and tenure: Community and socialization in academe.* Albany, NY: State University of New York Press.

Turner, C. S. V. & Thompson, J. R. (1996). Socializing women doctoral students: Minority and majority experiences. In C. Turner, M. Garcia, A. Nora, & L. Rendon (Eds.), *Racial and Ethnic diversity in higher education,* ASHE Reader Series, Needham Heights, MA.: Simon & Schuster Custom Publishing.

U.S. Bureau of the Census. (1992). *1990 census of population: General population characteristics, United States.* Washington, DC: Government Printing Office.

SECTION IV.

Conclusions and Implications for the Future

CHAPTER 11

Pull and Push Factors in the Educational Attainment of Hispanics: Current Realities and Future Directions

Abbas Tashakkori, Salvador Hector Ochoa, &
Elizabeth A. Kemper

Introduction

This book began with four general questions regarding the education of Hispanics in the United States:
1) What has been the historical nature of educational access and outcomes for Hispanics in the United States, and how has it evolved?
2) What is the status of educating Hispanics in the midst of recent controversies regarding minority issues in the United States?
3) Given current demographic trends, what educational outcomes can be predicted for Hispanics in the next decade?
4) What policy and curriculum changes are needed to improve future outcomes for Hispanic students?
The contributors to this volume examined these questions from a variety of perspectives. In this chapter, we attempt to re-examine the general issues related to educational opportunities and outcomes, and then try to identify current trends and summarize possible strategies to improve the status of education among Hispanics.

In our view, access is not the sole issue of concern. A variety of personal, family, and cultural factors also affect the degree to

249

which equality in access will lead to equality of outcomes, especially personal variables such as perceptions and educational plans. To complement the rich sources of information presented by our contributors, we will use the student survey data collected in the National Longitudinal Study of 1988[1] (NELS-88, see Ingels et al., 1994). This study focused on a large representative sample of eighth grade students from across the United States, and followed up every two years until 1996. The chapter examines issues pertaining to access of Hispanics to quality education, along with several moderating/mitigating factors and the education-related outcomes.

Access of Hispanics to Quality Education

The contributors to this volume discussed the issue of educational access and some of the resulting developments from varying points of view. Legal, policy, and political factors that enhance or serve as obstacles to access were discussed by almost all of the authors. Their discussions revealed that disparities in access start from the early years of schooling. As discussed by Carrasquillo in chapter 2, many Hispanic children do not have access to early childhood education. Even though elementary school is theoretically accessible to all children in the United States, Laija and Ochoa (chapter 1) demonstrated that the type of schools that many of the Hispanic children have access to do not provide quality education. Moreover, Carrasquillo (chapter 2) states that the quality of instruction that Hispanic children receive is often "substandard" when compared to non-Hispanic whites.

The gap between the access of the Hispanic and the non-Hispanic white populations to quality education widens as they grow older. Elementary school is the battleground between the proponents of English as the only language, and those who believe in bilingual education. Although some bilingual education programs are offered to Hispanic children in elementary schools across the country, the types of bilingual programs most frequently implemented are not of the type that yield high achievement outcomes. Weaver and Pardron in chapter 4 discussed the effectiveness of maintenance and two-way bilingual programs. In spite of their greater levels of success, these types of bilingual education programs are implemented much less often than other forms of dual language instructional programs. The good news is that the number of these more effective programs seem to be increasing. Encina (1997) cited work from the Center for Applied Linguistics that reported that "182 two-way programs were in operation in 100 school districts encompassing 18 states and the District of Columbia during the 1994-95 school year. Ten years ago, only about 30 such programs existed" (p. 1).

By the time Hispanic students enter middle and high school, if in fact they do, they are already substantially older than their classmates. But, as also discussed by Nora, Renden, and Cuadrez in chapter 8 of this volume, many do not reach this level because the proportion of Hispanic students who drop out of school is more than three times that of non-Hispanic whites. Although finishing high school does not guarantee social mobility, even limited mobility is almost impossible without it (Perez and De La Rosa Salazar, 1997). Furthermore, as Portales (chapter 9) and Nora et al. (chapter 8) discussed, without access to quality high school programs, it is impossible to have access to higher education, a gate keeper for most higher paying jobs in the country (Goldenberg, 1996).

Illusory Access

The select group of Hispanic students who finish high school face an "illusory" choice between entering college or trade school and joining the work force. Expanding on Nora et al. (chapter 8), we use the term "illusory access" because like those authors, we believe that choice does not truly exist for some Hispanic youth. Contributors to this volume (Portales, Nora et al., Garcia and Thompson) have pointed to some of the problems regarding the access of Hispanics to higher education. Recent political moves in California, Washington, Texas, and Louisiana against affirmative action comprise the biggest threats to access. Failure of the K-12 educational system to prepare Hispanics to graduate from high school and continue on to higher education is another. There are also personal and community-level obstacles, which seriously limit the access of Hispanics to prestigious colleges and universities across the nation.

Although the access to community colleges and two-year institutions seems to be readily available to Hispanics and other minority high school graduates, even that access is illusory.

Access to higher education is more probable if the following actions/events are present:

- the opportunity exists, at least theoretically,
- the student intends to continue his/her education,
- the student believes that he/she has a good chance of being admitted,
- the student believes that he/she is academically prepared for higher education and can succeed,
- the student has taken the necessary admission tests such as ACT or SAT,
- he/she takes all steps to apply for admission, and
- he/she is financially able/enabled to register.

In such a complex set of actions and opportunities, access is not simply having a choice to apply and subsequently enroll in a college if accepted. An illustration of this complexity might be found in the NELS-88, 1992, responses of twelfth grade students. When asked to specify their type of high school, 26% of the Hispanics identified it as an "academic" program, as compared to 55% of Asians, 44% of non-Hispanic whites, and 32% of African Americans; more Hispanics (46%) than members of other respondent groups mentioned "general high school" (as compared to 38% of the non-Hispanic whites, 39% of African Americans, and 32% of Asians). Since academic high school programs are actually college preparatory in nature, it might be concluded that Hispanics high school graduates are at a disadvantage. These results are consistent with De La Rosa and Salazar's report (based on De La Rosa and Maw's 1990 study) that Hispanic students "complete fewer 'Carnegie units' and fewer advanced math, science, computer, and English courses than Non-Hispanic white Americans, and are more often 'tracked' into non-academic courses that make access to college difficult" (p. 70-71). As also noted by Nora et al., not only does the tracking of Hispanics into general education courses have a substantial negative impact on their future access to quality higher education, it also limits their chances of employment in technical or other high-paying jobs upon finishing high school.

Another aspect of illusory access is high school students' preparation to apply to college. When the twelfth graders were asked if they had taken the ACT, 32% of Hispanic students stated that they did not think about it (as compared to 18% of non-Hispanic whites, 17% of Asians, and 26% of African Americans). Only 20% of Hispanics reported that they had taken the ACT, as compared to 36% of non-Hispanic whites, 28% of Asians, and 21% of African Americans.

Similarly, only 29% of Hispanics stated that they have taken the SAT (as compared to 42% of non-Hispanic whites, 64% of Asians, and 34% of African Americans), while 28% mentioned that they have not even thought about it (as compared to 16% of non-Hispanic whites, 10% of Asians, and 22% of African Americans). Based on these results, again, it is obvious that access to higher education is less likely for Hispanics than for other groups.

In sum, one might conclude that despite improvements in educational opportunities for Hispanics in the last few decades, complete access to quality education is still far from available. Furthermore, the disparity between the educational opportunities of Hispanics and others, especially non-Hispanic whites, begins in lower grades, increases in high school, and is most evident in higher education. Based on the current trends reviewed by the contributors to this volume, the gap between the access of Hispanics and the non-Hispanic whites does not seem to be decreasing.

Although legal change has affected educational access for Hispanics, it has not led to true equality in such access. Legal and policy changes in the direction of affirmative action have been threatened by the recent political and public opinion shifts in the United States (Darder et al., 1997). Where access is theoretically present, it is in actuality an illusory one for the Hispanic youth, especially with regard to four-year colleges and prestigious universities. It is probably impossible to transform this "illusory access" to true opportunity without more focused efforts towards (a) impacting the self-perceptions of Hispanic students, (b) preparing Hispanic high school students for college, and (c) educating the Hispanic youth regarding the process of preparing and applying for college. Data discussed above clearly point to this necessity. Supporting this conclusion, Vasquez (1997) suggests that differences between Hispanic youth and others in their planning for college "implies differences in the *development* of aspirations and expectations to attend college"(1997, p. 462, italics in the original).

Mediating and Mitigating Factors

All of the contributors to this volume discussed some aspect of educational outcomes for Hispanic youth. They pointed to a variety of factors that might explain the lower educational attainment of Hispanics. Despite this known under-achievement, there is no doubt that many Hispanics are highly successful both academically and professionally. There is no compelling evidence that the success of these Hispanics is due to differential access to educational opportunities. What are the factors that prevent universal success among the majority of Hispanics students? In trying to explain the educational underachievement of Hispanics, different authors have identified a variety of cultural, family, and personal factors. These include: low proficiency in English, poverty, low parental education, acceptance of one's ethnic minority status leading to lower perceived self-efficacy, and lack of learning materials at home (Perez and De La Rosa Salazar, 1997, Alva, 1995; Lindholm, 1995; see also Carrasquillo's chapter in this volume). Nora et al., in chapter 8 of this volume, reviewed a number of barriers to the educational attainment of Hispanics, among them were family culture, educational aspirations, social experiences, and environmental pull factors.

Some of the obstacles to educational attainment, such as poverty and adolescents' responsibility to take care of their families, can not be directly impacted by policy makers. Hence, we do not discuss them in detail. However, there are many other obstacles and mitigating factors that can be affected. An examination of attitudes and aspirations of high school students will provide some insight into this.

Culture

The Hispanic culture, specifically the norms, values, and beliefs regarding education, has been identified as a possible mediator of success and failure of Hispanic students (Trueba, 1989). The Hispanic family is usually a tight-knit, social, support group for its offspring. The impact of Hispanic parents on the educational motivation and attainment of their children should be an inherent part of investigations into this issue. In the 1990 NELS-88 national survey of tenth graders, more than 63% of Hispanics (as compared to 37% of non-Hispanic whites and 51% of non-Hispanic African Americans) considered being able to live at home while attending college as somewhat or very important to them. The same trend was also present in the 1992 survey of the twelfth graders (66% for Hispanics, as compared to 40% for non-Hispanic whites and 50% for African Americans). Although this strong family tie provides a source of support for the Hispanic youth, it also adds constraints on their choice of college.

This was also confirmed when tenth and twelfth graders were presented with a number of future life events and were asked to rate the importance of each. Hispanics, at both grade levels, rated living close to parents and relatives as more important than all other groups (84% of combined ratings of somewhat or very important in tenth grade, as compared to 78% of non-Hispanic whites and 77% of African Americans; in twelfth grade, 83%, as compared to 72% for non-Hispanic whites and 68% for African Americans). This closeness provides a very positive support environment for Hispanic children and youth. However, it might also have a negative impact on their willingness to move away from home in search of better higher education opportunities.

The strong ties that Hispanic youth have with their families has positive consequences as well. Hispanic parents are usually involved in their children's education, and solid family ties make it more likely for them to impact the educational outcomes of their children. Okagaki and Frensch (1998)[2] found that Hispanic parents, compared to non-Hispanic white and Asian-American families, reported that they placed significantly more importance on

> developing conformity to external standards. . . e.g., How important do I think it is for my child to do what the teachers tell him/her to do?. . . and parental monitoring of children's activities. . .e.g., How important do I think it is for me, as a parent, to know what my child does in school. (pp. 129-130)

These researchers also noted that Hispanic parents did provide assistance with their children's homework. Hispanic and Asian-American parents, however, felt significantly less confident than Non-Hispanic white parents with respect to their ability to assist their children.

Parental beliefs regarding higher education, and their support for the offsprings' educational attainment is a relatively uncharted research territory among Hispanics. Consistent with the current differences in enrollment, demonstrated by Portales in chapter 9,

Hispanic 10th and 12th graders were markedly different from Asians and non-Hispanic whites in their perceptions of parental aspirations for their higher education. Table 1 presents a summary of tenth and twelfth graders' responses regarding their parents' aspirations regarding their college education. As Table 1 shows, at both grade levels the percentage of Hispanics who reported that their parents wanted them to graduate from college was smaller than that of non-Hispanic whites regarding both mothers' and fathers' desires, but larger than African Americans and Asians (with the exception of 10th grade fathers').

Table 1. Percentage of 10th and 12th Grade Students Who Reported Their Parents Want Them to Graduate From College, by Race (more than 2 years of college).[a]

	Asian	Hispanic	Black	White
10th Grade				
Father	36.9%	36.4%	30.4%	43.7%
Mother	38.6%	39.2%	37.0%	46.9%
Respondents	1302	2751	2218	13837
12th Grade				
Father	20.6%	21.3%	14.2%	29.0%
Mother	31.6%	31.8%	28.0%	35.6%
Respondents	1406	2922	2260	1402

a - Respondents had a variety of other options not reported in the table (e.g., getting a full time job, going to trade school, etc.).

These results are not consistent with previous findings based on parental self-reports. Okagaki and Frensch's (1998) study compared the educational expectations of Hispanic, non-Hispanic white, and Asian American parents. Hispanic and Non-Hispanic white parents' expectations of their children's "expected educational attainment" did not differ (p. 130). Moreover, these researchers found that these three groups differed with respect to "minimum educational attainment" for their children. Asian American parents expected the minimum to be college graduation, Hispanic parents expected some college education, while non-Hispanic white parents expected only the completion of high school. A possible reason for the disparity might be sampling;

Okagaki and Frensch's study was based on a sample of 275 parents in one geographic location while the NELS study examined a national sample of more than 20,000 students.

Language of Instruction

Another variable researchers identified as causing Hispanic students not to take advantage of educational opportunities are difficulties related to language instruction. In Lindholm's (1995) words,

> the ability to succeed academically requires the acquisition of academic language skills that can be used in abstract, to refer to things removed in time and space, particularly the language required of reading tasks that enable a student to comprehend and critique text far beyond the contextual picture-supported and simplistic vocabulary-supported stories given to beginning readers (p. 275).

As discussed by Eugene Garcia in chapter 7 and Weaver and Padron in chapter 4, lack of a functional proficiency in English, might be one of the main reasons for Hispanics' educational lag, their frustration with schooling, and ultimately for their acceptance of the self-fulfilling prophecy that wrongly advocates their inability to complete schoolwork (Alva, 1995). Alva has reported that students' perceived stress regarding language was the most influential variable to differentiate the successful and unsuccessful students in a discriminant function analysis. Self-concept was the next best discriminator between the two types of students.

Obviously, language plays a major role both in access to education and in determining the outcomes. Without addressing the complexities and problems involving this issue, the gap in access and outcomes cannot be reduced effectively. According to McLeod (1994), data provided by the Council of Chief States School Officers indicated that approximately 93-95% of students who are eligible for Title Seven bilingual education services do not receive them.

Weaver and Padron (chapter 4) discuss critical issues concerning dual language instruction. Of particular importance is the work of Thomas and Collier's (1996) longitudinal study comparing different types of bilingual programs. The impact of exiting limited-English proficient Hispanic students from bilingual programs before they attain Cognitive Academic Language

Proficiency (CALP) (Cummins,1984) on their academic achievement cannot be overemphasized. The frequency of this occurrence is quite common. In order for access to truly begin to occur one must address the following two questions. Are limited-English proficient Hispanic children receiving the most beneficial types of bilingual programs available? Are they being given sufficient time to develop CALP before being discharged from bilingual programs?

Education Related Outcomes

A number of educational outcomes might be attributed to the schooling experience of Hispanic children and youth. Some of these outcomes are directly derived from educational experiences, such as performance on tests, drop-out and suspension, and graduation from high school or college. Almost all contributors to this volume examined at least one or more of these direct outcomes. There are, however, a variety of indirect (mostly psychological) consequences of Hispanic children's experiences in the educational system that bare equal importance. Regardless of the distinction between direct and indirect consequences of schooling, five types of educational outcomes might be present at one point or another in Hispanic children's lives: (a) academic/educational self-perceptions, (b) expected/aspired educational attainment, (c) educational achievement, (d) resilience/drop-out, and (e) actual educational attainment (i.e. higher education).

Some of these outcomes are the result of educational experiences at one level, but impact both the access and the outcomes of the next level. For example, repeated disappointment and frustration with elementary school might lead to low self-perceptions and educational aspirations, leading to low performance at the next level, and/or drop-out.

Academic Self-Perceptions

Marsh, Byrne, and Shavelson (1988) suggested that there is at least some association between academic self-perceptions and academic achievement. Although these self-perceptions are sometimes considered antecedents of achievement, prior successful experiences are assumed to be the major determinants of these self-beliefs (Tashakkori, 1993). Much has been said about the impact that the educational experiences of Hispanics have on their self-perceptions and self-esteem (Trueba, 1989; Vasquez, 1997).

Table 2. 10th Graders Mean Academic Self-Perceptions in Math and Reading, by Race (not available in the 1992 data for 12th graders).

Item	Asian	Hispanic	Black	White
Math is one of my best subjects	4.31	3.69	3.92	3.90
English is one of my best subjects	4.11	3.79	3.99	3.91
I get good marks in English	4.62	4.26	4.42	4.43
I have always done well in math	4.48	3.83	4.04	4.02
I am hopeless in English classes	1.88	2.04	2.05	1.93
I get good marks in math	4.52	3.90	4.09	4.18
I do badly in tests of math	2.41	2.83	2.67	2.65

Averaged values: 1 = false, 2 = mostly false, 3 = more false than true, 4 = more true than false, 5 = mostly true, 6 = true.

Table 2 summarizes the academic self-perceptions of tenth grade students surveyed in the NELS data collection efforts (1990 follow-up). As can be seen in the table, Hispanic tenth graders, collectively, had the lowest perceptions of their own competence in math and reading.

Expected Attainment
        In the NELS 1990 survey, when the tenth graders were asked how confident they were that they would graduate from high school, Hispanics, collectively, reported the smallest chances of graduating from high school. Among Hispanics, 74% were very confident, as compared to 89% of non-Hispanic whites, 87% of Asians and 84% of African Americans.
        It is interesting to note that Hispanics also had the smallest perceived chances of having a well-paid job in the future. This is in line with the conclusions of Nora et al. in chapter 8, that Hispanics being tracked into general education courses in high school leads to the curtailment of their being employed in high paying jobs. Table 3 shows a summary of the tenth and twelfth graders' perception in this respect.
        Although the majority of tenth grade Hispanics thought they had a high or very high chance of going to college, this percentage was lower than that of the other three respondent groups (Asian-Pacific, African American, non-Hispanic white). As a matter of

fact, only 38% of Hispanics thought that their chances of going to college were very high, as compared to 64% of Asian-Pacific, 40% of African Americans, and 55% of non-Hispanic whites.

Table 3. 10th and 12th Graders Perceptions of Future Academic Success, by Race.

Item	Asian	Hispanic	Black	White
Perceived chances of going to college:				
10th graders:				
Low and very low	3.1	14.8	12.5	11.2
About fifty-fifty	9.2	21.8	22.0	13.1
High and very high	87.7	63.3	65.5	75.8
12th graders				
Low and very low	2.9	9.7	8.6	8.2
Fifty-fifty	6.1	15.9	16.4	8.4
High and very high	90.9	74.5	75.0	83.4
Perceived chances of graduating from high school				
10th graders				
Low and very low	.3	1.4	2.0	.9
About fifty-fifty	4.2	12.8	9.6	4.2
High and very high	95.6	85.8	8.4	94.9
12th graders				
Low and very low	.8	2.2	2.8	.9
Fifty-fifty	2.6	6.9	6.3	2.1
High and very high	97.7	90.9	91.9	98.0

The striking difference between Hispanics and others respondent groups points to (a) the Hispanic youth's awareness of access difficulties, (b) their low evaluation of their own abilities, (c) their realistic evaluation of their lack of readiness. By virtue of being in tenth grade, these Hispanic youth were already a select group, as a substantial proportion of Hispanic students drop out of school before the tenth grade.

The twelfth grade students' prediction regarding their level of educational attainment is presented in Table 4.. Based on statistics reported by Carrasquillo in Chapter Two, the Hispanic group is much more selective than the non-Hispanic whites or other respondent groups. Many who did not perform well have already dropped out. Despite this selectivity, an examination of the responses indicates that a smaller proportion of Hispanics expected to finish college or attain higher degrees, as compared to other students.

Table 4. 10th and 12th Graders Projections of Educational Completion.

Percent responding:	Asian	Hispanic	Black	White
10th grade				
High school graduation or less	5.7	19.7	16.6	11.7
1-4 years of trade school	5.4	13.8	11.7	2.5
1-4 years of college	12.7	20.5	19.5	15.0
Finish college	33.2	24.8	26.1	32.8
Master's degree	17.2	8.9	11.6	14.9
Ph. D., M. D., other	25.8	12.3	14.4	13.1
12th grade				
High school graduation or less	2.1	6.4	5.2	5.2
1-4 years of trade school	4.5	11.5	11.1	10.7
1-4 years of college	8.6	17.2	12.9	12.5
Finish college	31.2	29.1	31.4	33.9
Masters' degree	23.3	14.4	17.7	18.5
PH.D., M.D., other	24.9	13.9	15.6	14.1
Don't know	5.4	7.5	6.2	5.0

Academic Achievement

Without exception, the authors in this volume discuss the lower academic attainment of Hispanic students. These students are shown to read below grade level, are placed in low ability groups, and perform lower on tests (Sosa, 1990, Perez and De La Rosa Salazar, 1997). As discussed by Figueroa and Artiles in chapter 5, a disproportionate number of these students are placed in special education programs. On the other hand, the proportion of Hispanics in programs for the gifted is considerably smaller than non-Hispanic whites and some other groups (see chapter 6 of this volume). A number of authors have suggested that some of this under-achievement is the result of inappropriate tests and measurement instruments (i.e., language problems). Regardless of the cause, research clearly points out the educational under-achievement of Hispanics.

Table5. 12th Graders Mean Achievement Test Scores (NELS, Second Follow-Up), by Race and Subject.

Percent responding:	Asian	Hispanic	Black	White
Reading	52.27	46.61	44.99	52.29
Math	55.72	46.35	44.22	52.65
History	53.53	46.91	45.30	52.32
Science	52.82	45.89	43.19	52.76

Hispanic underachievement is not limited to early grades. According to the Texas Educational Agency's, statewide data across third to eighth grades and tenth grade for the 1995-96 academic school year, only 54% of Hispanics passed all three sections (reading, math, and writing) of the Texas Assessment of Academic Skills (TAAS) as compared to 79.8% of non-Hispanic whites (Texas Educational Agency, 1997). Although the twelfth graders in the NELS project were clearly a select group due to the large proportion of Hispanics who drop out of school, their average test scores were much lower than non-Hispanic whites and Asian-Americans (see table 5).

Resilience and Drop-Out
As discussed by the contributors to this volume, Hispanics, overall, are shown to have the lowest degree of educational resilience, and are more likely to be suspended from school (Major and Stewart, 1991). Not only is the overall drop-out rate among Hispanics alarmingly high, as discussed by Carrasquillo in Chapter two, in some areas of the country this rate is as high as 70%. Low persistence and graduation rates are not necessarily limited to the immigrant Hispanic population. Among the twelfth grade Hispanic students who were born in the United States, the rate of graduation in 1990 was only 78% (see Nora et al. in this volume).

Actual Educational Attainment
Hispanics' alarming drop-out rate curtails their educational attainment for the future. Only a small proportion of Hispanic students who reach college age have the opportunity to enroll in

college. A smaller number of Hispanics actually enroll in colleges and universities, and an even smaller number graduate from institutions of higher education. Although this pyramid of selectivity is not limited to Hispanics, their rate of selectivity is much higher than that of non-Hispanic whites. The end result is that a very small group of Hispanics ever graduate from level "A" universities. Portales (chapter 9) provided ample examples for such a selectivity pyramid among Hispanics in Texas.

It should be noted that although educational attainment has a definite effect on the quality of adult life, the disparity between Hispanics and non-Hispanic whites with the same level of education continues. As discussed by Goldenberg (1996), in 1994 the net earning of Hispanics without a high school education was $13,733, as compared to $17,323 for those with a high school education, $21,041 for those with some college education, $29,165 for those with a BA degree, and $51,898 for those with higher degrees. Despite the drastic difference in pay between educational levels, at each of these levels Hispanics earned far below non-Hispanic whites. For example, Hispanics with high school education earned $3,588 less than non-Hispanic whites. The biggest disparity was at the BA level in which the Hispanics earned an average of $8,831 less than non-Hispanic whites. The only exception was found among those who did not graduate from high school. The difference between Hispanics and non-Hispanic whites was only $208. It is obvious, from the above discussions and from the contributors' presentations in this volume, that the issue of Hispanics' education in the United States is a very complex one. It is impossible to understand the issue or to change the status of Hispanics' education by simply focusing on the legal issues pertaining to access.

Conclusions

Based on reviewing the educational status of Hispanics during the 1980s and before, Meier and Stewart (1991) pointed to the need for a number of policy changes to improve the quality of education for Hispanics. Their recommendations included: changes in federal agencies, political recommendations, attracting more teachers, banning ability grouping, "effective" bilingual education, and using alternative discipline techniques at school. Recommended changes in federal agencies included: empowering the agencies that combat discriminatory practices by school districts, enhancing of data collection techniques regarding these practices, making such data more accessible to policy makers and scholars, and changing funding strategies such that the incentives to place larger groups of students in special education classes is reduced. Meier and Stewart also proposed changes at the local level. Following their finding that the "election of school board members had a critical impact on the educational opportunities afforded to Hispanic students," they concluded that " . . . the range of political pressures that the school systems respond to must be increased" (p. 222). They also proposed changes in teacher certification practices to increase the number of Hispanic teachers, as well as a concerted effort to increase the number of Hispanic students in colleges of education.

Their academic recommendations included abolishing the ability grouping in schools in order to reduce the over-representation of Hispanic children in lower track programs, changing the criteria for placement in special education programs when these programs are truly necessary, and replacing "harmful impacts of many bilingual programs as they are currently operated" with "effective bilingual education"(p. 220). They also suggest replacing out-of-school suspension with more productive discipline techniques such as in-school suspension under supervision, and behavior contracting. Most of the problems identified by Meier and Stewart in 1980s and their recommendations for policy change are still applicable a decade later. The contributors to this volume presented recent evidence pointing to the continuation of the problems that Meier and Stewart (1991) outlined almost ten years ago.

Most of the authors in this volume provide suggestions and recommendations for improving the educational outcomes of Hispanics. These suggestions might be classified in two categories, each including positive factors (facilitators) as well as negative ones (obstacles). One dimension includes the pull factors, those that attract and motivate Hispanics and facilitate their access to quality education. The second represent the push factors, those personal, family, and social factors that encourage and support Hispanic youth staying in school, and reach high levels of educational attainment. Obviously, this classification is for illustrative purposes, since many of these factors interact with each other in terms of their effect on educational outcomes.

The positive and negative pull (attracting/discouraging) factors include the macro-level laws and policies such as: (a) legal statues and changes in laws aimed at improving the educational opportunities of minorities, (b) federal, state, and local policies to provide access to quality education for minorities, especially for bilingual children, (c) political forces that affect these opportunities, (d) school and district level policies and practices that might affect Hispanic children's learning environment, performance, and resilience. Changing ability grouping practices, providing quality programs for all children regardless of their classification, and increasing the number of Hispanic teachers and principals were among the suggestions made by different authors in this volume.

The push (motivator) factors include: (a) the Hispanic culture and its' views towards education, (b) school climate as perceived by students, (c) Hispanic role models, such as Hispanic teachers and professors, (d) Hispanic parents and their impact on the education of their offspring, and finally, the most important element, and (e) Hispanic students and their educational aspirations, beliefs, self-perceptions, and behavioral intentions. There are, undoubtedly, many successful Hispanic students and professionals. In order to impact self-perceptions and aspirations, these successful students, teachers, principals, and other professionals should be introduced and utilized as role models from early levels of schooling. Furthermore, personal success leads to higher self-esteem and efficacy. Opportunities for success, even in small degrees, should be made available for Hispanic students at all levels. Socializing families and educators regarding the importance of this issue is a crucial part of any intervention strategy. Obviously, access to effective bilingual programs is needed to help Hispanic children experience such success and to prevent their feelings of inadequacy and lack of ability.

Portales (chapter 10) proposed a "school-centered partnership" in which the school systems partner with colleges and universities to cooperate in preparing students for higher education, and an "informational outreach" to inform parents and involve them in the education of their children. In an effort to improve push factors, urgent attention should be paid to preparing Hispanic youth for higher education while they are in lower grades. Also, given the high poverty level among Hispanics, it is highly unlikely that many families would have the financial means of supporting their children's higher education. New developments in Texas, California, and other states that curtail the access of Hispanics to financial assistance would lead to the widening the gap in access.

There is little doubt that education of Hispanics has improved during the last quarter of the current century. However, the next century will be highly technologically oriented. A high degree of literacy, strong background in math, science, and computers, and technical skills for the increasingly complex labor force are crucial for the survival of the next generation of youth. Given the high poverty level and the relatively low average educational level among Hispanic families, it is highly unlikely that a majority of these families will be able to prepare their children for the labor market of the future. The responsibility for such a preparation falls more than ever before on the shoulders of educational institutions. These institutions, however, need empowerment and improvement to face this challenge. Current political moves in the country exacerbate the problem by limiting remedial and bilingual programs, as well as accessibility of higher education to Hispanic youth. If the problems are not faced now the status of Hispanic education will be far from the level necessary for their future survival and prosperity. Are our policy makers and our educational institutions ready to take the challenge of improving the status of education for all minorities, Hispanics in particular?

Notes

1. The National Education Longitudinal Study of 1988 (NELS88) consists of data collected among eighth graders across the United States in 1988 (base year) and follow-ups of these students in 1990 (first follow-up, tenth grade), 1992 (second follow-up, twelfth grade), and 1994 (see Ingles et al, 1994 for details regarding sampling and other information). A large amount of information was collected about each participant, including past educational history, aspirations, attitudes, self-perceptions, demographic information, and performance on achievement tests. For the purposes of this chapter, the tenth and twelfth grade data were analyzed. The tenth grade data were available for 20,706 students. Only the data that was collected among Hispanics (n=2751, Asian-Americans (n=1302), African Americans (n=2218), and non-Hispanic whites (n=13837) were used for this chapter. The twelfth grade data included 2292 Hispanics, 1406 Asian-Americans, 2260 African Americans, and 14024 non-Hispanic whites.

2. The sub-scales used by Okagaki and Frensch (1988) were based, in part, on items adapted from Schaefer and Edgerton (1985) and Small and Luster (1990).

References

Alva, S. A. (1995). Academic invulnerability among Mexican-American students. In Padilla (ed.), *Hispanic psychology: critical issues in theory and research*, Thousand Oaks, CA: Sage Publications.

Cummins, J. (1994). *Bilingual special education issues in assessment and pedagogy.* San Diego: College-Hill.

Darder, A., Torres, R. D., and Gutierrez, H. (1997), *Latinos and education: A critical reader.* New York: Routledge.

Encina, E. (1997). Two-way bilingual education gaining in nation's schools. *Hispanic Link* [on-line]. Available Internet: www.latinolink.com/opinion/opinion97/0202H12E.HTEM.

Goldenberg, C. (1996). Latin-American immigration and U.S. schools. *Social policy report: Society for research in child development*, 10 (1), 1-30.

Ingels, J. S., Dowd, K. L., Baldridge, J. D., Stipe, J. L., Barot, V. H., & Frankel, M. R. (1994). *National education longitudinal study of 1988, second follow-up: Student component data files user's manual.* Washington, D. C.: U.S. Department of Education.

Lindholm, K. J. (1995). Theoretical assumptions and empirical evidence for academic achievement in two languages. In Padilla (Ed.), *Hispanic psychology: Critical issues in theory and research*, Thousands Oaks, CA: Sage Publications.

Marsh, H. J., Byrne, B., & Shavelson, R. J. (1988). A multifaceted academic self-concept: Is hierarchical structure and its relation to academic achievement. *Journal of Educational Psychology, 80,* 366-380.

McLeod, B. (1994). Linguistic diversity and academic achievement. In B. McLeod (Ed.). *Language and learning: Educating linguistically diverse students (*p 9-44). Albany: State University of New York Press.

Meier, K. J., & Stewart, J. (1991). *The politics of Hispanic education.* Albany, NY: State University of New York Press.

Okagaki, L., & Rensch, P. A. (1998). Parenting and children's school achievement: A multiethnic perspective. *American Educational Research Journal, 35,* 123-144.

268

Padilla, A. M. (1995). *Hispanic psychology: Critical issues in theory and research*. Thousand Oaks, CA: Sage Publications.

Perez, S. M.,& De La Rosa Salazar, D. (1997). Economic, labor force, and social implications of Latino educational and population trends. In Darder, Torres, and Gutierrez (Eds.), *Latinos and education: A critical reader*. New York: Routledge.

Schaefer, E.S. & Edgerton, M. (1985). Parent and child correlates of parental modernity. In I.E. Sigel (ed.), *Parental belief systems: The psychological consequences for children* (p. 287-318).Hillsdale, NJ: Erlbaum.

Small, S. & Luster, T (1990, November). *Youth at risk for teenage parenthood*. Paper presented at the Creating Caring Communities Conference, East Lansing, MI.

Tashakkori, A. (1993). Race, gender, and pre-adolescent self-structure: A test of construct-specificity hypothesis. *Journal of Personality and Individual Differences, 4*, 591-598.

Texas Education Annecy (1997). *Snapshot '96: 1995-96 school district profiles*. Austin, TX: Texas Agency.

Thomas, W. & Collier, V. (1996). *Language minority student achievement and program effectiveness*. Fairfax, Va: Center for Bilingual/Multicultural/ESL Education, George Mason University.

Trueba, H. T. (1989). *Raising silent voices: Educating the language minorities for the 21st century*. Boston, MA: Heinle & Heine Publishers.

Vasquez, M. J. T. (1979). Confronting barriers to the participation of Mexican-American women in higher education. In Darder, Torres, and Gutierrez (Eds.), *Latinos and education: A critical reader*. New York: Routledge.